GRAND PRIX

Tony Howard has travelled extensively and in 1976 was South African Motor Writer of the Year. He has worked for *Autocar Magazine* and *Daily Mirror Newspapers*, and won a Conoco Jet Motoring Writer Award in 1982. He has ridden in land-speed record car Thrust II, and is the only Briton to have driven three times in the Paris–Dakar Rally. Tony Howard is a freelance writer, and lives in London.

COUNTDOWN TO A GRAND PRIX

Tony Howard

ARROW BOOKS

For Anne and Claire
who must take much of the credit
but none of the blame

Arrow Books Limited
17–21 Conway Street, London W1P 6JP

An imprint of the Hutchinson Publishing Group

London Melbourne Sydney Auckland
Johannesburg and agencies throughout
the world

First published 1984

© Tony Howard 1984

Set in Linotron Plantin by
Input Typesetting Limited, London SW19

Printed and bound in Great Britain by
Anchor Brendon Limited, Tiptree, Essex

ISBN 0 09 935210 9

CONTENTS

ACKNOWLEDGEMENTS

Writing a book such as *Countdown to a Grand Prix* depends largely on the willingness of key people to answer questions and otherwise give a good deal of their valuable time, not to mention their encouragement. For this generosity I want to thank:

Derick Allsop, Andrew Andersz, Yvette d'Arcy, Kaspar Arnet, Elizabeth Aves, the Banking Information Service, John Barnard, Eric Bhat, Robin Bradford, Ann Bradshaw, Creighton Brown, Geoffrey Charles, Ron Dennis, Colin Dryden, Bernard Dudot, Peter Dyke, Neil Eason-Gibson, Richard Evans, Robert Fearnall, David Fern, Patrick Fitz-Gibbon, Malcolm Folley, Mike Francis, Graham Gauld, Yves Genies, Patrick Head, Frank Hemsworth, John Hugenholtz, The Institution of Mechanical Engineers (North Western Branch), Tony Jardine, Brian Jones, Jane Judd, Nobuhiko Kawamoto, Bob Kirwin, Robert Langford, Mark Lucas, Nigel Mansell, Anthony Marsh, Andrew Marriott, Patrick Mennem, Leslie Nicholl, Ian Norris, Derek Ongaro, Jane Partington, David Payne, Simon Pearson, Maurice Phillipe, Nelson Piquet, Dr Harvey Postlethwaite, John Redford, Michael Reid, Chris Rogers, Anne Routledge, Jean Sage, Ekrem Sami, David Simpsom, Patrick Tambay, Michele Tetu, David Thirlby, Kate Tillett, the Tobacco Advisory Council, Paul Treuthardt, Raimondo Corsi di Turri, Bob Tyrrell, Ken Tyrrell, Murray Walker, Derek Walters, Derek Warwick, Angela Webb, John Webb, John Weinthal, Mike Whitehouse, Don Whiting, Alec Whittaker, Frank Williams, Byron Young, Eoin Young; also Ray Hutton, editor of *Autocar*, and Peter Newton, editor of *Cars & Car Conversions*, for their kind permission to use extracts from material I had written for their respective magazines.

My apologies to anyone I have omitted; no slight is intended.

Photography by: John Townsend. Additional pictures by: Michael Cooper, John Dunbar, Ford Photographic Services, Tony Howard, Longines.

PROLOGUE

Like itinerant jet-setting jousters, grand prix drivers remorselessly travel the world in hot pursuit of the perfection that will wrest the most expensive and spectacular of sporting titles, the Formula 1 World Championship.

Seen from one angle, this is an intensely personal – and self-indulgent – endeavour by a small elite of extremely fortunate individuals. But, no matter how exciting and acclaimed are their roles, they are simply players on a vast stage, creatures of the media and under the sway of rapid technological advance and the often conflicting interests of big business.

Grand prix racing has been transformed from an esoteric activity, followed by relatively few afficionados. It is now worldwide mass entertainment with an enthusiastic, if sometimes bewildered, lay following. Its personalities, teams and sponsors are household names. Twenty years ago, there were ten grands prix a season. Seven were run in Europe, and about twenty cars started on each occasion. Since then, power has quadrupled.

Nowadays there are about sixteen races, of which eleven are in Europe, and maybe thirty drivers vie for twenty-six places on the starting grid. There are those in the sport who say the calendar is too crowded, while others would be quite happy if there were thirty grands prix a year, citing the success with which countries such as Britain and Italy have each staged two events a season.

The combined population of the countries in which grands prix are run is 650 million, of which half are English speaking. These races attract the third largest television coverage in the world, behind the Olympics and World Cup

Soccer; they are broadcast in more than forty countries, and the annual audience tots up to 935 million. Attendances as high as 200,000 are claimed over a grand prix weekend. Yet this is a far from cheap sport to watch – a family of four treating themselves to the best tickets would expect to pay £150.

The attractions of the grand prix circus are well summed up by this extract from an American tobacco company investigation: 'Motor sport at the Formula One level is sophisticated, cosmopolitan, and has an international following of intelligent and, in the main, up-scale males and females. It combines all the elements of twentieth-century mythology – i.e. speed, excitement, money, chic and celebrity.

'Grand prix motor racing attracts a great deal of publicity as a sponsorship vehicle. There are clearly a number of benefits: truly international events in four continents over nine months with a race every three weeks.

'The sport conveys an image of glamour, excitement, danger, internationality and success (big money). Formula One is highly aspirational. It attracts good media coverage. The TV audience is international and very large. It is a good vehicle for strong brand graphics, and it has massive opportunities for exploitation.'

There are myriad starting points along the complex critical path that leads to the start of each grand prix. The purpose of this book is to shed light on major elements individually, showing how they come together to form such an exciting whole.

The aim is to take the reader behind the scenes to meet some of the fascinating people who have made the sport their life. As a breed, many are an object lesson in how tenacity, enthusiasm and ingenuity can get you there in the end. For, though the circus does tend to be self-obsessed, it is a microcosm of the real world outside but with colours and contrasts much sharper.

Teamwork is undeniably what the sport is all about. But, in the end, a single individual must step into that racing car, and pitch all the skill and courage he can muster into the intense game of extracting the ultimate performance. This experience is so highly charged that many strive for years to be allowed it, risking death or mutilation. And, even after horrendous injury and the agonies of recovery, they keep coming back for more.

Their wives and girlfriends must live with that risk, and the knowledge that their men have another mistress beckoning all the time who offers something possibly better than sex.

For the driver, race day invariably begins in the usual five-star hotel bedroom. When he wakens, he starts to count himself down towards those concentrated two hours during which he will once more flirt with destiny.

He tends to become a very private person, contemplative, fending off anything that may disturb his routine, and trying to slip into the circuit as anonymously as possible. This is no time for a woman to cling, demanding protestations of undying love – poor bitch, she knows damn well she may never bed him again.

Dressing has a ritual quality. First he draws on close-fitting fire-resistant underwear – white socks, long-johns and polo-neck sweater – like a shrink-wrapped shroud.

The outer layer is a quilted fire-resistant overall, close-fitting at the neck, wrists and ankles, embroidered with name and blood group, and emblazoned at vast expense with sponsors' decals. The thin-soled boxing-style boots and long gauntlets he wears are of a similar material.

Over his head he draws a protective Balaclava helmet that exposes only his eyes, giving him the appearance of the Invisible Man. Then on goes the full-face crash helmet which, when new, should be virtually too tight for comfort. It has a hinged section under the chin which snaps shut to fully encase the head. And the vizor will withstand a blast from a shotgun. Built-in earphones and a microphone allows easy intercom conversation with the pit crew, and there is an inlet pipe for air from the emergency life support system. When he is ready to drive not an iota of the driver's flesh is exposed, for fear of fire.

Clambering into the car is an exercise not recommended

13

for the tubby or arthritic. He steps in over the high sides of the cockpit, first standing on the seat and then coiling his legs forward into the close confines between the front suspension, before lowering his arms from above his head to rest his hands on the chunky suede rim of the steering wheel, which is about 22 cm diameter.

Cocooned in his overalls and squashed into the cockpit which fits around him like an outer skin and has almost no elbow room, he is virtually helpless to do up the six-point safety harness. One of the pit crew has to do this for him.

Thus ministered to by his minders, his countdown is almost complete. Let the grand prix commence.

1

PENCILMAN

Engines scream, not in unison; twenty-six cars creep forward, restrained only by a red light. Spectators are transfixed by tension. Four seconds later, the green light unleashes a concerted, deafening howl. Wheels, scrabbling for grip, lay thick black stains on the track. Cars dodge and weave in a breathtaking rush towards the first corner.

This is sport, entertainment, show business – call it what you will – at its most exciting. But behind the glamour and clamour lie a diversity of serious technological exercises, as intensely competitive as anything that takes place on the track.

Grand prix racing often starts and finishes in quiet solitude, as the designer begins to work out or re-think his ideas from scratch on a blank sheet of paper. So much is at stake that determination, stamina and an ability to maintain a stream of fresh ideas are essential.

Some feel the pace of development has been forced too hard and too far, and they fear this may be burning out the top designers who scarcely have time to pause for breath. This is certainly true of the *garagistes*, as they are somewhat patronizingly dubbed by their counterparts employed by the *grandes marques*, Alfa Romeo, Ferrari and Renault.

These pressures run far deeper than the quest, at its most visible level, for race-winning performance which involves finding the best combination of tyres and settings of suspension and aerodynamic aids. There is the mental strain of being at the circuit, facing questions about why the car is not faster, why components are breaking.

All the time, the designer's mind is on the car today, tomorrow, next week, and even months ahead. He has to cope with the immediate problems as the start of the race looms inexorably closer, yet maintain a firm grasp of an expensive test programme, scheduled to run for many months.

With the end of a season comes a break of maybe four months before the next year's first race. For most of the team it is a time to slow down a bit, re-group, take a holiday, spend more time at home with the family. But not for the designer: he must get cracking to complete his plans for the new car so that it can be built and tested thoroughly before its first racing appearance the following season.

When he is not away at grands prix or testing, John Barnard of McLaren International works a punishing week. He is in his drawing office by 9 a.m. and seldom leaves before 8 p.m. For good measure, he puts in eight hours on most Saturdays. During the big push to finalize a new car, he won't leave until 10 p.m. for five or six weeks at a stretch. And, on Sundays, he will work an additional six hours.

'It is almost as though my family is geared to not having me there on Saturdays. If I am there, it can be a problem – they don't know what to do because the old man is home,' says Barnard wryly. 'Now, unless you are a racing-car designer, you just cannot understand what it means. I have a feeling that writers, novelists – from what I know of them – are most like us in that they work to absolute deadlines which cannot be moved. And they have to create, come up with something new, fresh, better all the time.'

The analogy is well chosen. If the designer fails to produce the goods on time, the race will still be run. If that failure is maintained for only a short time, his team may be finished. He cannot afford to lose his grip.

In a way, life is easier for the designer at the start of his career. He has a multitude of untried ideas buzzing around in his head, so he has plenty of options to pursue. Once he is established and has more experience however, these options are whittled down because he has a much clearer understanding of what is likely to work and what is not.

Then comes the increasingly difficult slog towards the

completely different approach, the real breakthrough. The underlying philosophy is that the rules are far from sacrosanct and must be stretched to the limit, even far overstepped – if you can get away with it.

Designers' ingenuity has probed plenty of loopholes over the years. 'The rule book was, unfortunately, written for gentlemen to interpret in spirit and not for the players to exploit to the letter', points out Dr Harvey Postlethwaite, chief of racing chassis design at Ferrari. 'Behind most of the problems of Formula One lie its regulations and its governing body. As Formula One has sprinted ahead technically and as a spectacle for vast worldwide television audiences, spurred on by big financial gains like many other sports, the international governing body has remained in the era of the blue blazer and the leather armband.'

And he claims: 'They are increasingly powerless to judge the relevance of the technical deviousness, and increasingly in the sway of the most powerful and vociferous competitors.'

From the time of the first grand prix, a 1239 km, two-day event, staged by the Automobile Club de France in 1906, the spirit and the intention behind the rules may well have been clear enough. But, like Topsy, they have just growed as successive governing bodies of the sport have sought greater safety or good order by attempting to tame what they saw as undesirable trends.

For the most part, rule changes have been responsive – plugging a loophole here, quashing a flagrant breach there – and not pre-emptive. And, as grand prix racing has never been more dynamic than in recent years, so alterations to the rules have come thick and fast.

Furthermore, the teams have, as we shall see, become increasingly litigious. If one car sprouts a bright new idea, maybe of dubious conformity to the rule book, the competition will invariably want the legality tested. Like rowdy children, jostling to be a top dog in the school playground, they all covet the new toy – but they want to be sure it won't be confiscated.

More than sixty pages of small print, in French and

English, are specific to the annual Formula 1 world championship and its sixteen-odd grand prix races. They provide not so much an absolute but a benchmark, continually changing, with which the designer has to work. They are as much a spur to his inventiveness as a response to it.

The world championship proper, intended to be the pinnacle of motor sport, came into being in 1950, admitting Formula 1 cars with engines of 4500 cc, normally aspirated, or 1500 cc, supercharged. The withdrawal of Alfa Romeo at the end of 1951 left Ferrari virtually unopposed at the top. So, in the interests of competitive racing, the championships of 1952–3 were run to Formula 2 – at that time 2000 cc un-superchaged. Meanwhile, a new Formula 1 was devised – 2500 cc normally aspirated, or 1750 cc supercharged – and this was used between 1954 and 1960. But, as speeds rose and accidents took their toll, those in authority grew nervous. From 1961 to 1965, therefore, a fourth Formula 1 was in force – 1300 to 1500 cc un-supercharged – and, for the first time, a minimum weight limit: 450 kg (992 lbs).

Authority regained its nerve, however. From 1966, the present engine Formula was introduced – 3000 cc normally aspirated, or 1500 cc supercharged. Minimum weight was 500 kg until 1969, but crept up in four stages to 585 kg in 1981, the aim being to allow greater leeway to make the cars safer. By 1983, the limit was down again – to 540 kg – in response to the increasing use of advanced lightweight materials.

At least there had been constancy in terms of engines – that is until Renault came into the fray in mid-1977 with a turbo-charged 1500 cc engine. This sowed the seeds of a revolution which grew until, seven races into the 1983 season, the normally aspirated 3-litre engine very likely won its last world championship F1 race.

In one sense, grand prix racing is like a banana republic – one revolution after another. Often cast in the role of Fidel Castro or Che Guevara was Colin Chapman, the legendary innovator behind so many Lotus successes, who died at the age of fifty-four in December 1982.

It was Chapman who led Formula 1 designers to use the monocoque, or 'tub', in which the driver sat and which formed the load-bearing chassis between the front suspension and engine. The monocoque was fabricated from sheet metal, and was lighter and stronger than the 'space frame' of steel tubes which it displaced.

At the inception of the present Formula 1, Chapman persuaded Ford to fund a new engine, and this led to the Cosworth DFV, the most successful grand prix power unit of all time. It made its debut in the Lotus 49 in 1967. Not only did it propel the car, it eliminated the need for a chassis frame by carrying the loads between the back of the monocoque and the rear suspension.

Soon after this, Chapman's cars began to grow wings. These were seen, in embryo first, on the Lotus 49B, and worked to counter the aerodynamic lift developed by a car at speed. Realising the potential of these wings – in effect up-turned aircraft-style aerofoils – to provide extra downforce and increase tyre grip for better acceleration and faster cornering, Chapman went straight to the point. Within months his cars were equipped with large wings which were carried high, out of the turbulence created by the rest of the car, and were attached by means of stalks to the wheel hubs. This meant the downforce acted directly on the tyres and not through the springing.

Everyone else quickly followed suit. Almost as quickly, such wings were banned after several breakages caused cars to crash out of control. When wings returned, shortly afterwards, they were firmly attached to the body.

The quest for better traction then turned to four-wheel drive. Once again, Chapman was in the forefront, but the concept did not live up to the original hopes for it.

He set them talking again with the Lotus 72, a novel car in many respects. It was very light, and had a sharp, wind-cheating wedge shape and big wings. Both front and rear brakes were mounted inboard to reduce unsprung weight, helping the suspension to work more effectively. The springing medium was torsion bars, saving weight and space, in place of more conventional coil springs. Suspension geometry was designed to counter the tendency to squat while accelerating and to dive while braking.

As much by accident as design, the significance of aerodynamics came to be recognized. Designers also began to understand that outright straight-line speed might not be the only answer, that it could be worth trading some of this off against higher cornering speeds which resulted from wings that necessarily increased drag while they intensified down force.

By the mid 1970s, most constructors were using wind tunnels to check out their ideas for shaping the cars. The aim was to get more downforce for less drag. This work continues to be a major preoccupation of the design teams.

McLaren International, for instance, tests scale models nine months a year in the 'moving ground' wind tunnel it operates at the National Maritime Institute at Teddington. Williams Grand Prix Engineering does the same at its Didcot factory, while Brabham has access to wind tunnels at Southampton University. Ferrari uses various Fiat facilities around Turin, working first with scale models and then the complete full-size car with all its systems installed.

The wind tunnel has given rise to a fascinating variety of approaches. Perhaps the most readily visible of these was the Tyrrell P34 that raced in 1976–7. A six-wheeler, it had two pairs of small front wheels. The reasoning was that this greatly reduced frontal drag while increasing the tyre-to-track contact patch of the steering wheels, thus improving the 'turn-in' to corners.

Then came the controversial 'ground-effect' era, sparked off by Colin Chapman after a spell in the wilderness trying out exotic, almost infinitely adjustable, suspension systems. The Lotus 78, which won five races in 1977, had undersides curved so that a venturi was formed between the car and the track. Air passing under the car thus created a depression, in effect sucking the car more firmly towards the track; encouraging air flow under the car in this way also helped to reduce drag, and so aerodynamic efficiency was better.

The Lotus 79; which dominated the 1978 World Championship, took these ideas a lot further. The competition followed the same route, also using sliding 'skirts' between car and track to seal in the vacuum underneath. These skirts should not in fact have been tolerated in view of a proscription on 'moveable aerodynamic devices' that was prompted by the wings on stalks of a few years earlier, but the rules were amended to accommodate them.

Brabham's Gordon Murray naughtily went one better, reviving an idea first tried on the Chaparral sports racing car in 1970. The Brabham BT46B sported a large fan at the back. This might well have aided engine cooling, but the primary effect was to exhaust air from under the car, creating a vacuum which was maintained with the aid of both lateral and longitudinal skirts. This car won first time out in the 1978 Swedish Grand Prix, but it was heartily disliked for blowing muck into the faces of other drivers. A previous ruling that the car was legal was quickly reversed, but the team was allowed to retain the championship points gained in Sweden.

At its zenith, the application of ground effect was creating about 2700 kg of downforce at 290 km/h (180 mph) in addition to the actual weight of the car. The effects were incredible. Tyres were pressed so much more firmly into contact with the track that their grip went up in leaps and bounds. Lateral forces on the car and driver increased from 1,5g to 3g, with peaks of 3,5 g at the tightest part of a corner – three and a half times the force of gravity.

If the human head weighs 6 kg and a crash helmet is 1,5 kg, cornering in a grand prix car increases this to more than 26 kg. Try walking around with an 18,5 kg weight strapped to the side of your head, and see how you like it. The drivers certainly didn't. And their troubles with neck muscles and backs were made worse by the very harsh ride that came with the stiff springing necessary with high downforces.

The implications didn't end there. Drivers' feet were being dragged off the pedals by high g-loadings, and they complained of blurred vision. Even the superstars could hardly believe how fast they were now able to drive into corners – often virtually too quick to see far enough round the bend to react in time, should anything be amiss. Also, braking forces were doubled to 2 g.

The most serious problem of all was the risk of those skirts losing contact with the track surface, either through breakage or because the wheels had ridden up the kerb. The instant the seal was lost, under-car vacuum and thus downforce diminished. The car no longer generated the grip necessary to sustain the speed at which it was cornering. A spin or big slide was almost inevitable and, with cornering forces doubled, the potential impact with the scenery was twice as hard.

There was a resurgence of concern about the safety of both drivers and spectators. And agreement was pretty general that a reduction in cornering speeds was desirable. But this aim fell foul of the highly politicized struggle between the Formula One Constructors' Association and the *Fédération Internationale du Sport Automobile* for control of grand prix racing.

Rule changes, intended to put an end to sliding skirts and thus ground effect from early 1981, contained more loopholes. A 6 cm (2,4 inch) minimum ground clearance was specified. But Gordon Murray realized that this could be got round by using non-sliding skirts and suspension that could raise and lower the ride height. When the car was checked in the pits, it would comply with the rule. Once out on the track, the driver flicked a switch, the car and its skirts sank into contact with the track – and there was the ground effect.

Almost reluctantly, Murray put these ideas to work and, inevitably, the rest of the pack followed him. The cars gave the driver a harsher ride and were, if anything, even more difficult to control.

At the same time another bright idea from Colin Chapman's team was hitting problems. The Lotus 88 was the subject of a long drawn out wrangle that saw it alternately pronounced legal and then illegal. It was too clever by half to escape the in-fighting of the times and was prevented from ever racing.

In effect what the 88 did was to return to the principle

of applying aerodynamically generated downforce direct to the wheels, instead of via the chassis and through the springs. As usual, monocoque, engine and gearbox were in one unit with front and rear suspension attached, but with softer springing than was customary at the time. Around this whole was placed a ground-effect producing body shell, moving independently and attached directly to the suspension wishbones. The ride for the driver was softer, while cornering speeds still benefited from big downforce.

That season, not controversially but much more significantly as it turned out, Ferrari had followed the Renault lead into turbo-charging. And the British Toleman team had made its debut with the Hart turbo engine.

Brabham started 1982 with BMW turbo power, and there was word of an Alfa Romeo turbo engine. The silliness of variable ride-height suspensions was dispensed with, while non-sliding skirts continued to be tolerated.

The next major wrangle was over water cooling of brakes, an idea first put to use by Patrick Head of Williams. This led to protests and then disqualifications on the grounds that it was a ploy to run cars under the minimum weight, making up for this at the end of a race by topping up with 'essential fluids' – in this case 30 to 40 litres of water.

Then disaster struck, bringing into question once more not only ground effect but also the use of super-sticky qualifying tyres with such short lives that drivers were increasingly under pressure to take extra risks when attempting a high placing on the starting grid. Gilles Villeneuve was doing just that while qualifying for the Belgian Grand Prix when his Ferrari glanced off another car, cartwheeled through the air at 240 km/h and broke up on landing. He never recovered conciousness, and died that night.

Villeneuve's team-mate, Didier Pironi, had two heavy shunts while testing, but was unhurt. It was to be third time unlucky for him. While practising for the German Grand Prix in the rain, his car also was launched off another, and his injuries kept him out of racing at least until the end of 1983.

In the French Grand Prix, two weeks earlier, Jochen Mass's March was knocked off a flat-out fifth-gear corner, ploughed through catch fencing and over a barrier, landing at spectators' feet and bursting into flames. Miraculously, no more than three people were hurt, and Mass was able to walk away from the incident.

It was enough. In mid-October, 1982 FISA president Jean-Marie Balestre announced 'exceptional measures' to put an end to ground effect. 'We are rushing headlong towards rolling bombs whose trajectories have more to do with ballistics than with motor sport,' he warned.

At the beginning of November, the move was ratified by all concerned – that is to say the *garagiste* and *grande marque* constructors. Even at such short notice, skirts and curved undersides were to be abolished from the first race in 1983. In their place, the bottom of a car would be completely flat between the front and back wheels. Furthermore, permissible rear wing width was reduced from 110 to 100 cm, while effectiveness was further decreased by 60 cm rear overhang instead of 80 cm. Minimum height of the wing went up from 90 to 100 cm to give the driver better rearward vision.

As a sop to those *garagistes* who would still be relying on normally aspirated Ford Cosworth engines, and had come to regard ground effect as an essential weapon in their battle to stay on equal terms with the increasingly powerful and reliable turbo cars, the minimum weight was brought down 45 kg to 540 kg. It would be difficult with a heavy turbo engine to get down to the limit, but much easier with the lighter Cosworth.

Many of the design ideas already well under way in preparation for 1983 had to be scrapped. It was time to go back to the drawing board, burn more midnight oil. Only one thing was sure – however long the new rules were to be in force, they would be milked dry and developed to the absolute limit from every angle.

Lap times had tumbled dramatically during the ground-effect period. Pole position qualifying time for the British Grand Prix at Brands Hatch, for example, came down from

1 minute 19,35 seconds to 1 minute 9,54 seconds between 1976 and 1982. Without the aid of ground effect, but with the benefit of extra turbo power, Elio de Angelis and the John Player Lotus 94T took pole position with a 1 minute 12,092 seconds lap of the same circuit, while qualifying for the 1983 Grand Prix of Europe.

Yet, at Silverstone, scene of the British Grand Prix on alternate years, pole time was still quicker – down from 1 minute 11,0 seconds in 1981 to 1 minute 9,462 seconds in 1983 (both times it was René Arnoux, first in a Renault, then a Ferrari). So it was impossible to make the sweeping generalization that the decline in lap times had been halted by flat bottoms. On some circuits, what the cars had lost through the corners they were more than making up for by gains on the straights, thanks largely to turbo power.

In any event, cars were now generating as much as 900 kg downforce at 290 km/h with the help of cleverer wings and by exploiting the fact that the rear part of the underside could be curved and faired in at the sides to create some downward suction. Renault even tried routing its exhaust pipes out into this cavity, using the high velocity gases to help draw more air through it. But, by consensus, the idea was quietly abandoned lest a new contentious bandwagon be set rolling, though it reappeared for 1984.

By the end of 1983, the power race was well and truly under way. A team was nothing without a turbo engine, and so the stakes were raised even further. High spending players were Alfa Romeo, Ferrari and Renault, each putting its engine in a chassis of its own construction, and Brabham powered by BMW, Ligier by Renault, Lotus by Renault, McLaren by TAG Porsche, Toleman by Hart, and Williams by Honda.

Thus, after winning 155 grands prix, the old faithful Ford Cosworth 3 litre V8 was abandoned, not without some trepidation, by front-running teams. The 1983 Italian Grand Prix was the first race, since the engine's first-placed debut in 1967, in which a Cosworth-powered car failed to finish in the top six places. Nevertheless, for reasons which will emerge later, there are those who believe it has by no means run its last successful race.

While power is now more than ever the name of the game, the quest for the ultimate aerodynamic form is unlikely to diminish. Also, as straight-line speeds continue on the up-and-up, brakes will be improved apace. Cars will approach corners maybe 50, 60, 80 km/h faster, and will turn into them just as quickly as ever.

They may now only be capable of pulling 2 g instead of 3,5 g. But, thanks to improving turbo response and increasing punch, they will be accelerating away ever more strongly. The net effect – time taken between entry to and exit from a corner – will very likely be much the same as it was before the demise of full ground effect.

Competitive pressures in grand prix racing have always forced designers to make use of the most advanced materials and techniques. This was never more true than today. Since the mighty Regie Renault put its prestige on the line by entering the field with effectively unlimited resources, Alfa Romeo, Ferrari and others have replied in like coin. 'They can't be seen not to be successful,' notes one engineer. 'So the competition amongst the accountants is intense. I don't know where they get the money from. But we keep spending it.'

As one peels the leaves off the grand prix racing artichoke, a plethora of motives, causes and effects is revealed. The outer layer is macho – the simple racer's competitiveness, the burning desire to be a winner, familiar to all sports. Close to this is corporate and national prestige in all sorts of manifestations.

As the major automotive manufacturing interests force the spending pace, the racers – the *garagistes*, largely reliant on non-automotive backing – must also find yet more cash if they are to have a hope of staying in the technology race, and thus among the pace-setters on the circuit. And, with this impetus, the amount of money being spent by the teams grew by several hundred per cent in the early 1980s.

One view of the sport sees it as a substitute for warfare as a technological forcing house. In a chicken-and-egg relationship with the automotive and aerospace industries, grand prix racing has eagerly exploited, at an early stage, materials such as aluminium, high-strength steel, magnesium, titanium, plastics, glass fibre, polycarbonate, bonded honeycomb laminates, Nomex, Kevlar and carbon fibre.

To be successful, the designer must draw together so many strands that he cannot afford to play the secluded boffin. His task goes much further than resolving all the complex elements of his racing car into a winning compromise. He must also keep abreast of new materials and manufacturing techniques, and be alert to ways in which they might suit his purposes.

One rationale often used for the grand prix car has been its relevance to the road car of tomorrow. This link is possibly less tangible, less obvious than twenty years ago, but it remains strong. And, arguably, a very real contribution is being made in helping Space Age materials on their way towards more affordable and down-to-earth applications.

The first use of carbon fibre on Formula 1 cars was in rear wing mounting plates. When one of these broke on Rolf Stommelen's Embassy-Hill during the 1975 Spanish Grand Prix, the car flew over a guard rail, killing three spectators. This gave carbon fibre a bad reputation, discouraging other designers from using it at the time.

During the ground-effect era, carbon fibre was employed in side skirts where, again, the requirement was for a light but strong material, but much more widespread use of carbon fibre had its beginnings in 1979 when Ron Dennis, John Barnard and Creighton Brown, now the shareholders of McLaren International, decided to combine talents in going grand prix racing. Barnard was to design a money-no-object car, a positive move towards improved performance. 'We were looking around for a new approach, a step forward,' he remembers.

For once, he had the luxury of time to go foraging for information – at this stage, a full organization had yet to be set up and sponsorship found. Barnard's researches led him into contact with British Aerospace engineers who had made much progress using carbon fibre for turbo fan engine cowlings, and had a lot of test data on composites. 'It was their thing. They told me how wonderful it was, how you could do anything with it. And I started thinking about it seriously.'

This odyssey led to Salt Lake City, Utah. Nearby is the aerospace division of Hercules Corporation which makes such exotica in carbon fibre as satellites, missiles, fuel cells for NASA space shuttle launch rockets, and many components for the F16 military aircraft.

The upshot was that when the Marlboro McLaren MP4 was first revealed to the media early in 1981, it had a carbon fibre monocoque, made by Hercules for around $50,000. The advantages are reckoned to be worth every cent. The new style of monocoque is one-fifth lighter than the conventional type, fabricated in aluminium. Yet it is twice as rigid, allowing the frontal cross-sectional area to be reduced by one-fifth, a considerable aerodynamic advantage.

The effectiveness of McLaren's new monocoque as a survival cell for the driver was dramatically demonstrated in the 1981 Italian Grand Prix when John Watson's car slammed into a barrier with such force that it broke in half and rebounded across the track. Twenty minutes later, he had walked back to the pits.

For some time now, McLaren has made all its body panels and many other parts entirely from carbon fibre, pre-impregnated with resin. It is easy to mould into complex forms but after curing in the oven it emerges very stiff – ideal for thin panels that will not distort under aerodynamic load, as well as for highly stressed pieces such as wings and their supports. Even the high-pressure air bottle for the engine starter is made from this weight-saving material.

Other teams – ATS, Brabham, Ferrari, Lotus, Toleman, for example – have also made extensive use of carbon fire, using varying methods and combinations with other materials. Some – Williams and Tyrrell – remained faithful to aluminium and honeycomb sandwich for the construction of monocoques, arguing that repairs were easier, as were changes to the front suspension mounting points, should a redesign prove necessary. Williams, though, was an early user of carbon-fibre wings, camouflaging the fact with paint, and Tyrrell has them too.

However, carbon fibre tubs have proved remarkably easy to repair, and maintain their rigidity – and thus their useful life – much better than aluminium ones. During one period of twenty-seven months, when Williams had fifteen monocoques built, McLaren procured only eight.

Remarkably little metal – engine, radiators, gearbox, suspension – is now used. And one prediction is that carbon fibre will largely replace the heat-treated high-grade steel used for suspension wishbones.

Already it is being increasingly used for brakes, with ventilated discs made of carbon fibres placed three-dimensionally in a graphite matrix and pads of similar material. The give-away is when a car's brakes can be seen glowing cherry red, even in bright sunshine.

Friction with these brakes is generally better, so the driver needs to apply less pressure on the pedal. And there is a considerable weight saving – 10 to 12 kg, compared with conventional iron discs.

However, careful attention must be paid to cooling, using scoops to force air into the disc centre and then out radially through its internal vents. If ambient temperatures are high, carbon discs may burn, either producing carbon dust or vaporizing. The problem is that racing car brakes are applied so hard and so frequently that they never cool down properly. The friction of carbon brakes can be very sensitive to temperatures as well as to the oxidation that occurs on the working surfaces.

There is an amazing difference in cost, too. Whereas a set of four ventilated iron discs costs about £500 and lasts through two or three grands prix, requiring only new pads, a set of carbon discs and pads may have to be discarded after qualifying and certainly by the end of one race, at a cost of £2500 to £4000.

Some would argue that it is better to seek weight savings elsewhere on the car than to put up with the teething troubles of carbon brakes. Others are convinced that these will be overcome fairly quickly, that prices will come down, and that, within ten years, carbon brakes will become commonplace on road cars.

'I'm going to plug away until we just bolt them on, and they are all we ever think about using,' says Barnard, who confesses to being one of the world's great optimists. 'And they are so much lighter than iron discs that unsprung weight ceases to be a problem, so we can leave the brakes where they are most convenient – inside the wheels.'

Formula 1 engineers make extensive use of computers; for instance, they can analyse structures so as to get the most strength for the least weight, check out ideas for suspension geometry, and greatly reduce the time taken to tool up for new design ideas.

Ferrari builds its monocoques from composites of several materials, using each where its properties will be most effective: glass for robust but flexible surfaces; carbon fibre for extremely stiff reinforcements; Kevlar, a lightweight and good all-round performer with tremendous impact resistance; and Nomex honeycomb light and fire-resistent.

Stress paths in the monocoque structure are predicted by computer, and can then be seen as a three-dimensional model on a video screen or are reproduced on paper by an automated draughting table. In this way 'cloth' pre-impregnated with resin, can be chosen with a preponderance of this fibre type or that, woven in the appropriate direction.

These cloths are then laid into a mould with a core of honeycomb and additional strands of carbon fibre where extra strength is required. Baking then takes place in an autoclave – high pressure oven – to ensure that everything remains precisely in position during the curing process.

The result is a one-piece monocoque, complete with integral outer skin, bulkheads, even non-metallic engine mountings and suspension pick-up points, ready to be built up into a racing car. And it takes half as many man-hours to make as a conventional aluminium tub.

Eventually all monocoques will have to be produced in this way, says Harvey Postlethwaite. 'There doesn't exist another way of achieving the stiffness and performance of this type of structure. Such is the pace of competition that Formula One has taken up what is really aerospace technology. And we have already outdistanced the aerospace companies, at least in the boldness and scope of what we are doing. We came later, but I think we are running faster.'

The process is bound to go much further, benefiting from Fiat's much-publicized know-how in robotics. The cars are relentlessly becoming more complicated, tricky to build and maintain. Yet the demands of competition put great emphasis on the ability to respond quickly, to try new ideas. 'If another team comes up with something that appears to really work, you must be in a position to investigate it, to use it yourself,' explains Postlethwaite.

By 1984–5, Ferrari will have a system in which engineering drawings will be translated by computer on to tape to control a robot machining an aerodynamic form three-dimensionally. Tooling can be shaped directly on this, ready to mould the part. This could reduce the time taken between making a drawing and attaching the completed part to a car from three months to two weeks.

More often than not, grand prix drivers are employed by teams not based in their native countries. This internationalism is seen among designers, too. It took Postlethwaite, an Englishman, to bring chassis design up to the mark at Ferrari, an Italian team whose main strengths lay in engines and reliability. John Barnard spent time in America, designing to win the Indianapolis 500. Gerard Ducarouge worked first for teams in his native France, then for Alfa Romeo in Italy, and latterly for Lotus in Britain. In fact his efforts for Lotus are remembered as one of the big Formula 1 achievements of 1983, though the man himself is quick to point out that it was teamwork.

In the aftermath of founder Colin Chapman's death, Lotus's showing had been uninspired. Ducarouge joined the team at the beginning of June, recruited by team manager Peter Warr to devise a competitive car. The decision was made to dispense with the overweight 93T built around a 250-litre fuel tank to enable its Renault turbo engine to run a full race distance – before refuelling pit stops came into vogue. Instead, Ducarouge and the design staff would pen a smaller, nimbler replacement, based partly on the Cosworth-engine car with which Elio de Angelis won the 1982 Austrian Grand Prix by a whisker.

The target was the British Grand Prix, only five weeks ahead. Ducarouge and the design team managed to complete the drawings two days early, in less than a fortnight. Their scheme was for a car with new suspension, gearbox casings and bodywork – only the Renault engine and the outer skin of the monocoque remained from previous types. Working two shifts, seven days a week, the team managed to complete a first 94T by 10 July, and it was tested briefly, first at Lotus's Hethel track and then the Donington Park circuit. Within the week, two of these cars were on the grid for the start of the grand prix at Silverstone where Nigel Mansell finished fourth.

In this rush to recovery, Lotus avoided a pitfall which has caught others. For some teams, creating a succession of cars has been a favourite pastime. 'If they're not competitive, then they go and make a new car. They don't bloody know why the other one didn't go. They just know they're going to make a new one,' observes John Barnard. 'And they could quite possibly build in the same problems.'

There is no point, he asserts, in completely re-engineering a car – unless it can be made lighter or stiffer, or there is some other definite performance gain to be had through, for example, a new monocoque with smaller fuel tank.

'If you can't come up with a completely revolutionary idea or some really good new overall design package, then you might as well get the car ready early and have time for plenty of testing,' says Barnard. Also, it helps clear the designer's mind as he casts around for his next breakthrough.

'The difficult part is that you can sit there, hands behind your head for two days, staring at the drawing board. That's one of the reasons I'm glad I work in a closed office,' he laughs. 'Otherwise people walk by, and they think: "He hasn't done a thing, produced anything." They don't say it, but I know what they're thinking.'

In all this, the driver represents the bottom line. First consideration is his safety. Frank Williams is very matter-of-fact about this: 'We – like nearly all other teams – are very sincere in our desires not to hurt our drivers. They are a big investment, and it would reflect badly on the company and motor racing. We take it seriously.'

The rule book, however, is not necessarily the best way or definition of making a car safe, considers Williams. 'Speaking for this company, our designer, Patrick Head, is not obsessive about his safety requirements, but he takes it most personally. It is his car, his reputation, his career. I needn't say more.'

Certainly, much has been achieved in this direction. There are those who feel that it has reached a point where, to build in another 5 per cent safety margin would be an exercise of disproportionate dimensions. More attention should be focused on impact absorption at circuits, they say.

In the end, it must be the driver who is best placed to assess the risks. 'You soon learn that, if you're going to do anything along those lines, you must start right at the bottom and work your way up,' says Barnard. 'It is not just anybody who can step out of a road car and into a Formula One car.'

So there is little point, he believes, in driving his own creations. 'Sure. I could manage one hundred and fifty mph, maybe one hundred and eighty mph in a straight line. But, as for lapping a circuit within ten seconds of any F1 driver's time, impossible. Forget it.

'Unless I could get within two seconds of their times, it would achieve nothing – except give me a thrill, I suppose. To get any real knowledge of what the car is doing, I have to feel it through the driver, sense exactly what he is telling me.

'With experience, you reach the point where, if he says

33

the car is not responding to the wheel, he means it had gone five yards deeper into a corner than he thought it ought to before turning in. That's understeer. It's not that he arrived at the corner, and sat there twiddling the wheel for an infinity before the thing responded.'

It takes time to learn. No two drivers are exactly identical in style, in their feel for the car or the ways in which they convey the car's behaviour to the designer. McLaren's Niki Lauda and John Watson were a case in point, distinctly different.

There is a lot of psychology involved here. The set-up of a car might well be the one that is theoretically best for achieving quickest progress through a corner. But if it has a little wiggle and the driver thinks that it is not responding to his every twitch, he will feel uncomfortable, and will not be as fast. However, once the car *feels* as though he can do anything he wants with it, the lap times will very likely start falling.

'Niki pictures an arc through a corner in his mind, and he wants the car to follow that path precisely. In other words, when he comes up to a corner, he likes to turn the steering and have the front wheels take the car exactly where he has pointed them,' explains Barnard.

'John is very different. He likes the car to be very stable at the rear so that he can do what he likes with the steering, and he won't lose the back end, spin. He will come hard into a corner, get right into it, and then give the steering a big whang. If the thing is set up correctly, the front end will tuck in, and that's virtually his corner. He now has the car pointed in another direction, and can put his foot down, balancing it out of the corner on the throttle and by making small corrections with the steering.'

Generally, the differences between these two men's cars were achieved through aerodynamic means. Usually, Watson prefers less downforce on the front than Lauda, and more on the rear. Then, depending on the circuit, the ratio of front-to-rear spring stiffnesses might be changed to retrieve some sensitivity. With less downforce and softer springs on the front, Watson got a less-precise car – something he could be more aggressive with, yet not be worried by.

What, out on the circuit, would be of only mild concern to the Niki Laudas and John Watsons of this world would scare the pants of most of the rest of us, leaving us gibbering.

Such is the pile-driver performance of the Formula 1 car that anyone who tackles it successfully is functioning on the outer limits, both physically and mentally, egged on by torrents of adrenalin.

Where even the most exotic of roadgoing supercars leave off, the grand prix car takes over. Even if you have experienced the full performance of Jaguar's superb XJ-S HE coupé, one of the world's fastest road cars, it is difficult to imagine the grand prix driver's very different realm.

The Jaguar weighs in at 1755 kg and has 295 bhp maximum power at 5500 rpm from its 5345 cc V12 engine. Two important statistics here are that this car has 0,16 bhp per kg of its weight, and the engine achives 55 bhp per litre of its cubic capacity.

For the purposes of this comparison a Formula 1 car weighs 650 kg, also with fuel aboard. It has maybe 750 bhp at 11,500 rpm from its 1500 cc V6 turbo-charged engine. That means 1,15 bhp per kg – more than seven times the power-to-weight ratio of the Jaguar – and the engine gives 500 bhp per litre – nearly ten times better.

To help provide the traction to cope with its immense power-to-weight ratio, the weight of the Formula 1 car is distributed about 40:60 front-to-rear while the rear tyres are of large diameter and with extra width to create bigger contact patches. Much less uncompromising, the Jaguar's tyres are the same size all round, and its weight is distributed 55:45 for stability to reassure the less-skilled driver. The heavier end of a car will always want to get to the front – if it is already there, the problem does not arise.

The Jaguar is a 240 km/h car – rivetingly rapid, even on a straight stretch of autobahn when there are no other cars to contend with – and exacts all the concentration you can muster, requiring you to anticipate very far ahead. It accelerates from a standstill to 100 km/h in less than seven seconds, half the time it takes an MG Metro, and to 160 km/h in about 16 seconds. If you over-ride the automatic transmission manually, it shifts from first to second gear at 112 km/h and into top at 190 km/h. All you have to do is grit your teeth, and keep that pedal on the right pressed to the floor. No trouble at all.

Now picture yourself at the wheel of a Formula 1 car. You wonder what on earth induced you to be strapped into this thing, like a monkey in a rocket. You nod dumbly at the instructions being given by your minders, feel the palms of your hands grow damp inside those thick gauntlets, and try to choke back a very dry throat.

Switching on brings a whirring of fuel pumps. This is followed by the shriek of the high-pressure air starter, plugged into the back of the car by a mechanic. With luck, the engine whoops into life immediately, giving you three very potent messages: strong vibrations through the thighs, posterior and back; a loud roaring, just behind and definitely audible, despite wearing ear plugs, Balaclava and crash helmet; and the way the rev counter needle zaps back and forth, like a lizard's tongue, around its dial.

The beast is alive all around you, menacing and raring to go. If the engine is already warm and all systems appear to be functioning properly, there is no reason to hang about. Problem number one is to get the thing to move at all, and there are only limited opportunities to do this before the engine overheats while at a standstill.

A Formula 1 engine doesn't really get into its comfortable operating range until maybe 7000 rpm, sometimes quite a bit more. So to get away from the line without stalling you need to be bold, bloody and resolute.

Unlike a road car, the clutch is either in or out, and bites fiercely. The pedal is quite stiff, its travel is short, and there is a lazy grinding sound from the back of the car as you snick the gear lever into first with a firm hand. Keep those revs up, and go for it. Don't slip the clutch for too long or you'll cook it. Progressively feed in the clutch while you squeeze on more power, balancing the revs around 7000.

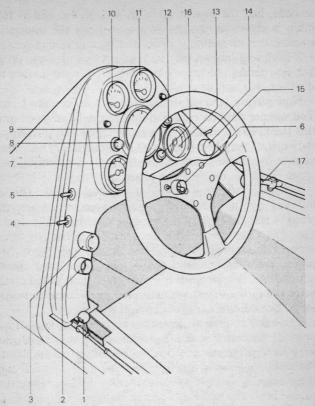

Controls in the cockpit of the McLaren MP4 are typical of the breed:

1   rear anti roll bar adjuster
2   driver operated fire extinguisher button
3   engine boost pressure control
4   switch – rear light for running in poor visibility
5   switch – for reading temperatures of left or right cooling systems
6   ignition cut off switch
7   combined twin needle gauge for fuel pressure and oil pressure
8   alternator charging light
9   rev counter
10 water temperature gauge
11 oil temperature gauge
12 oil pressure warning light
13 boost pressure gauge
14 electric fuel pump switch
15 brake balance adjuster
16 error lights for electronic engine management system
17 gear lever

Your head is snapped back with one and a half times the force of gravity. The car fishtails as the back wheels spin while you floor the throttle pedal. You fight to keep in a straight line with corrections on the steering, and the world becomes a wild blur.

The projectile lunges forward to 120 to 130 km/h in three seconds. The engine is fluffing – it's running against the electronic rev-limiter, fitted so you won't blow it up. It's time to bang the lever into second, flooring the throttle once more: 160 km/h comes up a couple of seconds later, and you should be ready to snatch third gear at 190 km/h.

Ten seconds away from the line, you hit 230 km/h, and grab fourth gear. This is more like it. Now you're getting up to racing speed. The adrenalin is really flowing, your mind is clear as crystal, working so fast the world seems almost to be in slow motion.

Zap it into fifth at 280 km/h, and on she sings to 320 km/h and more. That Jaguar is long gone, a chariot for mere mortals, but you are with the gods.

It's thirsty work for both driver and car – 4 mpg if you're to finish the race on a tankful. Maybe, back down on earth, the Jaguar's 20 mpg is more like it. But John Barnard is right: 'Seven-hundred plus horsepower in five hundred and forty kilos is pretty exciting, isn't it? And two hundred mph plus is beeloody quick.'

2
SHOWMAN

Diversity is the spice of grand prix life. Contrasts, seen from the outside, are in shapes, colours, sponsors' logos, sounds. Observed in close-up, the kaleidoscope of organizations and personalities behind the cars is yet more diverse, as are the paths they have followed to get where they are today.

Of the sixteen teams battling for places on the starting grid, eleven are based in Britain – mostly within an hour of London – three in northern Italy, and two in France – one outside Paris, and the other in Vichy.

Many of the team bosses have themselves driven in races, with varying degrees of success, before applying their talents to organization and to putting others behind the wheel. The hobby became a job. Youthful enthusiasm for the thrill of speed led to serious big business. It is a position which has been hard-won, and is jealously guarded.

Asked what advice he would give to a young man aspiring to run his own team, Frank Williams responds decisively: 'I wouldn't give anybody any advice on how to do that because he might be a competitor in a few years. If he's clever – if he's the right sort of individual – he won't need much advice. He'll make it.'

Williams Grand Prix Engineering is one of the slickest, best respected outfits in the Circus. Big sponsorship money makes it all look easy. The results speak for themselves – World Constructors' Championships in 1980 and 1981, and Drivers' Championships for Alan Jones in 1980 and Keke Rosberg in 1982. After Rosberg's fifth place in the 1983 South African Grand Prix, first time out with Honda turbo-power, there was obviously more to come.

It was 1969 when Williams first came into the grand prix arena with a Brabham, driven by his close friend Piers Courage who finished second in the Monaco and United States races. This encouraging beginning was to turn to dust. Courage was killed during the Dutch Grand Prix the following year.

For a long time Williams laboured on with insufficient budgets, running other constructors' cars and hardly setting the world on fire.

'I never had the feeling that I definitely *would* make it,' he remembers. 'But it was unthinkable that I should go back and start something else because I was doing what I wanted to do, and enjoying it. Even the struggle – and there was a struggle – had a great deal of pleasure because the end product was racing. And that's what I adored.

'I suppose, human nature being what it is, one is reluctant to give up halfway down the road. You want to get to the end, and prove that you can or can't do it.'

The present organization emerged in 1977. Patrick Head, now Williams's junior partner in the business, started work on designing a car for the following season. At the same time, Williams made the first contacts that were to lead to a long and mutually beneficial relationship with Saudi Arabia, a prize that is the envy of his rivals.

Saudia, the country's national airline, was the first big name to appear on the Williams cars. Then came the imprints of the city of Riyadh; Dallah Avco, an airport maintenance firm; Baroom, cement and steel traders; Bin Laden, roadbuilders; Siyanco, engineers; TAG, the Techniques d'Avant-Garde group. This Saudi cash fuelled the drive for success, and helped attract other backers such as Leyland Vehicles, Austin Rover Group, ICI Record Fibres, and Denim – a fragrance for men. And, latterly, space has been allocated *gratis* to the symbol of the Save the Children Fund.

Patrick Head and Williams share the running of the firm between them. Head controls design, the factory and testing – anything that results in hardware being produced. Williams's responsibilities are more ephemeral but no less vital.

They range across general management and leadership, selecting drivers, to the effort that goes into finding the sponsors who finance the operation. 'It's the most important single requirement of the whole company, of course, and it means that we are always able to pay our bills,' says Williams.

'Costs have gone up almost out of proportion since Renault put the squeeze on and really began to spend money on racing in late 1979 to 1980. Fiat matched them. Then Alfa Romeo came along. And so did BMW. Regrettably the turbo-charged engine took off, and that alone has pushed up costs enormously.

'While those teams are involved – and it's not going to change – you can do one of two things. Complain, do nothing, and be pushed and squeezed to the back of the grid and eventually out of racing. Or take them on.'

Hence the partnership with Honda, which first manifested itself in the second half of 1983. Rather than become a 'client' buying engines from Alfa Romeo, BMW or Renault, Williams preferred to hang back for twelve months. 'We decided to wait and marry into a major motor car manufacturer which was serious about winning, had the financial and technical resources to win, and therefore would save us the enormous cost of paying for our own turbo engines.'

Another bonus that accrues to Williams as a front-runner is that his is one of the few teams 'favoured' by Goodyear and gets all tyres supplied at no charge. This must be worth at least $1 million a year.

Putting together the rest of the act is Williams' financial responsibility. This is a daunting task, even with those first two heavy numbers already accounted for. In addition to the cost of tyres and engines, Williams admits to a 1984 budget of between $6.4 million and $6.7 million. Of this about $2 million is allocated directly or indirectly to research, development and track testing, a measure of the competitive pressures of the sport.

The overheads of the Didcot factory, plus the eighty-eight people on the payroll, account for $1.8 million. The most expensive employee is Keke Rosberg, his world champion status giving him the clout to renegotiate for the full million-dollar rate. And a further $1 million goes on carting team members, cars and all the other paraphernalia to sixteen races around the world.

It costs about $250,000 to construct a car, though it is difficult to put a price on such a thing because of the changes that are continually being made.

Income comes in from contract engineering work (undertaken on the team's high-precision machine tools), sponsorship, and prize moneys (about one-tenth of the total).

Williams's successes in involving first Saudi and then Japanese business interests with his team make him a pioneer in the sponsor-finding business. It takes, he says, a bit of imagination, some logic, and a lot of determination. For it is never easy to sell something new.

'The most difficult part was selling motor racing in Saudi Arabia. And, even now, I have only scratched the surface. A more organized person than me, who could spend a lot more time – six to nine months a year – in the kingdom and had a press and television campaign to generate interest, could make really large inroads into the funds available there.

'What has happened is that, not because of me but because of the team's success, mileage has been generated by itself. And that has helped. If we had not been successful, we would not have lasted very long in Saudi Arabia. So I'm saying you have to really go for it.'

It was rather different when it came to forging the Japanese connection. Honda was already in Formula 2 racing, and had had previous Formula 1 experience from 1963 to 1968. 'All we determined there was that, for technical and commercial reasons, we should be involved with Honda, rather than any one other company. Honda is resolved to race, and has terrific technical capability. And we would have an entrée to an extremely rich and export-oriented country, of which the biggest markets are the USA and Europe.'

In pursuit of these goals, Williams travels enormously,

some say excessively. 'I am a salesman. My prime job is to sell motor racing to our sponsors who are our customers,' he says. 'All of that is personal contact which means frequent visits to Saudi Arabia, mainland Europe and the United States – plus all the grands prix and some of our extensive testing programme. I like moving – I couldn't do a sedentary regular office job.'

It is just as well that he is an aviation fanatic, fascinated by aircraft as well as the technology and the organization behind them. For each year he spends at least 150 days out of Britain, logging about 500 hours in the air, getting there and back.

Fifteen times a year, and most frequently during the British winter, Williams goes to Saudi Arabia to husband his various sponsorships. He has dealt with most of his contacts for a number of years, and knows them well. 'I wouldn't say we are close, but the relationships are certainly cordial and informal – except with one or two of the most senior princes. Then it is most formal.'

He agrees that his reputation for leading an ascetic life-style may be helpful in the Middle East. But he is quick to point out that his neither smoking nor drinking is not high-principled self-denial. 'It's just that I never actually get round to enjoying the taste of one or the other.'

Nor would such indulgences really be compatible with the 80 to 100 km he runs each week, often round race circuits. 'I'm by no means an athlete, but I enjoy keeping fit. I'm vain enough to know that it helps, and I intend to live for a long time. Also, it makes a person just a little more remarkable. And I'm trying to sell something – including the personalities in the team – that is better than anything else.'

Somewhat surprisingly, then, Williams does not regard himself as an especially competitive person. However, he concedes that it hurts when his team doesn't win. 'I enjoy winning quite a lot. But Patrick Head is manifestly more competitive, in that, when he doesn't win, he becomes very badly behaved. I am older than him and wiser, I think, and perhaps I control my emotions a little better than him.'

The friendship between the two partners is part of their success. 'We all operate under a great deal of stress and strain – perhaps that's laying it on a bit thick, but we are certainly under pressure. Therefore, the chemistry is very important. Although we're two opposites, two different people, we have the same goal, and that helps.

'Patrick and I have our differences. Once every three months, we have a major row which, in a way, helps. And, next day' – snap of the fingers – 'that was just yesterday. Forget it.'

Race day is always a bit nerve-racking, even for an old hand. And winning, apparently, is never quite what it seems. 'Once the chequered flag goes down, it takes several hours for the adrenalin to disperse, for you to relax, and get back to normal. There is one hour of scrutineering after the race, and this can be agonizing if somebody is trying to make trouble for you.

'Next morning, it's just a bit of history. And thirteen days later, you're going to be exposed to winning or losing once again. So that becomes your prime preoccupation.'

In a way, it is easier clambering to the top than staying there. The Williams team began to show its mettle in 1979, when Alan Jones and Clay Regazzoni won five races between them during the second half of the season. This steamrolling momentum continued into the following year with Jones and Carlos Reutemann sharing seven wins.

Maintaining motivation is not as difficult as one might think, however – for Williams, at any rate. 'Once you have tasted success, you realize you want it very badly. Also, being successful does open a lot of doors financially. When you're on top, it's much easier to raise sponsorship than when you're sliding.

'From the time we hit the jackpot in mid-1979, we have been consistently at the top. I think I'm right in saying we have been there for longer than any other team at any other period of time. Most teams get on top for one or two years, then slide again.

'This has been the case with McLaren, Ferrari and Lotus. The only other team that approaches us is Brabham. They

44

were at the front in 1980, 1981 and, you could argue, 1982 – though they finished almost no races. They were certainly right there in 1983. That takes a *lot* of doing.

'But, what you have to remember is that Keke Rosberg won the 1982 championship, as well as most of his 1983 points, with a hundred and fifty to two hundred horsepower handicap.'

Picking the right drivers has been a key part of the team's championship-winning consistency. 'You always know who is good and coming up because you're around all the time, and you come to have a pretty good feel for who can get the job done. Patrick also has his own ideas, and we always consult. Sometimes we disagree. But, all of that said and all arguments aside, the fact is we were lucky with Alan Jones. I didn't know he was *that* good.

'We were lucky with Keke, too. I knew he was quick, but I didn't think he was that consistent, which he is. He's been off the road, broken a rear wing, once in two years. His car control is phenomenal, and he's arguably the fastest racing driver on the track. All the other drivers speak of him with somewhere between respect and awe – there's no doubt about it.'

There is no time to go talent scouting as such. But Williams and his competitors keep a weather eye on the results of the lesser formulae, and know who is consisently winning in a tough school where they have to be damn good to get ahead. Few of these hopefuls turn up at Didcot to plead for a ride in the big time. The cleverer ones know that results, not talk, are what count.

At this juncture Williams tells his mayfly parable: 'They mate above the sea, and drop two thousand five hundred eggs to the bottom which stay there for three hundred and sixty-four days. On the last day they come to the surface, and two thousand four hundred and ninety-nine get eaten by the fish. One or two get to the top, then live for twenty-four hours. It's the law of Nature, and there's no good in worrying about it. Wait for them – the good ones will get to the top.'

If he can bring in some cash – his own or a sponsor's –

and pass muster with the independent-minded Ken Tyrrell, doyen of the British team proprietors, the aspiring star may have a better chance of getting a start there than with, say, Williams.

For Tyrrell and for other teams this has been one means of survival – to stay in the hunt – after losing major sponsorship. This bodyblow can hit the best of them, usually resulting from an imbalance in the complex market forces at work within the sport. It could be that a sponsor decides to pull out, having achieved specific marketing aims. Or it could be a switch of allegiance as a result of nationalistic political machinations.

It may only take a surplus or a deficit of two or three sponsors wanting to be in the sport at any one period to dramatically affect the market price – what even a front-line team can command, and thus have at its disposal in the pursuit of success.

The Tyrrell Racing Organisation prospered from the time of its Formula 1 debut in 1968, its place assured by backing from Elf, the French petroleum giant. But the days of this support became numbered with the appearance of state-owned Renault on the scene in 1977. Hence Tyrrell's subsequent liaisons, first with Citicorp, then with Candy domestic appliances.

Then world recession began to squeeze sponsors' spending power, and the team was faced with lean seasons in 1981 and 1982. There was only one choice: to continue operating on next to nothing, hoping to stay in the market until further solid backing could be found once more; or to go away.

'How do you manage when you haven't got a sponsor?' Ken Tyrrell puts the question, and answers: 'With difficulty.'

In 1981, he kept going on less than $1.5 million. 'That year, we didn't bother with a budget because it wasn't necessary. If you don't have it, you don't spend it. But the trouble is you have to cut so many corners, stop doing anything that isn't absolutely necessary.

'The first thing that goes is testing. Next you chop your

labour force by ten. This means you can't produce bits for the car quickly enough to go testing anyway.

'Then you run your engines for one thousand miles instead of five hundred miles between rebuilds, make them go twice as far, take a risk on it, and hope like hell this is a viable economy. Sometimes you get a blow-up. Sometimes you don't.

'Next you take the minimum number of people to each race, and stay in the cheapest hotels you can find. We dispensed with our motor home and, instead, my wife fed the mechanics, using a kitchen table carried in the back of the transporter.'

To some degree, the team was able to live off the fat of previous years, dig into reserves. And there were a few *ad hoc* sponsorship deals – for one race or maybe three – to keep ticking over.

There was prize money too, relatively insignificant, but not to be sniffed at when every $3000 that comes in counts.

'If you had to go on like that for two or three years, you would be finished – simply because your performance would be so lousy that nobody would want to be involved in sponsoring you. To a certain extent, that's what happened. We had no sponsorship, so we had to cut back. The performance went right down, and we knew that was going to happen.'

A phlegmatic nature helps when riding such a storm. 'For some reason which I don't understand, I don't get highs when we're doing well. For the same reason probably, I don't experience the lows that other people have, I suppose.

'I don't feel I can go around, waving my arms about when we've won a grand prix, because that is what our sponsor pays us to do. But I am very disappointed when we perform badly because I don't think we ought to.'

Life for Tyrrell brightened once more when Michele Alboreto won the Las Vegas Grand Prix at the end of 1982. Then Ken and son Bob secured 1983 backing – a retainer plus performance-related bonuses – from Benetton, the Italian clothing group, repaying it with Alboreto's win in

Detroit, said to be worth $50 million in coast-to-coast US television exposure.

From the team's point of view, a sponsor should be prepared to put his cash 'up-front', and not make it conditional upon results. Explains Bob Tyrrell, whose main task is to bring in the backing for the team: 'If you don't have the budget, you're not going to get the results. It's a bloody difficult concept to put across, and quite unlike other sports. But there is no getting round it. If we have a bigger budget than Williams or Lotus have then we stand a far better chance than them of winning the championship.'

The bare minimum for a two-car team, buying in turbo engines, is reckoned to be $5 million for 1984, though $8 million is the sum more likely to give a smaller team the muscle it now needs to tackle the continental big spenders.

Ken Tyrrell, however, remains unimpressed by these Goliaths. 'Small teams have always blown off the big teams because they can adapt, change quickly. They don't have to hold a board meeting to decide to do something.

'Look at Brabham winning the 1983 championship. They just have a little factory up the road at Chessington, and employ sixty people. But Ferrari and Renault each employs several hundred. One is owned by Fiat, the other by the French government, and Alfa Romeo is owned by the Italian government. And look at the money they are spending – twenty to thirty million dollars a year.

'There is no way we ought to be beating those people. But Piquet is 1983 World Champion – so another small team has won again. All that money poured into the Renault effort by the French government is to no avail.

'If they don't win in 1984, they never will. No way are they going to be competitive in 1985 when fuel tanks are reduced to a hundred and ninety-five litres. They'll pull out then, and concentrate on the Indianapolis Five Hundred or something. Somebody on the Renault board will say enough is enough.'

Ken Tyrrell is right on target when he points out the disquiet of some teams about the new rules that ban mid-race refuelling and will progressively reduce tank size over two years. The aim is to curtail the race speeds of turbo cars, by forcing them to run less thirstily and less powerfully – with the boost turned down.

The view is, naturally, rather different from Renault's end of the spectrum. Team manager Jean Sage says there are 180 people on his payroll, but declines to disclose the budget. All he will admit is that the annual cost of Formula 1 to Renault is about the same as the amount spent on introducing a new car model to the media, dealers and public. He complains equably: 'Formula One is the top formula for racing. It has nothing to do with fuel consumption. If you don't allow technology and research for grand prix racing to advance, it doesn't interest so much the engineers and the public.

'We agree to limit the power of the engine. But, please, no fuel consumption regulations. That will be very dangerous because you will have very quick cars during qualifying, each looking for one clear lap. And, in the race, you'll have cars with maybe three hundred horsepower less than in practice.

'That will mean two different types of engine, so the drivers will have to adjust to a big change in the car, and the cost will be doubled. Also, I think it will be very boring to see people running out of petrol on the last lap. For the sport this will be very bad.

'These silly regulations are really crazy. In 1983, the Le Mans twenty-four hour race was a disaster with only eighty thousand spectators instead of two hundred and fifty thousand. What we saw on the straights were cars running at a hundred kilometres per hour to finish their lap because they had no more fuel. And there were other cars travelling at three hundred and seventy. The difference between them was terrible.'

Whatever the politics that continue to surround this issue, Renault Sport was committed to Formula 1 in 1984, regardless of whether or not it won the 1983 world championship it had striven so hard for; and it had been told it would carry on in 1985.

'But anything can happen – a very big European economic crisis, for example,' cautions Sage. 'This could stop everything, and other companies, too. However, Renault has found that Formula One is one of the best forms of promotion and publicity available now in the world. And, I think if we were to stop, it would be only to do something better than Formula One.'

In any event, a huge organization such as Regie Renault – with worldwide ramifications and following the dictates of corporate good housekeeping – must make this sort of decision well in advance. Budgetary commitments are made six months before the beginning of the next season, a luxury the less cumbersome privateer teams would no doubt revel in. In July 1983, for instance, everything was put in the pipeline for engines to be used the following year.

Renault does not reveal what it spends on its Formula 1 programme – 'for social reasons' – but there is an admission that its budget is comparable with Ferrari's. Quite possibly, no one within the organization has a very precise idea of the true figure. It would be one thing if it had to start from scratch, go out and buy everything in the shops. It is quite another matter when a team has direct access to a large car manufacturer's extensive research and other facilities already in existence for the development of new road cars for series production.

To everyone's relief, the principle of moving wooden dollars around within the corporation can be applied. This way, those sweaty moments – when directors have to be asked to sign cheques for huge amounts of real money – can usually be avoided. Instead a nod and a wink between department heads is sufficient to set things rolling. And, with a bit of good will, other departments – such as advertising, marketing, publicity and engineering research – can be persuaded that it is in their interests to bear a share of the action.

The rationale for Renault's Formula 1 involvement runs much deeper than the assumption that to go racing is a most cost-effective means of projecting a young 'high-tech' image on television than buying a similar amount of time to screen expensive commercials. The team works very closely with the research department, drawing on its know-how in areas such as turbo-charging, brakes, metallurgy, gearboxes and aerodynamics. In return, the pressures of race competition help accelerate the learning curves of those who are painstakingly concerned with less glamorous lines of investigation.

It is this intellectual stimulus that is as valuable as anything that comes out of Formula 1 – even if its practical application is not always immediately apparent.

3

PAYMASTER

August 1965 was a significant date for motor racing and other sports. It marked the deadline for the disappearance of cigarette commercials from British independent television. The tobacco companies had been spending about £8 million a year (£46 million at 1983 prices) on TV advertising – 44 per cent of their total budgets. Cigar and pipe tobacco commercials were allowed to continue, but this left nearly £6 million (£32 million today) burning a hole in the companies' pocket. And they, quite understandably, sought ways to make up for lost impact.

For motor racing, the tobacco companies did not manifest themselves immediately. It was not until 1968 that Colin Chapman, ever the innovator – and not just technically – sent shock waves along the pit road when his Lotus cars appeared in the red, white and gold colours of Player's Gold Leaf cigarettes.

Traditionalists were horrified at this American-style commercialization. Up to that point, backing for participants in the sport had come from within the motoring world – from car and component manufacturers plus the oil, tyre, brake and spark plug companies. Esso had previously been a big contributor to Lotus, while Shell did much the same for Ferrari.

There were many who thought that the cars should continue to be painted in the customary national colours alone – British racing green (the precise shade of which was a talking point for pedants), Italian red, French blue, German silver.

Endowing cars with ludicrous names – 'Dean Van Lines Special', 'Simoniz Special', or 'Sugaripe Prune Special' –

was something those brash Yanks did for their incomprehensible and tedious oval races, such as the Indianapolis 500. If they vulgarized the sport even further by paying telephone-number prize money, that was up to them. But we didn't need that form of intrusion at grands prix where European gentlemen raced. Greaseball mechanics were sometimes allowed to go, too, so long as they didn't become too uppity. It was most important to have the right crowd and no crowding.

This fellow Chapman – a bit pushy, don't you know – must have caught the disease when he set off in pursuit of the big money at Indy, creating cars to be driven by Graham Hill and Jim Clark, and entered under outlandish names such as 'American Red Ball Special' and 'STP Gas Treatment Special' – all just too ghastly to contemplate.

What had been a distant cause for condescending mirth or distaste was now a reason for shocked horror. And its ramifications were to go way beyond any that may have been foreseen at the time.

First to follow the Gold Leaf lead with another high-profile sponsorship in Formula 1 was not a tobacco company, but Yardley, the cosmetics firm, seeking to broaden its appeal to include contemporary youth. The Yardley colours appeared on the BRM cars, at a cost of £40,000 a season, in 1970 and 1971, and were then transferred to McLaren for 1972–73.

The Marlboro brand name replaced Yardley, first at BRM for two seasons and then, from 1974, at McLaren where it has been ever since.

Philip Morris's arrival in Formula 1 in 1972 was also marked by the formation of the Marlboro World Championship Team, an umbrella for the brand's personal sponsorship of individual drivers in grands prix, Formula 2, Formula 3, and motorcycle racing. Use of sponsorship to spread the Marlboro word has progressively been expanded to cover championships for the lesser formulae, as well as individual circuits and races. And the company remains 'totally committed to motor sport as an image building and promotional platform that has proved successful in terms of both visibility and awareness'.

The impact of sponsorship in shaping the burgeoning, if turbulent, fortunes of the sport has undeniably been immense. To begin with, it has helped popularize grand prix racing to the point where, in twenty years, the number of events on the calendar has grown from ten to sixteen, and there is pressure for more. And the sport is one of the hottest properties in television entertainment.

Annually, more than 650 hours of live or deferred race coverage is broadcast to a viewership of 935 million people in 41 countries. Additional material, such as documentaries and interviews with drivers, is watched by more than 201 million, while newscasts on grands prix reach 10,400 million people in 76 countries. In Britain alone, the figures are 20-odd hours of race coverage, watched by an average audience of more than 4 million per broadcast. Also, the sport is covered regularly in 97 of Europe's leading daily newspapers with a combined readership of 113 million.

A big factor in this has been the simple logic which suggests that, if a sponsor spends a large sum of money for the privilege of having his name painted on a car or a badge sewn on a tennis player's frock, he is mad not to put further cash to work telling the world about it.

Who is good at telling the world? The media. Public relations activity to attract media interest can range from a £250,000 thrash in the Albert Hall with free-flowing bubbly and superstar cabaret – for the announcement of a new Lotus, in case you missed it – to discreet arrangements for an exclusive interview with a driver.

Making the most of a sponsorship investment means bringing into play everything from public relations through advertising of successes or associations with teams to point-of-sale material in every kind of shop, and entertaining trade customers at races.

All the time the sport is being given the big build-up in every area of society by sponsors anxious to reinforce the excitement, glamour and machismo of grand prix racing and to enhance the benefits of being associated with it.

Ironically, then, the big commercial interests which pay so handsomely for the right to be involved are also largely the creators of the tiger they are so keen to ride.

One estimate is that the investment in the Formula 1 World Championship by sponsors and the major automotive companies totals more than $200 million a year.

The chain reaction is a classic one. The more money a team can attract, the more competitive it will be. The more successful a team is, the better the value it gives a sponsor, and the easier it becomes to attract money.

Tobacco giants are among the sport's most generous, visible and consistent backers. They put a lot in, and make sure they get a lot in return. They wield much influence, but they tread warily because they don't want to upset the applecart.

Britain's Tobacco Advisory Council points, with justification, to the value of the industry's sponsorship of the arts and sport. Motor racing as a whole is thought to soak up half of the $40 million sponsorship money spent by British industry and commerce and Formula 1 must take a lion-sized share.

Tobacco companies say they have delivered cricket from the doldrums, put British showjumping on the map, and turned snooker and darts into mass entertainment. More than sixty sports – from fishing and curling to hang-gliding and shove-ha'penny – have been recipients of such largesse.

The argument runs that, should tobacco sponsorship be banned – 'as a vocal minority insists' – the effect would be catastrophic. In the case of grand prix racing, there have been somewhat premature rumours of its death before. But the sport is so densely populated with survivors that a way through impending disaster has always been found.

Certainly, tobacco money has been largely instrumental in the transformation of the sport to what it is now, creating a lead that other sponsors have followed with increasing enthusiasm. But, probably, enforced withdrawal, while creating difficulties, would prompt some new initiatives – just as the tobacco companies themselves did when they moved in to fill the vacuum created as some of motor racing's traditional corporate friends began to shy away in the 1970s.

One of the loudest of that 'vocal minority' is David Simpson, director of ASH – Action on Smoking and Health. He calls smoking 'by far the largest preventable cause of illness, disability and death in the UK'. It accounts, he says, for four times as many premature deaths each year as road accidents, alcohol, fires, murder, suicides, poisoning and every other known cause of accidental death put together.

Simpson claims the tobacco industry uses sports sponsorship successfully to circumvent voluntary restrictions on ordinary cigarette advertising. Among his objections: any promotion of tobacco helps maintain the social acceptability of smoking, and helps to put across an image which is quite contrary to the realities of the habit. Also, the keen interest young people take in sport makes tobacco sponsorship of it particularly inappropriate.

In pursuing this cause, Simpson denies unfairly discriminating against tobacco while other products known to be harmful to health in the short or long term are not similarly picked out for vilification. Tobacco, he asserts, is a 'uniquely harmful product, not only in the unparalleled scale of the harm it causes, but because it is always potentially dangerous, rather than just dangerous if abused or consumed in excess – like, say, motorcycles, cars or alcohol.'

The counter-argument is that there is no evidence that tobacco sponsorship – or advertising, for that matter – causes people to smoke, or smoke more. The real reason for spending all this money on sponsorship, says the industry, is competition for shares of a contracting market. Manufacturers can only stay in business by maintaining brand loyalty, tempting users of other brands to switch, and generating awareness and goodwill. Sponsorship helps.

'It is not a convenient circumvention of existing controls on tobacco advertising,' claims the Tobacco Advisory Council. 'In any case, tobacco sponsorship itself has been restricted by voluntary agreement since 1977. These restrictions balance out the sponsor's legitimate right to recognition with the spectator's equal right to enjoy his chosen event without distraction.'

That agreement was the result of horse-trading between a British government, with a weather eye on the balance between the health problem and the implications of forcing the tobacco interests into a corner, and an industry under pressure but none the less holding some strong cards.

In the UK tobacco accounts, directly and indirectly, for more than 250,000 jobs and £300 million worth of exports. Smokers pay £4275 million a year in tax, nearly half the cost of the National Health Service. On the other hand, cigarettes cause 50,000 premature deaths and 50 million lost working days a year.

The industry undertook to cool it. In return, the government, much to its relief, was able to say that progress had been made, and that it was not now necessary to wave the big stick. However, a statement, issued at the time by the Department of the Environment, contained a paragraph making it plain that the companies had acceded to 'specific and strongly pressed government requests', and that doing so should not be taken as acceptance of the principle that 'one particular form of marketing activity should be subject to special restrictions . . . or . . . there should be any restrictions on company expenditure on any or all forms of publicity'.

The basis for the agreement and its successor that came into force at the start of 1983 – and runs until at least December 1985 – is that the industry's sponsorship outlay is limited to the amount spent during the 1976 financial year, but increased in line with the Retail Price Index. And returns must be made to the DoE every year – in strict confidence.

When televised, motor racing in the UK is restricted to four tobacco advertising signs, of no more than 11 square metres per 1,6 km. And the display of tobacco house or brand names on participants and their equipment is not allowed.

There was an exception in the agreement 'Any sponsor

of capital-intensive sports, namely motor racing, power boating and motorcycle racing, who currently displays a house or brand name or symbol on participants and their equipment, shall remove such displays no later than 30 September 1979.'

The revised 1983 agreement once again contains the requirement that 'the display of house or brand names or symbols on participants and their equipment, or on officials or their equipment actively involved and likely to come within range of the television cameras, is not permitted during the course of televised activity in the UK'. And that includes mechanics. However: 'Activities televised from outside the UK are not bound by this code.'

Such is the power attributed to fleeting images on the television screen that, in Britain and some other countries, tobacco-backed grand prix cars race with the main sponsors' names deleted from their usual distinctive liveries. And it's the same with the drivers' overalls. However, during pre-race practice sessions, the cars run with those names in place, and many of the photographs published in the press show this.

Also, these cars are registered with names such as 'John Player Special' or 'Marlboro McLaren,' and are mentioned as such quite legitimately in the commentary. It was interesting, though, to note that, during the JPS-sponsored Grand Prix of Europe in 1983, the John Player Specials were mentioned as such while the McLarens were given no Marlboro tag! During Nigel Mansell's mid-race stop for fuel and fresh tyres, the 'John Player Team Lotus' banner above his pit showed up nicely on the screen. And, in something of a coup for the race sponsor, television commentator Murray Walker spoke his introductory words to the coverage of the event sitting in the cockpit of a car: 'In a sponsor's dream position, Elio de Angelis in *this* John Player Special is in pole position.'

This is what emerges from the BBC's balancing act which tries to play it by the rules while recognizing that, in the words of Deputy Director General Aubrey Singer, 'without sponsorship of various types, this sport could not continue. . . .' He was replying to objections from ASH's David Simpson about the documentary *Inside the Monaco Grand Prix* in which the McLaren team was featured. Singer went on: '. . . part of the programme sought to make a fair assessment of the demands that sponsorship may put on the teams or individuals involved. To have avoided showing the sponsors' logos or any mention of their name would not only have been journalistically insincere but would have made a nonsense of what was a serious investigation.'

The complexity and sensitivity of tobacco involvement are of varying degree from country to country.

However those issues are eventually resolved, there is no doubt that the sport and many of its participants have benefited considerably from cigarette backing.

The Philip Morris company for example places its Marlboro name and money strategically, to help underwrite the cost of staging grand prix races, to back the McLaren International team (and Alfa Romeo/Euroracing, until the end of 1983) and has nearly half the drivers enrolled in the Marlboro World Championship Team. It also sponsors races and championships for the lesser formulae, as well as for motorcycles. And, in 1983, came the Marlboro Challenge, 'the search for tomorrow's champion'.

This operation is a good example of how a sponsor seeking exposure simultaneously creates publicity mileage for the sport. To kick it off, six million stickers and leaflets were distributed in March through clubs, pubs, newsagents, garages and accessory retailers around Britain.

From 11,500 correct entries, 1300 semi-finalists emerged. During ten test days at Brands Hatch, Silverstone and Thruxton circuits, these were whittled down to twenty who underwent training with the Jim Russell International Racing Drivers School before attending a final at Silverstone.

During a tense day, the finalists went through their paces in both Ford Escort XR3i saloons and Formula Ford racing cars, under the watchful gaze of former world champion James Hunt and other experts, until at last a winner emerged. One delighted face, nineteen glum ones; that's motor racing. It's just as well to understand that from the outset.

The prize, worth about £30,000, was Marlboro backing for a full season – in this case, the 1984 British Racing and Sports Car Club's 'Star of Tomorrow' Formula Ford Championship – plus a Formula 3 test with a view to an international drive during 1985.

The aim of it all is to put more Britons on grand prix starting grids where, not long ago, they predominated, and also help to create brand-awareness among enthusiastic patriots. However, that is but one national objective for a blockbusting cigarette. And the international 'snow-job' must be dovetailed with the marketing activities appropriate to each of the many countries where it sells.

Imperial Tobacco's John Player Special brand is also synonymous with the sport. It is almost a 'marriage made in heaven' – even the brand's black-and-gold colour scheme helps the Lotus cars stand out, aloof and rather up-market, in a world of garish colours screaming for attention. John Player Special is the name under which the cars are entered – remember Indianapolis? – and the theme is followed through in every stitch of clothing worn by team personnel – where he or she be main board director, driver or mechanic.

When JPS or Marlboro sponsor a race, it is as though it 'owns' motor sport. Brand identification percolates right through the whole scene, from the posters at the gate to the paint on the kerbs round the circuit – black and gold for John Player; red and white for Marlboro. So strong are their respective corporate identities that, even if you had forgotten how to read overnight, you would know at a glance who was running the show.

Though great emphasis is placed on the Britishness of the team, the aim goes much further than luring Britons, whether at home, or in duty-free shops in foreign airports. Imperial Tobacco International, an offshoot of 'Imps', sells JPS in European countries such as Italy, France and Spain. In Germany, it is franchised to R. J. Reynolds, a major manufacturer. In South Africa, as well as South American countries, it is sold under licence by British American Tobacco. When the circus hits town, John Player Team Lotus is right there, available to the local marketing company as an image builder, as well as pushing out on the track for a share of the worldwide television exposure.

'There is no way that one is able to realistically measure the value of any particular part of advertising, one against the other, and especially sponsorship,' comments Peter Dyke, head of sponsored events at Imperial Tobacco. 'It's part of the marketing mix. And – whether you're into motorcycling, tennis, golf or Formula One – it's creating awareness of your product. If you have success in a competitive activity, you have a bonus.

'We have a certain identity with motor racing. And our black and gold colours equate with the life-styles of many people – a bit pacy, and enjoyable in many respects. Whether you're selling motor spares like Unipart or clothing like Fila, you're looking to put them in front of the public. In our case, we hope that our involvement will influence existing smokers to buy our brand.'

The voluntary agreement between the government and the British tobacco manufacturers obliges them not to use personalities – in this case, the team's two drivers – in the promotion of cigarettes.

'The cars are registered as John Player Specials. But we do not feature the drivers as much as we would if we were selling potato crisps or strawberry jam because these are perceived by those who make the rules to be more acceptable than tobacco. And Imperial Tobacco has always been a responsible company,' says Dyke.

Cigarette company influence is known to have been at work behind the scenes, for instance, in the latter part of 1983, shaping the future of world champion *manqué* Alain Prost. In August, Renault Sport was admitting it could not – as matter of public policy, rather than one of access to money – afford to match Marlboro's inducements to Prost to join Ferrari. And, after the parting of the ways in October, it was Marlboro that was instrumental in placing the Frenchman with McLaren, unceremoniously displacing John Watson.

The emphasis at John Player seems to be different. 'We work on a policy that, whatever sport we're in, the business we know is producing and selling cigars, cigarettes and pipe tobacco. We like to be closely involved with governing bodies, discuss with them in great detail what our requirements are, and rely on them to provide what they believe is best for us,' remarks Dyke.

'Of course, talking specifically about Formula One, we would state a preference to have a particular nationality of driver. But that is all we would say.

'We would expect Team Lotus to exercise their very best judgement as to who is going to provide us with the best opportunity of winning. But you must always be mindful that they are governed by the amount of money they're given. In our case, we believe the money we put in is adequate for the team to field cars in sixteen grands prix and hire drivers of world championship class, given that all things break their way.

'We all know it's the luck of the draw. You have to accept that, when you put your company's sponsorship money into a competitive area, you have to take the good with the bad. If you win, it can be very good. If you lose, you get nothing. That's why you have to be running with the right people. Certainly there is no question that, over the years, John Player and Team Lotus have been a very harmonious and successful partnership.'

Be that as it may, Imperial Tobacco is one of the sponsors getting restive about aspects of the sport's overall organization, particularly the random way in which the grand prix calendar fluctuates. Criticism voiced by the company's marketing director, Brian Wray: 'Those seemingly, allegedly, in charge of this sport should do something about its unpredictability.

'Formula One suffers in a way shared by no other sport we're involved with. There is too much money involved in this business for it to suffer from such a lack of even short term planning.'

This quite understandable complaint stems from the complexities of putting the calendar together, dovetailing it with other motor sport, and trying to avoid clashes with other widely televised sporting events. Staging a grand prix on the same day as the Wimbledon tennis final, for instance, decimates its television potential and thus its value to sponsors.

The problem is compounded by attempts to initiate races in new venues. Often enough, the continuation of established races is touch and go, dependent on whether the local business community can be persuaded to stump up the necessary financial backing.

Add this to trying to put on a grand prix in a city such as New York where, even with the backing of Mayor Ed Koch, finding a venue, building a suitable circuit and overcoming objections from local pressure groups is a long-drawn out task. Yet, unless the race is given a date on the calendar, there is little apparent commitment from the Formula 1 circus. So why should New York bestir itself to pursue the dream expressed on the telephone by a man 5500 km away on the other side of the Atlantic?

'Fine,' says Peter Dyke. 'But it would be rather nice when you read the sixteen races planned for 1984, to be absolutely sure they are going to take place. Then it would be all well and good to learn that the intention was to add races in Australia, Japan and Dallas in 1985, but not 1984.

'It drives sponsors out of their minds, particularly if they're international – and most are. The calendar is released to the media, and it's worldwide news. The manager of your Dallas office reads that he's going to have a grand prix on his doorstep. He goes through the roof, and rings head office in London. Next thing you know, we're all spending a lot of money – even wasting a lot of money chasing rumours.

'There was all that nonsense about the New York GP – it was on, it was off. There was uncertainty about the Las Vegas race. The South African Grand Prix was going to be at the beginning of the season, and was changed to the end.

'At Imperial Tobacco, we spent two hundred thousand

pounds on literature at the beginning of 1983 to send round the world telling supporters of our black-and-gold cars where and when to look out for them. But it was actually nonsense because a lot of those dates didn't materialize.

'Yet we had hundreds of representatives calling with this literature on customers who could not understand why it was wrong. I'm supposedly employed as a professional by my company to advise the sales force about what's going on. Then it comes back through internal meetings that I don't know what the hell I'm doing. It's got to stop.

'It's not good enough for the Formula One Constructors' Association to say: "Well, we had a little problem." And, while we support the sport, we really have to start saying to those who run it: "For God's sake recognize that, over and above the money we put into sponsoring a team, we spend many thousands of pounds in actually promoting our involvement – which means promoting Formula One." '

Unless this happens, warns Dyke, there are many major sponsors likely to move in other directions. The same considerations, he says, are exercising the minds of the heads of television sport with whom he has talked. They have to plot the races into their schedules up to a year ahead, and are faced with a considerable dilemma as to whether they should take grands prix as regular features when they are unreliable.

'It's one hell of a good sport with all the excitement, all the ingredients,' enthuses Dyke. 'It's the top end of the business. But it does need to be pulled together.'

The problem for sponsors wanting to make the most of their investments runs far deeper than the added cost of having to reprint literature. If a race fails to materialize, this can force a company to cancel hundreds of hotel rooms and airline seats, booked for valued customers or sales staff who have won incentive competitions. Then, to retrieve some bruised credibility and make up for disappointment, a frantic scramble begins to place these people at an alternative race, for which hotels and flights will have been heavily book by others.

With so much big money focused on extracting maximum

media exposure from the sport and using it as a prime entertainment for VIP guests, it is small wonder that the paying spectator has taken something of a back seat, even though he still makes a vital direct contribution to the finances of individual promoters staging the races – as opposed to maintaining the circus in the style to which it has become accustomed. But there are signs that the sponsors once more appreciate that 'bums on seats' have as much place in the equation as the need to reach the wider television audience.

'I go to most grands prix. And I walk about, looking and listening – which is what any responsible sponsor should do to assess what sort of sport he is involved with,' says Dyke. 'During 1983, it suddenly struck me that maybe the spectator was not getting what he thought he'd paid his money to see – particularly if he had bought a paddock transfer ticket which can be very expensive in some parts of the world.

'It's a difficult question. As a sponsor, I recognise the need for mechanics to work in some privacy, and I would not want them jostled by the public to the detriment of preparing cars to win races. Also, drivers under pressure must have their comfort and rest, which means motorhomes. However, all that is in conflict with the spectator's quite natural desire for a close-up look and the chance to ask for autographs.

'Mind you, each driver has his own approach to his responsibilities to the public, which includes signing autograph books. But you have to accept that, first and foremost, he is there to drive the car to the best of his ability.'

To be able to produce the race results is one thing. Combining that with the right attitude, a presentable personality, makes for what is known in the trade as promotability – a difficult characteristic to define, except insofar as it means added sponsor-appeal, which in turn equals greater earning power.

Non-tobacco sponsors are, in many respects, more at liberty to employ a driver to good effect when he is not in the cockpit. So, for instance, Unipart's contract with

McLaren – until the end of 1983, at any rate – included access to Niki Lauda and John Watson, using them for product endorsements, television advertising and public appearances.

Personalities are certainly important to a sponsor like Unipart, which sells replacement car parts in 144 countries. 'We need intelligent promotable drivers who speak English. But, in theory, it's immaterial whether they come from the Isle of Wight or Venezuela,' says public relations manager Patrick Fitz-Gibbon. 'However, if a team picked two drivers who didn't speak English and were pretty unpresentable, we'd say hang on, let's look at our objectives.'

These are varied, though well defined, and linked with exclusivity, glamour, image, technical progress and excellence.

Unipart has its own television network, 'Channel 5', to communicate with dealers. And Watson made regular appearances, giving updates on Unipart's involvement in Formula 1.

Watson and Niki Lauda also featured frequently in company hospitality to its customers, doing the rounds and shaking hands. Typically, the two drivers and a Unipart calendar girl were the drawcard for 600 of the company's guests, entertained two nights before the Dutch Grand Prix. An expensive party? Yes. But it gave rise to £1.5 million worth of sales.

It is this kind of result that prompts marketing services director Frank Hemsworth to remark: 'Wattie as an individual is a fantastic ambassador for the sport. If there were more drivers like him around, I think Formula One would attract more sponsors – certainly in Britain.'

Unipart, Hemsworth declares, gets back everything it spends in the sport and a lot more. 'Too many companies think that simply sticking their name on the side of a car is the answer to everything. Then they are disappointed with the results. We decide whether or not we are going into the sport. Then we map out a plan of activity which justifies every single halfpenny we put in.'

Probably more important than just using Formula 1 to

get visibility for the Unipart name, the company's products are actually used in the construction and running of the cars. Items achieving a pedigree in this way include spark plugs, filters, oil coolers, radiators and oil.

In 1978, Unipart entered the engine oil market where long-established brands such as Castrol and Duckhams predominated. Rather than spend millions chasing them fruitlessly, the company came up with a concept for establishing a reputation for its oil, using McLaren. 'We knew there was a lot of myth and legend surrounding Formula One oil. But we suggested they put our high-quality 15–50 super multigrade in their racing engines,' recalls Hemsworth.

'Of course, they immediately choked, and said the idea was utterly ridiculous. "Obviously you know nothing about motor sport. Go away." But we got them to give us the specification for an oil necessary to do the job, and we married this with our own.

'After one engine test, I remember, the chap starting to strip it down said he'd now show me why our oil couldn't be used – because it would give extra wear on a particular part. But, when he took it out, there was less wear than there would have been with the oil they had been using for years.

'Having established that we could take our oil – exactly the same as you can buy in the shops – and put it in a McLaren racing engine, we started to advertise the fact that Niki Lauda and John Watson used identical oil in the cars they drove to work and those they drove on the track.'

As a result, in less than two and a half years, Unipart took over as the leading own-brand oil, selling eleven million litres a year, twenty-five per cent of the market sector.

Keeping sponsors happy is what keeps sponsors, as McLaren International is only too well aware. When the men from Unipart arrive at a circuit they know that their banners will already be in place over the team's pits, so they will feature in photographs. Decals are placed, not only on the outer skin of the car but on the chassis too –

pictures taken when mechanics are at work also carry the sponsor's message.

No sooner had the TAG Porsche-engined McLaren been wheeled out for the first time in public, surrounded by swarms of photographers, during practice for the 1983 Dutch Grand Prix, than the body was removed. Out came the Unipart products which featured in many photographs of the new engine.

That's a detail, maybe, but it means a lot to a backer who has much at stake. 'We genuinely feel we work harder than any other team at making it happen for the sponsor,' says Ron Dennis, commercial director of McLaren International, who describes his main pressure as 'financing the animal that eats the money'.

'The bottom line says McLaren International deals in media exposure and a service to its investors,' declares Dennis. 'I hate the word sponsor – to me, it suggests a charitable act – and they're not in it for love.

'We are pitching for the same budgets as the advertising agencies. We have to do as good a job, if not better than them. In this game, you must realize that you're not going to make it if you don't deliver to the letter, or deliver plus.'

The amount of money now being spent in Formula 1 is not the result of teams like McLaren going after it for its own sake, he says. They have been forced to in order to remain competitive with Renault and Ferrari. 'We'd love it to be half as expensive because it would take half the effort to generate the money and make it work. However, we do have an important strength – single-mindedness – which allows decisive black-and-white, yes-no thinking.'

The Achilles heel of those continental factory teams, thinks Dennis, is that their people are less willing to step forward and make controversial decisions and stand by them. 'Their cars look as though they have been designed by a committee, whereas a Brabham, a Williams or a McLaren looks as though it's been designed by one man – even if that isn't entirely true, at least there is one guy saying this is the way. That is why, hopefully, we can continue to win world championships against Renault and Ferrari.'

To do so demands excellence, consistency and continuity. Those qualities can only be attained through financial stability, which means maintaining sponsor – or investor – loyalty, and making sure you always have some more waiting in the wings, just in case.

If the worst came to the worst McLaren could survive – though not necessarily pull the results – on far less money than while it has been pushing out the technological boat. As much as 70 per cent of a team's spending goes on research and development. A lot of this would have to go, should a major sponsor pull out overnight, before a replacement could be installed. However, a high-profile international company is unlikely to do so precipitately – if only for fear of creating waves that could un-nerve shareholders, customers and suppliers with a move that is bound to attract wide publicity.

A wide-awake team should be able to see the writing on the wall in good time. And, anyway, commonsense dictates not filling the sponsorship basket with identical eggs. As a rule of thumb, the predominant 'name' on a team's cars is funding no more than half the budget.

That way a team avoids becoming a vulnerable corporate plaything, and so McLaren actively develops a multi-sponsor line-up. It aims to have something to offer backers, large and small, by no means all of whom achieve 'visibility' on the cars.

One of the problems familiar to anyone who has sought motor sport sponsorship is that it is relatively easy to persuade companies to contribute a warehouseful of hardware and tinned food. But it is much more difficult to attract the hard cash essential to make an operation tick. That's not to say there is no place for contributions in kind, in even a top-line team.

Formula 1 needs a lot of high-quality hand tools, for instance, and is also very preoccupied with weight – too much, and you are not competitive; too little, and you are disqualified.

McLaren satisfied these two requirements by forming associations with Beta Tools, whose equipment is used both in the headquarters workshop and at the circuits where it is prominently displayed, and with Salter Industrial Measurements, which supplies precision weighing bases for the workshop as well as portable scales to be taken to races.

That level of contribution, worth possibly $60,000 in cash, 'buys' an association with the team, useful in publicity material, entitlement to bring a few guests to a couple of races a year, maybe two personal appearances by drivers during the season, but no identification on the cars. In fact, McLaren reckons to offer a value-for-money involvement for as little as $15,000.

To have your 'Brand X' decal placed on a car would cost a minimum of $300,000, while sewing a badge on a driver's overalls would set you back at least $75,000.

A serious attempt is made to relate space allocations on the car to a proper commercial 'rate card'. However, the market fluctuates considerably in response to supply and demand. And it usually won't make sense to price space on cars at $5 million when less successful teams, living hand-to-mouth in their struggle to continue, would be only too happy to accept $1 million.

'Some of the smaller teams will sell for anything they can get, and they do make things a lot more difficult in some respects,' affirms Creighton Brown, a McLaren International director/shareholder whose main role is to look after sponsors' interests. 'Having said that, they are teams that cannot generate the TV exposure the bigger ones can. So you're looking at almost a different market. The kind of sponsors they may pick up on a race-by-race basis are not those who will come on our cars for a season.'

McLaren lays claim to being unique among the teams in that it maintains a full-time marketing services department. It had three principle tasks. The first is a continual search for new sponsors, in preparation for the day when an existing sponsor pulls out, objectives achieved.

The second aim is to market the team more extensively, promoting the sponsors primarily, but also to build up the mystique of McLaren. For the sponsors are paying for an association with a prestige team that projects a good image. The third task, probably paid least attention by teams that pitch for million-dollar backing, is 'servicing' the sponsorship.

Rather than sitting back and hoping that front-running race performances will produce media coverage, McLaren diligently tries to create additional interest – which is where having personable drivers helps a good deal.

During 1983, the team collaborated in making a feature film, starring former world champion Alan Jones, for television in his native Australia. British Channel 4 screened *The Englishman . . . the Irishman . . . and the motor race*, a film made by Unipart on John Watson's 1982 victory at Long Beach. Next, BBC's *Inside the Monaco Grand Prix*, focused on McLaren and Renault.

'We've tried to gear ourselves so that sponsors with us get much more than just identity on the cars,' says Ron Dennis. 'They get a complete package which we're developing all the time. It's much more than handing over a few anoraks. It's contact and preparedness to listen to marketing problems and trying to come up with answers. It's also having the balls to admit to a backer that an idea didn't work, and being willing to do something about it.

'As a result our sponsors feel part of the team to such an extent that, when we failed to get into the race at Monaco in 1983, they came and asked why didn't *we* qualify – not why didn't *you* qualify? That's a completely different approach from ninety per cent of the teams. Even Renault's top management would have turned round to the people in their team, wanting to know why *you* didn't qualify.'

The logic, too, is that the more a team is instrumental in putting a sponsor's name in the public eye and is used in the sponsor's advertising, the greater the mutual dependence. 'It's a quite conscious effort,' admits Dennis. 'The more you suck them in, the harder it is to sever the link. That's what it's about, and we try very, very hard to deliver. But we're not being evil, laughing sinisterly behind our hands.'

Formula 1 is still only scratching the surface, Dennis believes, when it comes to generating media exposure, understanding the needs of present and possible sponsors, and in being paid properly for the value the sport provides. 'I feel that the current investors in F1 are not paying the rate card. The fact is that they're paying only a small percentage at the moment, if you equate that with the exposure being generated for major sponsors in the higher levels of the sport.

'Anyway, we're not saying it's a horrible, horrible world in a big economic squeeze – there's no money. At least we're doing something to understand the problem, what the next step has to be.'

Even a sponsor-rich team such as McLaren must be prepared to throw its net wider to procure the $6 to $8 million it needs to operate for a season – excluding drivers, which are paid for by Marlboro.

Probably unique in this respect, McLaren turns over $225,000 a year on fringe activities not directly linked to sponsors' contractual requirements – personal appearances by drivers and providing show cars. A racing car, with slightly de-tuned engine, is kept ready for use in television commercials, for hire by film companies, and even to be driven by journalists looking for something really frightening to write about.

Another source of revenue lies in selling off cars when they come to the end of their useful racing life. A used one-owner Tyrrell will set a collector back $75,000. Two of the P34 six-wheelers are in Japan, one kept in running order by an enthusiast who likes to run it up his drive. The market value of these vehicles also provides the team with some useful collateral as it retains one example of every type it has raced, and these are on loan to museums.

It is the job of Bob Tyrrell, son of Ken, to find sponsorship for the team his father started. He makes the point that, in a way, one of grand prix racing's main strengths can also be a hurdle for the teams. As the sport's only rivals in terms of international coverage are of the magnitude of

World Cup soccer or the Olympic Games, multi-national names – such as Coca-Cola – are obvious target sponsors.

However, very few of these companies operate with centrally controlled world advertising and promotions budgets. Generally, these budgets are handled autonomously by national subsidiaries or franchise holders in individual countries.

'If a company does not have central control from somewhere, you can write it off your list of potentials, because you'd have to persuade too many people. There is no machinery for the budget to be shared out. It would take a massive effort, if only because of getting all the people together to talk to each other about it. Or you would have to make a different pitch in each country. The guy in the UK is only interested in his market – not what happens in America.'

The process of selection goes still further because Formula 1 is a marketing weapon not necessarily suited to all products. 'First of all, it's a fairly masculine sort of sport, but it does have a wider appeal than things like cricket. But there is no point in getting on the phone to Persil, even if Lever Brothers do spend thirteen million pounds a year on advertising in the UK. There is no way that you can persuade them that putting the Persil name on an F1 car is going to help them because it isn't. They're aiming at the average housewife who wants her clothes to be whiter than the woman's next door.'

So the Formula 1 teams' shopping lists of big spenders are considerably shorter than one might at first imagine. And there are well-beaten paths from one to another. 'Everyone knows that the tobacco companies have to be prime targets because they can't advertise on TV,' says Bob Tyrrell. 'Or one of the big Japanese companies would be ideal because they have international budgets, and most allocate them centrally. They all have ten million dollars set aside for things like the World Cup and motor racing.'

Tyrrell's main 1983 sponsor, Benetton, the live-wire Italian clothing group with a turnover of more than $300 million and exporting half its production to the USA, Japan,

South Africa and throughout Europe, is one of a number of firms in the apparel business that is using the sport to enhance a snappy image for its gear.

At an earlier stage in the clothes manufacturing chain is ICI – Imperial Chemical Industries – which has been using grand prix racing in interesting ways to promote its 'Record' range of synthetic fibres.

Between 1970 and 1980, ICI Fibres Division was faced with rocketing prices for oil-based raw materials, a levelled-off market and fierce competition from state-owned and subsidized rivals on the continent as well as increasing cut-price capacity in the Far East. It responded with plant closures and a slimmed down management which reduced the numbers on the payroll from 23,000 to 8500. This slashed costs and put the firm in a position to invest in the new technology it needed to produce better quality at higher speed.

There was a shift of emphasis towards more profitable up-market speciality fibres which nobody else could make, and the company dropped out of much of the more basic materials because earnings on them were low.

ICI Fibres also decided to move into the Continent in a big way; and to concentrate on better quality sportswear. With increasing leisure time, it's a growth market – young, fashion-conscious and free-spending. The need, then, was to find means to project a message of world leadership in newer and superior-quality fibres with which to capture new customers.

At the start of 1982 the attack was launched, low-key at first. A comprehensive sponsorship programme, covering half a dozen sports and twelve big names, was rejected on the grounds of the huge cost. Then ICI's European sports-wear marketing executive Mike Francis was briefed to build a plan around Sebastian Coe, the athlete. But he argued for retaining a spread of sports, without spending in-depth during the first year. Coe was included because athletics is a good spectator sport, and cheaper for a sponsor than soccer or tennis. In February 1982, the ICI Record insignia was worn by the Norwegian cross-country and Swiss downhill ski teams – big draws for spectators in key markets such as Germany, France, Italy, Switzerland and the Nordic countries where a lot of ski wear is sold.

In the wake of other ICI divisions' involvement in Formula 2, the decision was made to go into Formula 1. A personal sponsorship package was put together with Keke Rosberg, driving his first – and, as it turned out, championship-winning – season with Williams. Space was also taken on the noses of the Rothmans-sponsored Marches.

It all came together nicely. ICI Fibres' programme was gathering momentum, and the firm had backed a winning driver. March departed from the scene, the firm transferred its decals to the Williams cars, and began putting its grand prix involvement to work at the circuits.

The problem for a fibre manufacturer is the complex chain of events its products go through before they reach the public. So, the question for ICI Fibres was twofold: how to establish the 'Record' label as a symbol of quality and *chic* in the mind of the public, the high-street customer; and how to ensure that the resulting demand worked its way back through the chain of production, translated into demand for the company's fibres.

The answers, of course, had to come in reverse order. And this is reflected in the progression with which the brand name has been presented in Formula 1. First the label appeared on Rosberg, the driver, and the two March cars. And observers, if they were wide awake enough, wondered what the hell 'ICI Record' might be.

Step two was to use grands prix as an attraction, an opportunity to entertain ICI Fibres' direct and indirect 'downstream' customers, bringing them together to form liaisons beneficial to themselves and their host, subtly directing them all to 'think Record' in a congenial ambiance projecting the pacy image they wanted in the finished product.

The opportunity for a ringside seat at one of the world's greatest spectacles – with the possibility of meeting some of the main protagonists face to face – is often irresistible. Whether or not you're a motor-racing fanatic, it's a knock-out, a great weekend – surrounded by the beautiful and famous. You may be deafened and confused by the frenetic scene, but your buddies will be impressed to know that you were there.

The point is that when you have got to know a business contact over a few beers, exchanging anecdotes as you watch those lunatics dicing with death, you're more likely to be willing to make deals over the telephone. And, having accepted a VIP invitation to a race and taken the trouble to travel there, a knitter, weaver or garment-maker is hardly likely to be so churlish as to not attend a presentation – even alongside some of his fiercest rivals – to hear Keke Rosberg extol the virtues of their host's products – in fluent English, German, Swedish or Finnish.

Contact, initiating relationships is what it's all about. And, if this seems a pricy way of going about it, ICI's Mike Francis disagrees: 'Our customers like it because they can see at first hand how we are creating a market for them, establishing a profile for them in key countries.

'It gives us credibility. And it increases the amount of times we are in contact because they are happy to come to see us at the races – we can meet many more of them in a single weekend than we could in a month, travelling round Europe, seeing people individually. So, when we do visit them, it is to do serious business rather than just show our faces.'

The next – and most public phase – comes once all the behind-the-scenes effort has worked its way through the 18-month textile industry pipeline, and the goods are in the shops.

Undeniably, the grand prix circus has become an important catalyst for world trade. But, before that process had ever got under way, for a country to stage a race had become an essential symbol of its prestige – a sort of totem, a credential furnishing proof of acceptance into membership of the community of advanced and civilized nations.

South American countries – Argentina, Brazil, Mexico –

have battled on to satisfy the Latin passion for speed by staging grands prix, in the face of political turbulence, outrageous inflation and horrendous indebtedness to foreign banks. In such circumstances, who can blame them for a yearning to prove they are wanted? Mexico dropped out after 1970 and was replaced by Brazil from 1973. Argentina missed its 7 March 1982 date and, a month later invaded the Falkland Islands.

Tennis, soccer, rugby and cricket players face the prospect of being pilloried if they appear in 'Fascist' or 'racist' countries – though not nearly so often, one notes with interest, for going to the Eastern bloc where repression of dissenting points of view is a tradition going back well before 1917. However, fortunately for motor racing, it has largely escaped such scrutiny. Perhaps it is regarded as so much a plutocrat's playground as to not merit egalitarian scrutiny.

One country glad of this is South Africa whose apartheid – separate development policy has made it unacceptable in most international sporting arenas, and it has clung to its grand prix through thick and thin. It must be twice as expensive to stage as a grand prix in Europe. In addition to the prize fund of maybe $850,000 – the 'fee' paid to the Formula One Constructors' Association for staging the circus at Johannesburg – the organizers have to meet the cost of providing the teams with more than 200 air tickets as well as flying in the cars and 50 tons of equipment – no mean bill for a 19,000 km round trip.

Motor racing has yet to capture the imagination of the black people of the country, so spectators are drawn largely from among the whites who account for only 4.5 million of the 30 million population. It is remarkable, therefore, that 60,000 people – of whom maybe 40,000 pay to get in – are claimed to attend the grand prix at Kyalami.

On the face of it, the economics just don't make sense for local sponsors – twice the cost and half the crowd of a grand prix in Europe – notwithstanding the international television exposure. But a closer look at South Africa's taxation laws helps it all fit into place – so neatly – that is until changes that came into effect in February 1984.

Until then, if a company was classified as an exporter and could persuade the Department of Internal Revenue that sponsoring the grand prix was an export promotion, it was entitled to double deduct tax against the money it put up. Company tax is 46 per cent; twice that is 92 per cent. If the sponsor of the race paid the organizers 1 million rands, the government was, in effect, providing 920,000 rands of that.

For a hotel group – such as Southern Sun which backed the 1983 South African Grand Prix – the deal must have been even more attractive. For it was bound to sell a lot of accommodation to the visiting teams and journalists. If they spent, say, 300,000 rands, hey presto – the grand prix had not cost the hoteliers a cent. That is what well-deployed sponsorship is all about.

4

HIRED HAND

Job security is not one of the strong points of life as a grand prix driver.

Great physical risk presents the continual danger of being laid off for considerable lengths of time through injury. And it is an immensely difficult sport to break into, while alarmingly easy to be squeezed out.

This is an occupation where – like the stage – many are called, few are chosen, and there is always a long queue of eager would-be replacements banging at the door. So much so that drivers have been equated with light bulbs – if one fails, you have only to unscrew him from the car, and insert a new one. Don't put your son into motor sport, Mrs Worthington.

The light bulb analogy may overstate the case, but it brings home the point that this is a world where there are few second chances. Just as a journalist's worth is reckoned in terms of the quality of his latest news story, so the grand prix driver is only as good as his last race or championship season.

This is, of course, not only a matter of absolute ability, but of getting the best machinery with which to do the job, and of fate helping out with the opportunities of which to make the most.

In such a competitive job market, the employer can – indeed, he must – be ruthlessly selective as he casts around for drivers who can not only succeed in races but make the sponsor happy in other ways.

During the often fickle game between teams and sponsors, drivers are frequently played as pawns. Quite understandably, the sponsor wants drivers who can race high up the field where the television cameras concentrate. But he also seeks that elusive characteristic – promotability.

It is important that a driver be, in the words of Webster's Dictionary, 'capable of being promoted for consumer acceptance especially through advertising'. This is a hard-to-define amalgam of sex appeal, instant high-street recognition, and an articulate and congenial personality. It also pays to be of a nationality that matches the sponsor's target markets.

Best of all is the ability to transcend frontiers. For instance, an American who can win races and is fluent in English, French and Italian goes to the top of the queue. And to have a world championship or two under your belt assures a prime seat on the gravy train, though not a lifetime season ticket.

During any one year, there are probably only half a dozen drivers in the world who are genuinely capable of consistently winning grands prix. Such are the demands of the exotic hot house these superstars inhabit that it is small wonder they are tempted to believe they are indispensable and are paid solely to drive cars faster than anyone else, and win races.

Such delusions of grandeur are scornfully debunked by the hard-nosed men who control the teams. They recognize that a top driver must command a considerable sum on the grounds of his physical talent. But the real money is paid to those who are internationally famous, and thus highly promotable by sponsors.

One rule of thumb is that, out of every $100 a driver earns, $99 are for that promotability, and only $1 is for what he does behind the wheel. And that is because there are so many outsiders more than willing to come and do the job for nothing, simply for the enjoyment. It must be said that this view is hotly disputed by others who believe that a driver's worth is directly related to his talent, and that very few are of the required calibre anyway.

In fact, of the thirty-odd drivers in Formula 1, three or four are not paid at all, and some of them buy their way in, helping to finance a team out of their own pockets or with the aid of backers or personal sponsors.

Somewhere in the middle, relatively modest sums, averaging maybe $300,000 are paid. Only in the top third of the pack do the telephone-number fees begin.

Michele Alboreto, for instance, joined Tyrrell from the 1981 San Marino Grand Prix. He brought with him enough finance to run in three races, and signed a contract giving the team an option to retain him for three seasons if all went well initially.

Ken Tyrrell was so impressed that he took up the option, and Alboreto began to be paid. There followed two wins – Las Vegas in 1982, and Detroit in 1983 – and an offer for 1984 from Ferrari that Alboreto couldn't refuse, especially in view of uncertainty about Tyrrell's sponsorship and supply of turbo engines.

How a driver gets paid varies from team to team. It is a matter of how much clout an individual can bring to bear, market forces, personal relationships, sponsors' objectives and strong nerve during the brinkmanship of the annual round of 'musical drives'. While every contract is different, most teams pay a retainer plus a percentage of prize money won.

At Ferrari, the retainer used to be relative peanuts, but the team allowed its drivers considerable latitude in terms of personal sponsorships – selling space on their overalls. Now Marlboro pays Ferrari's drivers' retainers, and even has deals on the cars, a departure from the team's tradition that came about in 1984. Tyrrell's drivers wear the colours of the team's main sponsors, as do Brabham's. McLaren actively markets space on both the cars *and* drivers' overalls, paying the driver package fees.

Some drivers and the agents acting on their behalf prefer to negotiate one-year contracts, reasoning that successes will increase their bargaining power for the following season. Others prefer the security of a two or three year signing, and a few of these have the muscle – the promotability – to pull deals of such magnitude that a longer-term commitment is more than worthwhile.

81

The latest world champion is not necessarily the top earner. For much depends on how eager he is to exploit his position. He must be prepared to strike fast, undergo tough negotiations, and hit the promotional trail before the publicity momentum decays.

Nelson Piquet, champion in 1981 and 1983, appears happy enough with the $1 million plus Brabham pays him for his achievements on the track. Virtually unique among the drivers, he does not particularly like publicity. And, rather than rush about in a scramble to double his money after winning his first championship, he disappeared for a month's holiday. Very much his own man, he opted not to take the first jet home to a hero's welcome in Brazil and the start of at least six months of hectic and lucrative advertising and promotional appearances.

It is one of the sport's ironies that Piquet is of such stature that he appears relatively free of the pressures of this kind of exploitation while employed by Brabham, the team owned by Bernie Ecclestone who has been influential in bringing grand prix racing to its present highly commercialized and vibrant state.

More apparently at home in this world is Niki Lauda, proof of how promotability aids earning power. The forthright Austrian made his debut in his home grand prix in 1971. During his second year with Ferrari, 1975, he won his first world championship at the age of twenty-six.

The following year, he was well on his way to a second championship. Then at Nürburgring, ten races into the season, his Ferrari crashed at 240 km/h on the second lap, and burst into flames. Trapped in the cockpit, Lauda was critically burned and, even worse, his lungs were damaged by inhalation from the inferno that enveloped him.

During the ensuing fight for life, a priest was called who said the last rites, and press photographers pulled every trick to get the sensational picture of the champion who had been given up for dead. Yet, less than six weeks later, Lauda was racing again – in the Italian Grand Prix where, remarkably, he finished fourth.

But discretion proved to be the better part of valour

during the final race of the season. On the second lap of the Japanese Grand Prix, run through blinding spray, Lauda withdrew, feeling conditions were unsafe. It was a brave decision, made all the more emotive because it meant that James Hunt became champion, just one point ahead of Lauda.

In 1977, he returned to dominant form, won four races, and topped the final championship table by a handsome margin. Then he joined Brabham, coming fourth in the 1978 championship, but 1979 results for the team were pretty abysmal. Suddenly, fresh out of motivation, Lauda retired from the sport in the middle of practice for the penultimate race of the season. For two years he was completely out of racing, concentrating on building up his airline, but this began to falter in face of world economic problems.

The man still had influential fans, however, and pressure for a comeback mounted. Lauda eventually agreed to join a revitalized McLaren from the start of 1982, signing a three-year contract for an annual retainer held to be $2.5 million.

The logic behind paying such a sum is that putting a household name such as Lauda in a car helps to attract much more sponsorship than would otherwise be available, and the team's net revenue is that much greater.

Though none of the Lauda magnetism had been lost, it was in fact team mate John Watson who did better during the two seasons to the end of 1983, scoring sixty-one championship points and winning three races to Lauda's forty-two points and two wins.

As 1983 went on, Watson's chances of a sixth season with McLaren seemed secure. He was a proven winner with 151 races under his belt, more than any other current driver. And, although the oldest of them at thirty-seven, he still had a while to go before the onset of senile dementia would make him a danger to other competitors!

But, with a contract to be renegotiated from year to year, Watson was to prove highly vulnerable to the domino effect that suddenly rattled through the grand prix circus at the end of the 1983 season.

This came from a quite unexpected quarter, and had its origins back in the middle of the year and even earlier. During 1982 relations between Renault's drivers Alain Prost and Réné Arnoux, had become increasingly strained. This acrimony had come to a head in an all-Gallic way at the French Grand Prix. Prost had led the championship for the first six races, and his chances then still looked reasonable. Yet, in front of their home crowd, Arnoux had declined to concede his race lead to Prost who, at the time, lay fifth in the championship while Arnoux was sixteenth.

At season's end, out went Arnoux – to Ferrari. Prost remained as top dog at Renault for 1983. But, as early as July, while leading the championship, he began telling the team he wanted to leave in response to an enormous offer from Marlboro and Ferrari.

Renault was not impressed. For one thing, Prost was acting as though he was already a champion, pushing for a champion's rates he had yet to earn by a long chalk. And, in any event, there was the underlying feeling that the drivers were already paid too much, thanks to big profits in the tobacco industry.

None the less, the team wanted to retain this particular driver for another season: he looked well placed to be the first French world champion, and in a French car. But matching the offer – which Renault says Marlboro and Ferrari denied making – was seen as 'a question of principle and morality'. Renault could lay its hands on the cash. But what would be the reaction to such extravagance by a state-owned company from a socialist government and the French public, beset by recession?

However, in August, it was agreed that Prost would stay with Renault for 1984, but his contentious statements to the media continued. The firm's management began to feel enough was enough, even though Prost had certainly proved to be a talented driver. After all, they made no secret that they were in Formula 1 to improve Renault's image. And the man was proving to be a waste of money on that score.

Hence a clandestine decision to cancel his contract not long after it had been made.

Final though this was, the dispensing with Prost's services was to be handled more subtly than the way in which Ferrari unceremoniously leaked the dumping of Patrick Tambay in favour of Michele Alboreto *before* the South African Grand Prix at Kyalami – Tambay, to his credit, responded with characteristic cool, putting his car on pole position for that race.

Prost would not be told until *after* this final round, so as not to undermine his morale, but he was to be given the push, whether or not he emerged as world champion. When Prost was told, after his world championship defeat by Nelson Piquet, he quickly contacted Marlboro, McLaren's largest sponsor.

Watson had yet to re-sign with the team. And, just four days after the South African Grand Prix, television viewers heard him describe how he had been ousted by Prost. However, as it turned out, another two and a half days passed before the Frenchman signed for what is thought to be $1.3 million, made up from the Renault payoff and additional money from Marlboro.

Patrick Tambay had been snapped up by Renault – for $1,125,000 – when news of his departure from Ferrari broke. Also talking to the team at about that time was Derek Warwick who, a month later, joined the strength as 'equal number one' driver, but for $750,000.

Tambay had raced in seventy grands prix, scoring seventy-nine points in all by the end of 1983, when he was placed fourth in the championship. And he had won two races. Warwick, five years younger, had run in only twenty-seven races, scoring his first nine points in 1983. And, in line with the adage that 'mileage makes champions', it was natural that Tambay should be in a position to command the lion's share of the money.

After the shenanigans of previous seasons, Renault was purring about its new driver line-up. Tambay was an obvious choice – a Frenchman of established talent and with a reputation as the gentleman of the sport and one who thinks internationally. Articulate in English and urbane in manner, he is known in the USA, and maintains a base in London.

Thus he matched the team's philosophy that the driver's role should be made up in the proportions of 70 per cent skill on the track and 30 per cent human contact and public relations. Where Prost had disappointed, Tambay was confidently expected to excel.

The choice of Warwick was more difficult, especially when it came to explaining him to a French public that had scarcely heard of him. But the team had observed him at close quarters, doggedly driving his first three seasons with Toleman, and had been impressed. 'That team has never been successful,' says Renault's Jean Sage. 'They had some very hard moments, but Derek never lost his enthusiasm and his will to win. He is still the same.

'He is a straight guy without any problems, and we never heard of any trouble inside the Toleman team. They have been very nice to us all the time, and we were in good connection. So it's a bit of a pity that we steal one of their drivers.'

The man to take the decision to lure Warwick away was Gerard Larrousse, director general of Renault Sport, and a friend of Sage's for twenty-five years. 'I know very well the drivers, maybe better than him,' Sage says of Larrousse. 'He ask me what I think. And I was really pro Warwick since 1982. There was a balance between him and De Cesaris, but I don't trust this guy – he is risky. He could be very quick, or do a big mistake.

'But, when you see Derek, when you see what he has done with Toleman, you trust him. He's steady, consistent, determined. That's why I pushed Gerard to choose him.'

It was a tough choice, too, for Warwick, torn between loyalty to the team that had given him his start in Formula 1 and the desire for a really competitive drive. 'The most difficult decision was not whether to go to Lotus or Renault, but leaving Toleman. I had been talking to some great teams. But that meant leaving what, to my mind, could probably be one of the greatest as well, if they could get it all together.

'The problem was there was so much uncertainty. It wasn't certain they could get BMW engines. They had the budget to buy them, but not necessarily to further develop the Hart engines we had been using. That was the most important question, not that I didn't have faith in Brian Hart – I really rate the guy.'

Such was Warwick's allegience to Toleman that his dilemma had him close to tears a number of times. 'I don't think we would have had as much success as we did, if we hadn't been together for so long – three years. We worked one thousand per cent as a team. They were my greatest friends, and that was the most important thing.'

The deed done, they parted friends, says Warwick. 'In fact everyone in the team advised me to go to Renault. Though they also knew that would mean – and I'm not patting myself on the back because that would be too big-headed – they were losing somebody they rated.'

Just ten days after Renault and world championship leader Alain Prost had 'snatched defeat from the jaws of victory' at Kyalami, the team appeared to have bounced back. In preparation for 1984, it was out testing with the new drivers at Imola in Italy.

Autumn sunshine cast a golden aura across the Autodromo Dino Ferrari, sited slap-bang in the middle of the town. Onlookers crowded the pits grandstand, unconcerned it seemed, that neither the cars nor the drivers were Italian.

A laid-back Derek Warwick confided that, after the stress of negotiation and decision-making during the previous month, to come to Italy and start driving – learning the Renault for the first time – was like a holiday.

The pressures on him to move had begun seriously while he was in Spain for five days to finalize purchase of a house. The telephone had hardly stopped ringing. 'Toleman phoned six times, Renault three times, and Lotus three. It blew the estate agent's mind – he felt ten feet tall himself. There he was with this Derek Warwick being pampered by all these racing teams.'

Why choose Renault and not Lotus? One suspects tyres had something to do with it, but the man himself declines to be drawn on that one. Certainly, going to a French rather than a British team was daunting. 'I was frightened of the language barrier and, of course, you read in the press about the French being anti-British. So I thought maybe I would get rubbish treatment.

'But, from going over there, talking terms and getting more or less what I wanted, I felt that the most important thing for them was not whether the driver was French, English, Italian, Japanese or an Eskimo. It was for Renault to win the world championship. Maybe that was the problem Prost had – he thought *he* was winning the championship. But no driver does that on his own. A *team* wins it.'

Renault's declared strategy has been to give Tambay and Warwick identical treatment from the outset, both having equal access to the spare car. From mid-season, whichever of the two had most championship points would become *de facto* number one. That was not to say their cars would no longer be prepared equally. But it would mean following race tactics so as not to undermine the leader's advantage.

'I don't think I would have come in as number two,' says Warwick. 'If, right away, they wanted to put some restraint on you, they couldn't be serious about winning the championship.

'They agreed to equal status without any "umming" and "ahing". And I know Patrick agreed, too – he doesn't need any advantages. As long as he gets the same, that's good enough for him and, for sure, it's good enough for me.'

Out in this macho high-speed arena, you might expect to find yourself surrounded by extrovert hell-raisers, but there are few. Many more are to be found out in the spectator enclosures, letting off steam over a few beers. In fact, a high proportion of grand prix drivers today are relatively quiet, mild-mannered people. So perhaps it should not come as such a surprise when an unaffected racer like Warwick, with the world at his feet, tells you he's a family man really.

'My wife and children mean probably more to me than motor racing. There is no way I would do anythimg to jeopardize them. Both children have been brought up among a lot of family and friends. To take them out of that environment might hurt them psychologically in some way. And, at the end of the day, what's more important? Money or stability?'

That is a question bound to exercise a driver all the more as he joins the ranks of the top paid. And, although Warwick is loath to become a tax exile from Britain, he has given it some thought, considering, for instance, taking his family to live in Spain for a trial month to see how the children adapt.

'I really don't understand the British tax system where I would have to pay such a colossal amount that it could force me out of the country. And I think it should be reviewed. I know people will say: 'Oh, God. What's he moaning about? What's he got to worry about? He's wealthy now. But it's not as simple as all that. I may earn a million dollars today. Tomorrow, I may break both legs. I know it looks easy now I'm with Renault. Yet people just don't realize the years of sheer effort, the aggravation, you have to put in to be a racing driver.'

Having won a place with a top team, the effort must continue unabated. The first objective is to really get to know the new car during a four-month winter test programme, covering a full season's mileage at locations such as Paul Ricard, Kyalami and Rio de Janeiro. And a driver must keep in good physical and mental shape so as to maintain the stamina and concentration that are vital on the circuit.

He need not be an Olympic athlete, but he does have to be fit, fairly strong and have a lot of endurance. Warwick, for instance, denies being a fitness freak. But he does plenty of weight training and running, and plays squash a lot. 'If I have problems I want to think about, I go out for a five-mile run. When I'm hurting myself, I can then relax, and think things through.'

The right mental approach is essential in anyone aspiring

to be champion. He must keep this up, not only throughout each race or testing or practice session, but consistently from start to finish of a calendar of races on widely differing circuits that runs from around February to October, a long sporting saga.

The number one quality sought in a driver is speed – what Frank Williams calls talent, the ability to control a car better, closer to its limits, than his colleagues. 'Then he must have a good head because there are lots of drivers who are very brave and very quick. But, for every twenty like that, there is probably only one who has a good head to go with it.

'The best example is Nelson Piquet. For me, Nelson is the most complete driver. Keke Rosberg is a very intelligent man, but he doesn't understand racing cars as well as Nelson. He makes up for it by being quicker as a driver, and by having Patrick Head to bully him into giving answers about how the car is behaving. This is not to imply any criticism of Keke. He is very good with his car, and has good mechanical sympathy.'

Choosing a driver can be as complicated as the balance of characteristics of which he is comprised. The checklist need hardly begin with sanity, physical fitness, two arms and two legs. Probably the most important single physical characteristic in anyone wishing to be a top-class driver is extremely sharp eyesight, while a fine sense of balance is also a must.

Before he even gets a sniff at Formula 1, he must emerge at the top of the rough-and-tumble of the intensely competitive lesser categories: Formula 2 (engines of up to 2000 cc and six cylinders giving about 320 bhp in cars weighing no less than 515 kg) or Formula 3 (2000 cc, four cylinders, 170 bhp, 455 kg).

Having done that, he must contemplate vaulting into a completely new dimension where he will have to begin learning all over again – to handle maybe four times more power than he is used to. And he is a novice once more. Also, he has to face the stark fact that none of the grand prix teams really wants the hassle of a new driver because, for the first two or three seasons, he will very likely be next to useless – unless he is quite exceptional.

Even twice World Champion Nelson Piquet spent his first full year with Brabham just finding his way round, doing bloody stupid things, having accidents, and only picking up three championship points. He survived all that, however, and in 1980, his second season with Brabham, he won three races, and came second in the championship. But there are not many who can do that. Now, he is quiet, controlled – the man to watch who keeps his nerve right to the last lap of a championship-clinching race.

To find a way in, the would-be grand prix driver must have the absolutely unerring determination to get there, come hell or high water. This personal dedication must be combined with the intelligence to handle the financial and other complexities of the sport, as well as to capitalize on his racing experience. For he should never cease learning.

Ken Tyrrell says modestly that his reputation as a top spotter of driver talent is something of a myth, notwith-standing Jackie Stewart's three world championships under his tutelage. None the less, Tyrrell receives dozens of approaches from grand prix hopefuls seeking his advice on how to make the big break.

Tyrrell feels that the question as to what makes a grand prix driver is not easily answered. 'You're looking for one who is quick enough – not just now and again, but consis-tently. And a driver who is not always going off the road. All those things are obvious, and can be found out in a few hundred miles of testing, generally speaking.

'But, in fact, it's not as simple as that. I've found, over the years, that it's quite surprising how, just by talking for an hour with a man who wants to be a grand prix driver, you find out that he doesn't *really* want to – that he is not really prepared to make the effort that is necessary to become successful. Just not quite the right attitude, and I don't know how you define that,' he laughs.

Aside from having the innate ability, he must be hyper-competitive, but have this under control? 'Oh, yes. And he's got to be intelligent. Generally speaking, there are no thick world champions – never has been one. Of the current thirty-odd drivers, two or three, I suppose are thick. But that's not a very nice expression, is it?'

Though Frank Williams does not receive that many calls from aspiring stars, he does read the specialist magazines. 'You're always aware of what's going on. You know that so-and-so is always winning in Formula Two or Three and, if he is, he must be bloody good. But what we don't want to do is teach people. We just haven't the time.'

However, a first Formula 1 break may come in the form of an invitation to undertake some testing for a team like Williams. 'When Patrick Head and I decided that Jonathan Palmer could be very talented, we gave him a testing contract. We've operated that very happily for two years. Ideally, we would always like to have two British drivers, but we're not going to give him a drive in 1984, though he now has a lot of experience. We might have if he was brilliant and irresistible – which he isn't quite yet.

'But he's a very clever driver, and I think he'll get there by hard work rather than by brilliance. He's a very clever man – a bit like Nelson. He thinks all the time about how to improve things, and he's always talking to Patrick. Drops in here a lot. If, in a couple of years time, Jonathan has had an apprenticeship with another team, and the guy is a winner, we'll go into the market place, and try to buy him back.'

That is by no means faint praise from one of the most successful grand prix operators of the 1980s, but not enough for the much dreamed-of open sesame. Nevertheless Palmer's reward was to drive the third Williams car in the 1983 Grand Prix of Europe at Brands Hatch where he finished thirteenth. After the chance of a 'shop window' like that, the most likely course of action is to put together a package with one of the lesser teams, and move up the learning curve for one or two seasons in the hope of being offered a place by one of the top outfits.

No doubt the process of becoming a grand prix star begins when he falls out of his cradle, fascinated by an object that goes vroom-vroom and has four wheels. Certainly, psychological influences at an early age are decisive in forming the sort of extremely competitive character that feels a strong urge to take up motor racing or some other dangerous activity.

According to Dr Malcolm Carruthers, author of *The Western Way of Death*, once such a person has taken up his or her chosen competition, it can become an addiction. This is explained, he says, by secretion in the body of a hormone called noradrenalin which 'can become a self administered drug of addiction'.

Noradrenalin combines with adrenalin to be known collectively as adrenin. This is released into the bloodstream during a wide variety of states of emotional arousal. It accelerates the heart rate, increases blood pressure and blood coagulability, dilates the bronchioles, alters distribution of the blood in the body, and releases doses of oils into the bloodstream to provide extra fuel for high levels of activity.

There is considerable evidence to suggest that adrenalin release is associated with anxiety while noradrenalin is associated with aggression. Noradrenalin is released at and stimulates the 'pleasure centres' of the brain. In other words, it makes a person feel really good. So it is very easy to become a 'noradrenalin junkie'. The same influence is behind high-pressure business people who become 'stress seekers'. Noradrenalin is also a pain reliever which may explain why a rally driver with a terrible hangover starts to feel human once more after a long blast along a special stage. And it is also one reason why a soldier wounded in the heat of battle may not feel pain for quite a time after he has been hit.

The body's response to the incredible speeds and high g loadings of a Formula 1 car brings with it not only an overall glow of pleasure but a greatly heightened awareness – which is just as well.

Observing the British speed limit, it takes 32 seconds to cover 1 km. At 370 km/h almost twice the velocity at which a sky diver will hit the ground if his parachutes fail to deploy, a grand prix car travels 1 km in 9,7 seconds. This is about the time it takes an Olympic athlete to sprint 100 metres.

Assuming the grand prix driver's reaction time is really sharp – about 0,3 seconds – his car will have travelled 31 metres before he can respond – hit the brakes or swerve to avoid a hazard. Compare this with an average harassed motorist droning along at a hypnotic 110 km/h, less than one-third of the racing car's speed. And with a reaction time of as much as 1,7 seconds, he may cover 54 metres before taking evasive action.

The grand prix driver, very wide awake and concentrating so intensely, is thinking about six times as fast as the average man in the street, and this tends to happen off as well as on the track. 'You make decisions very quickly,' says Nigel Mansell. 'People can't understand when they ask me about something, and I give them an answer pretty well straightaway. If it isn't the answer they want, they say you haven't even thought about it – think about it for a day.

'You turn round and say: "Look, pal. I don't need time to think about it. That's it." You can make a decision – bang. It can create problems in your personal life sometimes – even with your wife. But I reckon a Formula One motor racing driver's brain – with the job he does at such speeds – can compute a lot more things and a hell of a lot quicker than the average guy can.'

This is a year-round phenomenon. 'The only days it doesn't happen are when you're absolutely shagged. After a race, you tend to crash out for one or two days, depending on whether or not you've been on a trans-Atlantic flight as well. In one particular instance I was on a plane for thirty-two hours straight after a race. When I got home, it took me about three days to come round, know who or where I was, and feel reasonable enough to even have a conversation with anyone.

'It's much easier to get over if you've had a good result, you enjoyed yourself and you're happy, than if you've had a bad drive and something's gone wrong for you.'

Mansell is pretty sanguine about the perils of grand prix

racing and efforts to make it safer. 'I don't hide from the fact that the sport is dangerous, but I don't dwell on that too much either. We're paid to do a professional job. That job is dangerous. If you're a professional, you calculate the risks, go about your business, and do it to the best of your ability. If anything goes wrong, that's hard luck.

'Just as there are always improvements that can be made in any sport, I don't think enough can be done to make racing safer. But I feel that, as long as people are still trying to make the sport safer and build better as well as faster cars, then it's a risk every driver will take if he's a racer. And I'm paid to drive these cars, not write the rules.'

There is, of course, a limit to the risks a driver is prepared to take and, for this reason, Monza is not one of Mansell's favourite places. At the end of the race maybe fifty thousand fans spill on to the track. In 1982, four of them almost bounced off Mansell's car during the slowing down lap. In 1983, he lifted right off before the finish line, ceding seventh place to Bruno Giacomelli. 'I'm not bothered about killing people if they want to run on the track. But they'll kill you if you hit them. I don't want to pass away because some stupid Italian runs across the circuit where cars are still doing a hundred and sixty miles per hour.'

A balance between courage and common sense means survival. If a driver cannot feel fear, he will probably kill himself, because that is all there is to prevent him overstepping the limits of his own abilities or the situation he finds himself in. Bravery is what it takes to overcome fear and explore those outer limits. Having said that, a grand prix driver concentrates too much to have time really to be frightened – even during an accident where everything is measured in split seconds.

During the 1981 Italian Grand Prix John Watson's McLaren slammed into a barrier, breaking in half and rebounding across the track. Seeing this on a pit lane television monitor, his team's blood ran cold. They were appalled, wondering if he could possibly get out alive, and sensed immense relief when they saw him being helped out of the monocoque.

Twenty-five minutes later, Watson walked into the pits, looking hot and flustered. All he said was that he was sorry he'd made a mistake and that it would be necessary to build him a new car. That was his only outward reaction. He seemed to accept the shunt – and the fact that he might not be there at all – as part of the job.

Ask a grand prix driver to compare his racing car with a family saloon in detail, and you'll most likely tax his powers of description. Among the answers: 'Just like a road car but with all the sensations writ large'; 'Fantastic – the best thing in my life'; 'Shit, there's just no comparison at all – for Joe Bloggs to get into an F1 car would just blow his mind.'

Even when the adrenin has caught up with the car, the job, seemingly a succession of contradictions, still takes a lot of doing. 'You have to have a tremendous amount of feeling for the car. You must be very gentle with it, but also very aggressive. You have to be fast but slow,' says Derek Warwick helpfully. Then he's off again: 'People often ask me what it's like doing two hundred miles per hour. Well, I don't know because you don't think you're doing two hundred.

'What you're doing is a one-minute thirty second lap or whatever. That's the important thing. You're looking at the oil temperature gauge, water gauge, boost pressure, boost temperature, rev counter. You're thinking about how good it is in slow corners, fast corners, the tractions, the turn-in, the oversteer. There are a million and one things to think about. So the concentration you have to apply just for one lap is tremendous. And I think one of the difficult things is not being fit enough to drive the car but being able to concentrate for the length of a Grand Prix or a test session.'

No two grand prix cars behave identically, as Warwick found when he made the transition from Toleman to Renault. The first differences he noticed were that the latter feels much softer and its engine is more torquey. 'It comes in very low, and has a wide power band. The most important thing is how gentle the car is. But the Toleman jumps about, you have to be aggressive with it, and you're at nerves end all the time.

'They must have done a lot of work on the Renault, and it's really quite nice to drive. Physical effort is low, whereas the Toleman was always quite hard work. And the Renault is one hundred per cent more forgiving.'

Apart from that first drive in a new car, one of the best sort of days during a grand prix driver's scramble up the slippery slope must be when he calls at the factory to be fitted for a seat. For this is when he quite literally makes his mark with a team. A block of damp clay is placed in a mock-up monocoque, and the driver climbs in, complete with overalls, to work the clay into shape around as much of his body as possible, also making sure he is within comfortable reach of the pedals, steering wheel and other controls.

Once that impression in the clay is set, a form-hugging seat can be reproduced from it to hold the man secure in his machine. This is surely the moment that purges all the paranoia, doubt and uncertainty that characterize the weeks or even months of haggling before a contract is signed. 'Welcome to the team. First, please stick your bum in that goo.'

5

PICKING UP THE PIECES

A grand prix driver must always be reconciled to the possibility that he will fall prey to a violent accident. This may result from his own or another driver's error, some change in the car's behaviour, mechanical failure, a rapid diminution of grip because of rain or oil on the track, or visibility being wiped out by blinding spray.

Once control is lost, the driver becomes a passenger in his projectile. As the milliseconds tick by, he is quite probably calculating coolly what the impact and its consequences may be. For others, the blackout of unconsciousness or death is instantaneous.

The likelihood is that a driver will crash once in every ten grand prix. And one in three of these accidents will be severe enough to incapacitate him for a short while at least.

Of the 200-odd drivers who participated in the 388 world championship races run between 1950 and 1983, more than 60 have met violent deaths, though only half of these occurred during a grand prix or practice beforehand. During these 33 years, the drivers collectively have raced 7500 times in grands prix, and there has been one fatality for every 214 'driver-starts'.

The sad balance of deaths among the fraternity is accounted for largely by other categories of racing. However, six are recorded as having been killed while testing, four in road accidents, and four in air crashes.

Running the gauntlet of such hazards in pursuit of the intense satisfaction there is in the sport is perhaps justified by the statement that 'the mere act of being alive is a risk'. In fact, of the 57 million people in the United Kingdom, around 1.2 per cent die every year. Of those deaths, 25,000

Green light at Brands Hatch...
19,000 horsepower streaks away
from the line at
Osterreichring...
15 seconds later at the end of
GP racing's longest straight,
Kyalami

Left: Wired for sound: McLaren's John Barnard hears how it is

Below: An Englishman from Italy: Dr Harvey Postlethwaite, part of the motor racing brain drain and designer of Ferrari's high-tech chassis

Facing page:
Above: Firing up the team: Frank Williams in his element

Below: Best of friends, only hours from deciding who will be champion (left to right): Nelson Piquet, Brabham designer Gordon Murray, and Alain Prost

Above: Williams team mates Jacques Lafitte *(left)* and 1982 Champion Keke Rosberg sign autographs to please the sponsors

Below: Britain's Derek Warwick, at Imola the day he first drove a Renault, with *Countdown* author Tony Howard

Above: Laid-back
– Nigel Mansell

Right: Ditched by
Ferrari, snapped up
by Renault, Patrick
Tambay repaid
ingratitude with pole
position for the last
race of 1983

Magic mouthpiece – Niki Lauda. If only he wouldn't swear on radio

Left: Darting eyes – René Arnoux

Below: Cocooned in high technology – John Watson

Left: Not the Klu Klux Klan — just race marshals, sensibly fire-proofed

Below: The price of inexperience. Andrea de Cesaris marks his debut with a first Formula 1 prang during the warm-up session before the 1980 Canadian Grand Prix

Facing page:
Above: Jacques Lafitte heads for the catch fences

Below: Danny Sullivan makes the same slip as Derek Warwick

Right: Getting it taped – Tambay tests telemetry festooned Renault

Left: Power to pull the sponsors, McLaren's Ron Dennis with the TAG Porsche turbo engine

Below: Another turbo self-destructs

Above: Bullying the information out
of the cockpit – Williams designer
Patrick Head with Keke Rosberg

are violent, including 6000 road deaths and 4500 suicides. And, when the subject is broached, people close to the sport tend to point to these examples and others, such as the perils of fox hunting or even cooking supper in the kitchen at home.

It was Bruce McLaren, killed in 1970 while testing one of his own cars, who came out with the thought that to live to do something well is so worthwhile that to die trying to do it better cannot be entirely foolhardy. A real conversation stopper.

On the other hand, Clay Regazzoni, paralysed from the waist down as a result of spinal injuries received during an accident in the 1980 Long Beach Grand Prix, has written that he would rather be a nobody, forgoing his past and all the satisfaction he has had from motor racing, if he could be a normal human being today.

Perhaps the most bizzare fatal accident in the sport befell Tom Pryce during the 1977 South African Grand Prix. A car stopped beside the main straight, on the opposite side of the track to the pits. Two marshals prepared to leap over the barrier with a fire extinguisher and dash across the track to help the driver. And, when given the signal that it was safe, off they went.

However, Kyalami's straight runs up an incline to a crest where the starting grid is. When the marshals began their sprint, they had not seen that, in the depression on the blind side of the crest, a tight group of cars was approaching flatout, building up speed to 290 km/h.

The time it took for them to arrive was insufficient for the two young men to run across the track. By chance or quick reaction three of the drivers managed evasive action. However, Pryce's car hit one of the marshals who was tossed 10 metres in the air like a rag doll, and fell to the ground dead.

Pryce was struck in the face by the 9 kg fire extinguisher with such force that it was flung over the top of the main grandstand. Pryce, now dead at the wheel of his Shadow, continued flat-out down the straight, T-boned Jacques

Lafitte's Ligier as he turned into Crowthorne corner, ploughed through catch fencing and smashed into a wall.

Among the quickest to respond to the tragedy was the television helicopter which, with inane lack of consideration, was kept hovering overhead, blowing dust into the eyes of those making a frantic rescue bid.

Later the same year, another Briton, David Purley, endured an even heavier shunt during qualifying for the British Grand Prix at Silverstone. But, miraculously, he emerged alive from what is reckoned to be the most severe racing impact to be survived.

Before the incident, a powder fire extinguisher had been used to put out a small petrol fire on his car. Although mechanics had cleaned up meticulously, there were still traces of powder – set hard like cement – in the engine throttle slides, as examination after the accident revealed. These were the cause of Purley's misfortune. As he lifted off during the approach to Beckett's corner, the throttles remained stuck wide open. The car careered straight on into a bank at 290 km/h, and came to a dead stop within inches, subjecting Purley to a peak deceleration of 180g.

The impact dislocated both his shoulders, broke seventeen ribs, fractured his pelvis in seven places, his right leg in seven places and his left leg in ten. Then followed seven months in hospital fighting through the pain to regain initial mobility, followed by more months of operations to lengthen a shattered leg – it was 65 mm shorter than the other.

What characterizes this, and many similar tales of recovery against the odds, is the determination and the initial physical fitness of the drivers. The latter does give them a head start, even in overcoming more mundane ailments. A grand prix driver who catches a bad cold or hurts himself falling out of bed will probably recover two or three times as quickly as the average person.

By the standards of today, anyone who went racing in the grand prix cars of the 1950s and even 1960s was definitely asking for trouble. There they sat, wrestling with the steering, not restrained by seat belts, and their heads protected only by rudimentary crash helmets. Roll-over hoops, when they started to be fitted, were not up to much, and there was always the danger of a driver being crushed under his up-ended car, or of being flung out.

Whether or not an accident rendered the driver unconscious or immobile, the next immediate hazard was fire. And a high proportion of the deaths that have occurred may well not have done so but for this. All too often it was recorded that rescuers were inadequately equipped to tackle the flames or arrived too late to do so, and stood helpless to avert calamity.

Even today, designers, drivers and team managers admit that enough can never be done about safety. For, in the nature of any evolution in an imperfect world, it is impossible to foresee every eventuality. And, almost by definition, there must be conflict in the sport over safety.

Building better driver protection into the cars means more weight, which clashes with the competitiveness that is the object of the whole exercise. Improving circuit safety standards entails expense which is bound to be passed on to the paying public in one way or another, and it often means they are pushed further and further away from what they have come to watch. So why not stay at home and see it on television?

Inevitably, there is a degree of fatalism – both among the drivers who take the risks and those who prepare their cars for the fray. This is not to suggest unfeeling disregard. It is all too clear that this is not the case when Ken Tyrrell's voice becomes almost inaudible as he recollects what 'a terrible blow it was to all of us' when his driver Francois Cevert was killed during practice for the 1973 United States Grand Prix. Hearing this ten years later, one still has the feeling of having strayed into the privacy of grief.

Frank Williams makes the point that more than 130 people are killed every year, falling off Swiss Alps. 'Because most of them were unknown, and usually did it in private, it was no big deal. But if someone well known is burned to death in front of a hundred thousand people, that makes news. That's the difference.

'The time it really hurt me was when Piers Courage was

killed – and he truly was a close friend. I've buried quite a lot of people in my time – not all drivers – and it's something we all have to get used to. It's very sad when they go down below the earth. But it's part of the deal, like engines – if that doesn't sound too callous. Engines blow up, and cost a lot of money. Once in every two years, a great driver gets killed – but he's doing what he wants to do. We could go bankrupt in the next three months and lose everything – it would be one of those things. No one made me go racing, and no one is forcing me to go on. It's a very callous answer, but that's it.'

Certainly, safety measures have come a long way in response to many painful lessons. Arguably, however, the trend to rear-engined designs that took hold from the late 1950s was a retrograde one from the safety standpoint. To begin with, there was less car between the driver and the accident. And frontal area was kept to a minimum to reduce drag. This entailed cramming in fuel wherever there was a bit of space that would otherwise be wasted.

Often, the driver's backrest was a wedge-shaped fuel tank between him and the front of the engine. He had a tank slung in the space frame along either side of him, and another in the scuttle above his knees. These tanks were skilfully fabricated in aluminium, and the driver literally shoehorned himself into the tight confines of a rolling bomb.

The prospect of being trapped by the legs while gallons of petrol gushed out of ruptured tanks did not bear contemplating. But a driver stood more of a chance if he had not been knocked out cold or impaled on the steering column. As this came to be better understood in the late 1960s safety belts began to be used, notably by three times World Champion Jackie Stewart who devoted considerable energy to the cause of safety in the sport.

In Britain, fitting seat belts for both front seats became compulsory for all new road cars registered from April 1967. The following year, the year book of the *Fédération Internationale de l'Automobile* included the rule that seat belt mounting points be fitting to racing cars. Only from 1972 were grand prix drivers required to wear a full safety harness – two shoulder straps, two between the legs, and one around the abdomen. Posthumous World Champion Jochen Rindt had been wearing shoulder and lap straps when he was killed during practice for the 1970 Italian Grand Prix. But he might have survived if he had also had the benefit of crotch straps to prevent him being wrenched in a sliding movement out of his upper harness.

Also steadily making progress was the transformation of the cockpit from a coffin equipped for instant immolation to today's survival cell. Multiple tanks continued to be used to optimize distribution of the weight of the fuel, but these became aircraft-style rubber bladders, protected by crushable structures. Aviation specification fuel lines with self-sealing breakaway couplings were also adopted.

Nowadays, a Formula 1 car has a single fuel cell protected within a hollow box structure behind the cockpit and integral with the rest of the monocoque. This practice came about when the need arose to use the structures along the sides of the monocoque for the creation of ground effect, now banned.

Oil tanks may not protude from the back of the car where they could be damaged by contact with another car, and spill on to the track.

An important requirement is that the driver should be able to get out of the cockpit in no more than five seconds without having to remove the steering wheel – which anyway is generally removable by means of a quick release device. Minimum dimensions are therefore laid down for the cockpit opening which must be 60 cm long and 45 cm wide for at least 30 cm forward from the backrest.

Some humorist has also managed to have written in the rule that 'Sitting at his steering wheel the driver must be facing forward.'

Two roll-over structures are demanded, one ahead of the driver and above steering wheel height, the other behind him and above his helmet, so that, if the car flips, he should not bang his head or hands on the road. These hoops must be able to withstand loads of as much as 7.5 times the weight of the car with driver and full fuel load.

Minima are also stipulated for the structure protecting the driver longitudinally, and this must extend to at least 50 cm forward of the soles of his feet. The front 40 cm can be a separate piece, firmly attached to the main monocoque, the idea being to provide a deformable structure that will progressively absorb the load occurring during a head-on impact.

In this survival cell, the driver is secured to his custom-formed seat by a full safety harness with a central quick release and wide webbing to spread the load of an impact.

Use of carbon fibre and other new materials now means that, generally speaking, a survival cell can resist impacts of more than 50 g before breaking up. And a driver subjected to loadings of such magnitude for even half a second would most likely be finished by the trauma anyway.

The hopeful assumption is, of course, that the driver does survive the crash itself, and then the rest of the belt-and-braces approach may be brought into play. First, there is a 'kill' switch – a spark-proof circuit breaker that shuts off all the car's electrical circuits and can be operated by the driver inside the cockpit and from outside by a rescuer, using a pole with a hook if necessary.

Two inert-gas fire extinguishers are fitted, and are triggered simultaneously. One, of 2,5 kg minimum, discharges into the engine compartment, mainly around the fuel and induction system. The other, of at least 5 kg, feeds into the cockpit for 30 to 60 seconds.

As a precaution against the on-board extinguishers failing to quench any fire that may have begun, the car is also equipped with a life-support system. This is to prevent the driver being suffocated if fire consumes all the oxygen in his vicinity. It consists of a medical air bottle that, when set off, discharges for at least 30 seconds along a flame-resistant pipe into the driver's helmet, creating a pressurized 'micro-climate' there and also saving him from inhaling toxic fumes that could damage his lungs.

Careful attention has been paid to protecting the body

from burns. First layer, next to the skin, consists of socks, long johns, polo-neck sweater and balaclava helmet, all knitted from Nomex, a fire-retardant aramid fibre, evolved by Du Pont for the US Army in the early 1960s. It is inherently flame retardant, unlike conventional fabrics which have to be specially treated. And it can be washed or dry cleaned without losing its properties.

A development is Nomex III, with 5 per cent Kevlar. This is widely used to give defence against severe and even fatal burns to tank crews, riot police, military pilots, firemen and industrial workers, as well as racing drivers. Desirable properties of such a material are that it should not break open, exposing the skin to flames, nor should it melt, drip or give off toxic vapours. Nomex III retains 70 per cent of its strength after 30 minutes exposure to 260°C dry heat, and only starts to char at 370°. When subjected to flames, the fabric thickens, and its pores close, giving the wearer further protection.

A professional racing suit, made up of five layers – Nomex cloth outer, Kevlar knit, Nomex felt, Nomex felt, Nomex knit – can make the difference between life and death by insulating the wearer from the heat of flames enveloping him.

In such a suit, while the exterior flame temperature shoots up to 200°C plus, it takes ten seconds before the driver feels any increase. After 20 seconds, interior temperature has risen to 40°. And it takes another 40 seconds to reach 90°, at which point second-degree burns begin, though the pain threshold comes earlier – at 70°.

By this time, anyone wearing a single-layer suit of treated wool or cotton would already be dead. However, assuming he is not injured or stunned, the modern grand prix driver should have time to hit both the kill switch and the quick release of his safety harness, and spring out of the car like a jack-in-the-box, with nothing more to complain of than a hot posterior.

In any event, matters should be so ordered that, by then, rescue procedures are already well under way. A vital objective is that, if there is an accident anywhere on the circuit, at least two trained firefighters with portable extinguishers should reach the car within 15 seconds of an accident. This is known as first intervention.

Second intervention is by a fast vehicle, equipped completely to extinguish a 180-litre petrol fire as well as to resuscitate and free the driver, and it must arrive within 30 seconds. Emergency vehicles and marshals' posts must be furnished with cutting tools to deal with tangled catch fences or crushed bodywork, gear to right an upturned car, asbestos blankets to smother a fire, and fireproof clothing for the rescuers themselves.

If the driver is reported as injured, grand prix racing's official doctor is immediately alerted. He is Professor Sidney Watkins, one of the world's top neurosurgeons, who attends every race in the championship, and waits on standby in a fast car parked in the pit road.

As soon as he reaches the stricken racing car, he minutely examines the driver to assess the full extent of his injuries, and then sets about stabilizing his condition, using an intravenous drip to compensate for blood loss.

Then, and only then, it may be safe for the other rescuers to begin the circumspect process of extricating the driver while his broken body is held together by the professor to avert further damage that could result, for instance, in permanent paralysis. Cutters and hydraulic rams are used to unpeel the car from around the victim, like shelling a super-fragile pod of peas. And then he is whisked to hospital by helicopter.

In an ideal world, none of this would be necessary, of course. It is argued with considerable cogency that safety measures within the cars themselves have now reached such high standards that the effort required to make further improvements is out of all proportion to the results attainable. If this view prevails, the focus on circuit safety must intensify, giving more clout to those most involved in promoting it.

Their brief is to see that the ever present possibility of a car flying off out of control is mitigated. Ideally, this would entail power, at the stroke of a pen, to sweep away all immoveable objects – such as concrete walls or barriers perpendicular to the direction of travel – within likely range of the track.

But, while the circuit operators should not be cast as villains in the piece, resistance to draconian measures is bound to come from them, mindful of cost and the fact that most of their lifeblood comes from spectators who pay to *see* their heroes at work. Which leads us back into the ebb and flow of grand prix politics – the art of the possible.

What is advocated, however, is that, with a bit of thought, far better energy absorption systems could be devised for deployment around circuits without incurring outrageous expense. And a continual spur to this is the requirement that circuits be re-licensed every three years, following an inspection that covers not only track safety but aspects such as lavatories and the possibility of overcrowding in the paddock, denying access to a firefighting crew.

In the good old days when racing drivers were real men and not a lot of overpaid namby-pambies afraid of taking a few knocks or singeing their eyebrows, it was quite good enough to mark out the circuit with a few 220-litre oil drums and maybe dump the odd bale of straw in front of a tree or lamp post.

Then came steel Armco barriers to prevent cars from leaving the track and being smashed to smithereens as they ricocheted from tree to tree. And catch-fencing, following the same principle as arrestor nets on aircraft carriers, was erected where there was space to cushion head-on thumps into walls around the outsides of corners.

Such fencing, however, is not unreservedly admired. Drivers are concerned lest they become ensnared in it and fire breaks out, or they may be struck on the head by one of the supporting poles. And then there is the cost of replacement.

FISA circuit safety inspector Derek Ongaro – he is the official grand prix starter too – points out, though, that catch-fencing is gradually being phased out. 'We've had a fair amount of success in substituting gravel pits – and nothing seems to slow a car down so well because it sinks

107

in. Drivers, motor cyclists and karters prefer them. They are cheaper from the circuit owner's point of view, and only need a bit of raking over.

'At Hockenheim, we persuaded them to put a gravel pit outside the Ostkurve. They said it wouldn't work. But we got the circuit director to try to drive his car across it. He had to be towed out. It's little things like that that start to get the message across.'

Most important of circuit safety criteria is to protect against head-on collisions. The Eau Rouge corner at Spa-Francorchamps illustrates how Ongaro can help in consultation with the drivers. 'For years there was a problem there. I looked at the corner, read some books and watched films of accidents there. It's quite obvious, when you really sort it out, that the accidents were happening there because the car came down the hill, and left, then right, uphill. If it was out of balance at the bottom of the dip – if another car touched it or there was water on the track – then there was a big accident on into the grandstand.

'After chewing this over for a while with some of the drivers, I suggested taking that kink out, pushing the road as far over to the right as possible. So you could just go down the hill and then up. First reaction was that this would be a lot faster. That was true, but you wouldn't have an out-of-balance situation at the bottom. And, if a car went out of control it would go further up the hill and come into a sliding contact with the barrier instead of head-on.

'We carried the old pits guardrail all the way down the hill, so a car out of control would only be in sliding contact right the way down both sides. It was a little bit faster, but it was OK.'

Causes for drivers' concern can be more imaginary than real. 'Often, they get psychological blocks about things. For years, we had a drama at Monza about the tyres around the end of the guardrail after they pass the start and go onto the new circuit where the old high-speed section turns off.

'The precise statement was: "You must do something about those tyres." In fact, there were an awful lot of tyres there already. If you have too many and they are hit, they're no good because they fly in all directions. So we simply painted them yellow. And we never heard another thing.

'It's something that I can understand. The driver gets it in the back of his mind that something is wrong. It may not be. But, if he sees that you've tried to do something, then usually his mind is relieved. Sometimes their complaints are justified, sometimes not.'

The degree of control over the circuits is probably greater than it is over the cars. For the terms of reference are clearer and easier to implement. 'If we want something done, and it isn't, we can stand in the middle of the track, and tell them: "You don't start practice, you don't start the race."

'On many occasions, we have held things up for a couple of hours because an ambulance is missing, or some guard-rails need tidying up. On that side, we can really wade in, and say no. We took the licence away from Jarama for that very reason. They just wouldn't do things that were required. Without that licence, they're not insured. Do they want to take a chance? Oh no.'

However, there is not a lot that can be done about accidents where cars collide, or one is launched off the wheel of another. 'I just don't know how you deal with that because you never know where it's going to happen or why or how. You can't have a thirty-foot high barrier down each side of every circuit to stop the cars flying off – because the higher you build a fence, the weaker it gets.

'So it's a compromise. Generally speaking, this launching doesn't happen in a sweeping turn. Usually, this sort of contact takes place when they're in a straight line, trying to pass on the way into a corner or sweep.'

Just as unpredictable is the kind of catastrophe that befell Ricardo Paletti at the start of only his second grand prix, in Canada in 1982. Didier Pironi's Ferrari, on pole position, stalled just as the green light went on to start the race. And there was nothing to be done to stop the race during those frantic moments as the twenty-five others burst forward, swarming along the track.

Most, though intent on getting a good start, were just able to duck around the static obstacle so unexpectedly presented by the Ferrari that should have been on its way at the head of the field. But, accelerating to more than 160 km/h by the time they reached it, drivers coming from the back of the grid were less fortunate, their chances of avoidance diminished by their greater speed and the confusion of cars ahead.

Three cars became involved in a mêlée, thumping the barrier. The inexperienced Paletti, his head down, charged up the grid along the right-hand side, and slammed into the back of the immobile Ferrari. It is doubtful if he even saw it. Pironi immediately dashed to his rescue, but was forced back as Paletti's Osella burst into flames. It took a seeming age to free the young Italian who later died in hospital.

'I looked at the tape time and time again,' remembers Ongaro. 'And you had to put that accident down as inevitable. I know it sounds callous. But you've got to accept that these people are in a very dangerous game. The law of averages dictates that, sooner or later, something that isn't very nice is going to happen.

'Once they get themselves warmed up to gallop for the starting light, I don't think you can change anything. They're triggered very easily at that stage. It's the time when they're really on edge and try to gain half a tenth of a second on everybody else.'

One move that has met with mixed feelings is the ban on mid-race refuelling effective from 1984. The objectives are twofold. First is to curtail the amount of fuel available and thus the power of turbo engines, reducing speeds. Second is to avert the dangers arising from such frenetic activity in the pits.

Objections to the ban come from those who regret the loss of some of the spectacle in the sport and others who feel that placing such an artificial limitation on engine power is anathema to the sport. There is always the possibility that such opinions may one day hold sway once more.

However, among those who firmly believe that refuelling

stops will stay banned is Bob Tyrrell. 'If they don't, sooner or later there is going to be an inferno in the pit road with a lot of people running around burning. It's not like Le Mans or Indianapolis where the fuel is fed in under gravity. This stuff is going in at a hundred pounds per square inch – seven times atmospheric pressure. The whole bloody lot goes in in four seconds.

'Sooner or later, a pipe is going to be ruptured. Or somebody is going to put the fuel in before they plug in the vent for the vapour to come out. The whole thing is going to go up. And there are going to be twenty-five people running around, screaming, with their hair on fire. And it will happen.'

6

MOTIVE FORCES

Power is now, more than ever, the name of the game in Formula 1. And three key events have led to this state of affairs.

First was the decision in favour of the present engine formula that came into force from 1966 onwards. After a good deal of bickering, the rule makers opted for 3-litre engines, naturally aspirated, and thus doubled the maximum capacity allowed. But they also threw in a limit of 1,5 litres supercharged, not really thinking anyone would be bothered to go to all the trouble and expense that that would involve. If they had settled for 1,3 or 1,4 litres, things might have turned out very differently.

Second was in early 1977 when the directors of Regie Renault gave the green light to Renault Sport to race in Formula 1 with a 1,5 litre turbo-charged V6, derived from a 2-litre sports car engine with which the team was to win the Le Mans 24-hour race the following year.

Third was the ruling, towards the end of 1982, that finally banished ground effect. This meant that teams running naturally aspirated engines could no longer compensate for their power deficit by applying great ingenuity to aerodynamic means of cornering more quickly and thus maintaining lap times on a par with the turbo cars.

At the time of Renault's debut in mid-1977, the 3-litre Ford Cosworth V8 had increasingly been the mainstay of the sport for ten years. And, then, only three makes of engine – Alfa Romeo, Ferrari and Matra – challenged the Cosworth. By 1983, the number of engine builders involved had risen to eight, even though Matra had pulled out the year before.

First to follow Renault's challenge was Ferrari which tested a V6 turbo at Imola towards the end of 1980, and raced this engine from the start of 1981. The reward was a win at Monaco, sixth event of the year.

Next came BMW's four-cylinder turbo which appeared in a Brabham during practice for the British Grand Prix in mid-1981, but was not raced until the South African Grand Prix, the first of 1982.

In a sense, the Hart turbo, also with four cylinders, beat BMW to it, by being raced in Toleman chassis from the 1981 Italian Grand Prix onwards. A year later in Italy, the Alfa Romeo V8 turbo made a fleeting appearance during practice, but it was not raced until the Brazilian Grand Prix in March 1983. Honda's V6 turbo was run first in the Spirit from April 1983, and then in the Williams cars from the South African Grand Prix, last race of the year. The TAG Porsche V6 turbo ran its first race with McLaren in Holland at the end of August 1983.

Between 1967 and 1983, the Ford Cosworth V8 won 155 grands prix. This compared with 89 wins for its nearest rival, Ferrari, between 1950 and 1983. During its life, nearly 400 of the Cosworth DFV were built, and it powered 12 different grand prix teams to victory: Lotus, McLaren, Tyrrell, Brabham, Williams, Matra, Ligier, March, Wolf, Hesketh, Penske and Shadow.

Power was progressively increased from 408 bhp at 9000 rpm to 510 bhp at 11,200 rpm, while weight was reduced from 161,5 kg (356 lbs) to 154 kg.

Provoked by modifications that Williams had made to further improve the power of its DFVs, Cosworth Engineering came out with the DFY in early 1983 – possibly a last naturally aspirated resort in face of the turbo onslaught. It was a short-stroke descendant of the DFV, and latterly had different cylinder heads. It was lighter – 132,5 kg – and power was up to 520 bhp at 11,000 rpm. (There were those who thought there was more to come with water injection, as used in turbo engines and declared legal after protests.)

The price of a DFY was £37,000, so to buy ten engines

for a two-car team meant a bill for £370,000, a lot of money, no doubt. But this was a snip when compared with the cost of turbo engines, £50,000 to £60,000, depending on how the accountants did their sums.

Michele Alboreto's Tyrrell was powered by a version of the DFY when it won in Detroit in 1983, the last Cosworth grand prix win of the year, and maybe of all time.

Such a demise is always sad to contemplate, but the DFV had an incredible run for its money. And nobody involved at the time when, in early 1966, Ford paid Cosworth £100,000 to develop the engine, could have dreamed they were creating a show that would run and run.

(It was therefore not surprising when, in December 1983, Ford announced that it was to collaborate with Cosworth Engineering to produce a 'year 2000' grand prix engine and 'certain associated power units.' This Formula 1 engine involves 'materials experts from Ford Aerospace, our advanced electronics operation, and other appropriate research support', and is expected to race in 1986.)

In any event, Ford gained immense kudos from its investment over the years. Noting this, Renault decided to pursue the same goals. It was a matter of national as well as corporate prestige for the state-owned company. To win at Le Mans – trouncing the foreigners in front of the home crowd – was a first objective. That done, the firm would switch its efforts and concentrate on the world arena – grands prix.

It was a brave gamble to take on the unknowns of turbo power though the principle behind it is simple enough. A naturally aspirated engine, relying on atmospheric pressure alone to fill the vacuum created in its cylinders by the downward stroke of the pistons, can never, in practice, achieve 100 per cent volumetric efficiency. In other words, the actual volume of mixture sucked in is never equal to the true capacity of the cylinder.

So the bang when the spark plug ignites the charge of mixture in the combustion chamber is not as big as it might be in theory. One way to get more power is to increase the rate at which these explosions take place – increase the revs.

But this is partly countered by a decline in volumetric efficiency – there is less time for the cylinders to fill, and they take in less charge on each occasion.

Using a blower to force the air/fuel mixture into the cylinders is a means of overcoming the problem. For increasing the pressure means there is a greater weight of air and fuel present, and the bang is bigger.

Exhaust gases, going to waste, account for 35 per cent of the energy consumed in a piston petrol engine. Directing them through a turbine that drives a compressor – turbo-charging – in effect does the job for nothing, because the energy thus used has already been discarded by the engine.

However, maximizing the performance in this way brings with it massive problems. These are largely associated with the huge amounts of additional heat that are generated – first in the compression of the air being fed to the cylinders, and secondly in creating a bigger explosion in the confines of a smaller combustion chamber.

Air compressed by the turbo-charger to three times atmospheric pressure, as it commonly is in today's Formula 1 engine, rises to a temperature of more than 200°C, twice as hot as boiling water. This air is then routed through intercoolers. These function on the same principle as an ordinary car radiator through which exterior air is passed to cool the engine coolant being pumped through inside.

In the first intercooler the compressed air temperature is reduced by the circulation of the racing engine coolant which then passes on through conventional radiators to be cooled by external airflow. Next, the compressed air feed passes through an air-to-air intercooler where it is further reduced towards the ambient temperature.

The reasons for cooling the compressed air are (1) its density is thus increased, and so a greater weight of oxygen is introduced to the cylinders (?) a cooler charge lessens the risk of detonation (an uncontrolled explosion before the piston has risen to the top of its compression stroke which can blow a hole in its crown), similar to the pinking that takes place when a road car is run on too low a grade of petrol; (3) thermic problems inside the engine are reduced

– after combustion, less heat has to be dissipated through the piston, cylinder walls, valve gear and combustion chamber envelope; (4) helping to contain exhaust gas temperature to a level that the turbo-charger turbine can survive.

The turbo-charger itself is light and compact. It consists of a single shaft, at one end of which is the turbine in its chamber, fed by the exhaust manifold. At the other end of the shaft is the compressor, connected by complex trunking to the intercoolers and then the induction manifolds. The turbine is subjected to temperatures of 1100°C, and spins at around 160,000 rpm, all of which demands the best of ceramics and metals technology.

As the turbo-charger is always spinning freely – it is not connected mechanically to the rest of the engine – its continuing momentum would cause the induction system to blow up the instant the throttles were shut.

To prevent this – as well as over-pressurization of the cylinders during full-throttle operation – a wastegate is incorporated in the plumbing for each turbo-charger. This is a spring-loaded pop-off valve, fed by a bleed pipe from the induction manifold. When pressure in the system rises above a predetermined level, the valve is forced open, allowing air to escape. Simultaneously, this opens another valve in the exhaust system, diverting the gases through a by-pass pipe around the turbo-charger.

Having solved that problem, the next is to get the turbine-cum-compressor whirring quickly again when the throttles are opened. Inertia of these revolving parts mitigates against this. Hence 'turbo lag' where, when the driver puts his foot down, nothing happens immediately. And this is followed by a sudden and huge surge of power, making the car tricky to drive with the fine balance necessary.

This is less serious on circuits with long straights and fast corners where the driver is hard on the power for the most part. But it could lose a lot of time against a more flexible naturally aspirated engine on a track with a lot of slow corners and short straights where the turbo lacks the time to get into its stride.

For this reason, most engines are equipped with two turbo-chargers – one for each bank of cylinders. As those spinning parts are smaller and lighter than in a single larger turbo-charger of similar total capacity they speed up more rapidly. And throttle response is snappier, though more progressive and controllable.

Also the turbo-chargers are changed to suit the circuit. Larger ones are used on fast circuits where the engine runs at full power most of the time. Smaller ones are attached where throttle response out of slow corners is at a premium.

It is the wastegate that is subjected to 'screwdriver tuning' when more power is sought for a super-quick qualifying lap. This is done simply enough by increasing the spring pressure that air in the induction system has to overcome before the pop-off valve will open. But, by intensifying pressure and heat in the cylinders, it shortens engine life.

A cockpit control for the wastegates is also fitted to allow the driver to turn up the power when overtaking, or even to turn it down to conserve the engine to the end of the race. As important, it was realized, was the use of this means to reduce consumption in face of smaller tanks – down from 250 to 220 litres from 1984 – and the impending ban on mid-race refuelling.

These rules are supposed to use the considerable extra thirst of the turbo engine as a lever to reduce power outputs during races. Not only is the 1,5-litre turbo motor inherently much more powerful than a naturally aspirated one of twice the capacity, but it requires more fuel to produce each horsepower. The reason yet again is heat. And additional petrol is squirted into the engine to help cool the charge and counter those thermic problems.

The greater thirst that results is counter-productive, and not only because it jeopardizes a car's ability to run a full race distance on a tankful. Whereas a Cosworth car, averaging 5 to 6 mpg (47,0 to 56,5 litres/100km), would go from start to finish on 150 to 170 litres, the turbo cars have been 60 per cent thirstier. With refuelling, they could get away with 3,0 to 3,5 mpg (80 to 94 litres/100 km).

But, even using every last drop of the 220 litres allowed for 1984, they must do better than 4 mpg (71 litres/100 km). And still they incur a fuel weight penalty of almost 50 kg, a lot to lift off the floor at one heave.

Significantly, Renault reiterating a discovery first put forward by Colin Chapman, has found that, for every additional 0,7 kg (the weight of a litre of petrol) in the car, the lap time on the short (3 km) loop at the Paul Ricard circuit is increased by one hundredth of a second. That means a 0,7 second penalty with a full tank. And this problem is obviously magnified on a full-length grand prix circuit with twice the lap distance. Also, extra weight in the car may mean it has to run on tyres with a harder compound if these are to go the distance. And this, too, contributes to slower lap times.

This is where the water injection systems, used first by Ferrari and Renault, come in. The water introduced into the combustion process absorbs a great deal of heat as it is converted into steam – it takes 540 calories to vaporize one gramme of water, once it has attained its boiling point, 100°C.

The significance of substituting water for extra fuel flow as a charge coolant is even greater than it at first appears. For it takes only 100 calories to vaporize one gramme of premium petrol, required by Formula 1 rules. The implication is that, for every gramme of water injected, more than five grammes of petrol need not be wasted in charge cooling but are conserved for the production of power.

Renault has been using a system that injects water at 2 bar (30 lbs/sq in) into the pressurized induction air, just downstream of the intercoolers, at the rate of about one gramme of water for every 100 grammes of air, or 10 grammes of fuel.

Ferrari's more complex system mixes between 4 and 10 parts of water with 100 parts of petrol just before it passes into the fuel injection metering unit. One purpose is to allow an increase in turbo boost without causing the detonation that would destroy the pistons. And it is admitted that there is also significant potential for saving fuel.

The problem for Ferrari is that racing cars have a re-circulatory fuel system with a spill return to the main tank – the aim is to counteract vapour lock. But the water-petrol blend must not be allowed to return to the main tank because it would separate out. Sometimes the pump would be drawing up very watery fuel to the injectors, and the engine would not run. And it is impossible to start under such conditions.

So the injection pump is designed to suck in its own spill before it draws in fresh petrol. And the driver has a cockpit switch with which to stop the water flow and clear it from the system before he comes into the pits, making it easier to restart the engine.

Water injection gave rise to what was possibly the sport's most significant legal battle of 1983. Ken Tyrrell first contested the legality of the Ferrari and Renault systems before the British Grand Prix, and he was joined by Frank Williams in a second protest before the German Grand Prix.

Both were rejected, and so the case was taken before a *Fédération Internationale de l'Automobile* appeals tribunal in September. The members considered themselves unqualified to make a ruling, and asked Professor Hans-Peter Lenz of Vienna University for his opinion. And, in November, as a result of his findings, the tribunal ruled that water injection was legal.

Tyrrell's motive for litigation that cost £8000 in legal fees was plain enough. FISA, quite rightly in his opinion, made a decision at the end of 1982 to reduce the power of Formula 1 engines by limiting the amount of fuel available. This was to be done by reducing the maximum size of fuel tanks, and abolishing refuelling stops.

'Of course, this applies particularly to the turbo-charged cars – normally aspirated ones use a lot less fuel. If water injection is allowed, it completely circumvents the reduction in tank size because they are chucking in water to cool the charge instead of pumping in a lot more fuel to do it.

'All the competitors and the FISA agreed that we should restrict the horsepower to between five hundred and fifty five and the new engine laws are due out to take care of that in 1986. For the interim, everybody signed a document agreeing that we should reduce tanks and there would be no refuelling. If we now have water injection, that's thrown out of the window.'

Premise for the protest was that water should be ruled to be an additive that increased power, and thus contravened Article 14 – dealing with fuel – in the Formula 1 Technical Regulations. This says that the only fuel permitted is petrol with a maximum octane rating of 102, and 'consisting exclusively of hydrocarbons and not containing any alcohols, nitro compounds or other power boosting additives'.

However, Professor Lenz decided that as no energy was released from water, it did not of itself increase engine power.

Frank Williams was party to the protest because he wanted clarification on the issue once and for all so that his engine partner, Honda, would know which course to pursue. Before the outcome of the case he said: 'If our appeal is turned down, they will have to use water injection because it definitely gives an advantage. It helps with the thermal problems inside the engines, so they are more reliable. And you get more miles per gallon.'

Had the appeal succeeded, it might have left the naturally aspirated 3-litre Cosworth firmly in a position to continue competitively against the turbos, at any rate during races, if not while qualifying. And this may yet be the outcome.

Certainly the Cosworth is noted with more than passing wistfulness by teams that abandoned it in favour of turbos. For the latter are not only much more costly. The complex plumbing is bulky and difficult to package within a slippery shape, and it adds weight. Also the aerodynamics are complicated by the need to pass air through intercoolers.

A brief comparison between the early lives of the Cosworth and Renault engines is illustrative of the magnitude of the technological leap from one to the other.

Ford commissioned the Cosworth at the beginning of March 1966, though designer Keith Duckworth did not begin his drawings until the end of June. Less than a year later, at the Dutch Grand Prix, his new engine made its debut, powering the Lotus 49s of Graham Hill and Jim Clark. And, almost too good to be true, Hill started from pole position while Clark went on to win.

For Renault, it was a different story. At the beginning of 1975 a pair of test engines were commissioned. These were of 1,5 litres, and were derived from the 2-litre V6 turbo which had first run on the bench in late 1972. Within a year, this 1,5-litre V6 turbo was giving 483 bhp at 10,500 rpm on the bench with boost of 2,5 times atmospheric pressure. It was installed in a 'laboratory' chassis and first run at Clermont-Ferrand and Jarama during March and April 1976.

All that glistens on the dynamometer does not necessarily turn out to be golden once it's propelling a car round a track, as Renault found. The engine had a narrow operating range – between 9000 and 11,000 rpm, compared with 6500 to 11,200 rpm for an unblown 3-litre. And turbo lag was such that the car would run 30 metres out of a corner before boost built up.

By this stage, the engine was producing 512 bhp at 11,000 rpm, but only 128 bhp before the boost came in. It was all or nothing with a finger-drumming wait between the two, and it must have been a real pain to drive. But the engineers kept plugging away at it.

In Renault's first twenty-eight grand prix starts – during 1977, 1978 and 1979 – the team managed only five finishes. Of the retirements, fourteen were attributable to engine or turbo failure. Then came the first win, with Jean-Pierre Jabouille at the wheel in the 1979 French Grand Prix. Between then and the end of 1983, the team's cars started a hundred and twenty-one times, suffered sixty-eight retirements, won ten races, and came within an ace of winning the championship.

Durability of the Renault Formula 1 engine has greatly improved over the years. At the beginning, its life before blowing up or between rebuilds was only 500 km but this has been extended to 1000 km, on a par with the Cosworth. Power is up also. The team has admitted to 600 to 640 bhp at 11,000 rpm, 'depending on configuration', and the engine is designed to run up to 12,000 rpm.

Its weight during 1983 was 170 kg complete with ancillaries – that is 38 kg heavier than a Cosworth DFY, but a 10-kg reduction was expected to result from use of more lightweight materials for 1984.

Renault began supplying engines to other teams from the start of the 1983 season – first to Lotus and then, from 1984, Ligier. Each pays more than $1.7 million a season for a complete power package, regardless of the number of engines used. These remain the property of Renault Sport, and rebuilds are the firm's responsibility. Though they are not for sale, the cost of each Renault engine is reckoned at about 500,000 francs ($68,000).

The deal is that the two customers get engines identical to those fitted to the works cars. 'It's the policy of the company that we cannot cheat with the engines,' says Renault team manager Jean Sage. 'They are exactly the same. It can happen that we have a new development to try, but they will get it a week later.'

However, the two latecomers in the turbo race, McLaren and Williams, ever sceptical in such a competitive business, preferred not to follow that route. It was partly a matter of money, and partly of wanting absolute priority when it came to engines.

Williams bided his time, and came to a deal with Honda that looks disarmingly simple. 'Instead of paying Cosworth, there is a different type of engine in the cars, and we don't get a bill for it. That's the only external difference, except that, because it's a turbo-charged project, the amount of money our partners will have to spend will be enormous.

'We are delighted it's their problem, and not ours. But they are not doing it for charitable reasons. They have their own very good, very Japanese, very well-considered reasons for going GP racing. And I think both parties will get what they expect from the other.'

What the initial two-year agreement could not guarantee was instant race-winning form, though the presence of twelve Honda personnel for the Williams-Honda debut at

Kyalami and a fifth place for Rosberg looked promising. 'What it takes,' says Williams, 'is the resolve and expertise of the two partners involved. If you're not resolved in racing – if you're not determined – forget it. You're a non-starter.'

McLaren also decided for exclusivity. After casting around, it concluded that there was only one company not then involved in grand prix racing but with the credentials to create a brand-new engine that would be a front-runner. It was Porsche which, surprisingly, had not been propositioned before.

'It was like the most beautiful girl at a party,' remembers McLaren director Creighton Brown. 'Everybody assumes she belongs to somebody else already. And they're all dead scared of going up and asking her for a dance.'

What emerged in October 1981 was that Porsche would develop a 'no-compromise state-of-the-art' engine for McLaren. And later it became known that the project would be financed by TAG – *Techniques d'Avant Garde* – a Middle Eastern group with interests in 'peak industries' and involved first in Formula 1 as a sponsor of Williams.

It took only eleven months before the new V6 twin-turbo first ran on the test bed. Then followed an intensive test programme, including 6400 km of track work. By the time the engine first raced in August 1983 – several million dollars later – it was giving 650 – raceable – bhp. This was 25 per cent up on a Cosworth; and torque was 40 per cent better. And there was 700 to 730 bhp on tap for qualifying.

However, the car was very difficult to drive below 7500 to 8000 rpm, as that was where the power really came in, and turbo lag was considerable. The aim through the winter was to get it to run progressively from 6500 rpm.

Other teething troubles occurred with the engine's electronics that operate the ignition and fuel metering. So complex are they that, when the engine refused to restart after twenty laps of tyre testing at Brands Hatch, engineers could do little about it until their testing equipment, delayed by Customs at Heathrow, was 'liberated'.

Living with this sort of frustration should pay dividends though. For the system has the capacity to ensure that the engine runs at a perfect air-fuel ration over a wide range of operating conditions. At the click of a 12-position switch, it can be changed from one programme to another to provide a combination of ignition and fuel injection characteristics to suit, say, the high speeds and 1900 metres altitude at Kyalami or the tortuous streets of Monaco at sea level.

Also, cockpit instrumentation will include a form of 'econometer' to tell the driver how hard he can drive if he is not to run out of fuel before the finish.

In any event, McLaren seems to have less worries than some other teams about how a refuelling ban could affect its ability to run competitive power during the race.

However, should the rule makers take the limitations of fuel tank capacity further than the 195 litres proposed for 1985, and minimum weight is further reduced, there could be an opening for a Cosworth comeback.

Even with a full tank, it could be difficult to run the distance with the turbo turned up to much more then 570 to 580 bhp. And, with a turbo engine, it is harder to get down to the weight limit than with the less complex and lighter Cosworth.

Extracting 540 bhp from the latter is feasible. Propelling a fundamentally lighter car and starting with less fuel lead, it could be very competitive again – if it could get a place on the starting grid. But that is less likely if qualifying continues the way it has been going.

With the increasingly fierce battle between turbo teams has come the 'hand grenade' qualifying engine with the boost turned right up to 3,5 or more atmospheres to produce maybe 800 bhp. And 900 bhp is predicted, possibly before 1985. Also, 1000 bhp has been seen on the dynamometer – albeit in flash readings, and then – bang! – it's all over the wall: Formula 1 engine test cells are peppered with shrapnel, signposts on the rough road of progress.

Qualifying engines, running absolutely at the limits of their endurance, are good for only a few super-rapid laps. However, it has been confidently predicted that, but for fuel restrictions, development would soon produce 800 bhp engines capable of running a full race.

And therein lies the rub. For the gap is widening between the amount of power available for qualifying and the race. So the sport is confronted with the spectre of drivers not only having to cope with a 300 bhp power variation, equivalent to maximum output of five family saloons, but of costs rocketing still further from an already high base.

With race engines 'tuned for economy', and qualifying engines set up for absolute power, regardless of thirst, two different types have to be built. Not only that, but the permutations of tyres, suspension settings and wings required to cope satisfactorily with the two engine variants are widely divergent.

That adds up to one sort of car for qualifying and quite another for the race. The price goes up, not only because two sorts of chassis have to be built, but each has to be developed to its optimum. Taking this to extremes renders the relationship between qualifying and the race almost meaningless.

The dilemma for the driver will be whether to devote his attention to getting his race car right and learn how to be quick in it, probably sacrificing his chances for a high grid placing. Or should he concentrate on qualifying and let the race take care of itself?

No doubt, however acrimonious is the round of argument about how the script should be rewritten, the show will go on. Certainly, now that the majority are so expensively committed, lobbying will be intense for allowing the turbo engine's advantages to be fully exploited.

As the teams departed for a tyre testing session in Rio de Janeiro in January, 1984, at least one of their number bravely faced the prospect of soldiering on for another season with the Cosworth V8. Tyrrell could have had turbo engines, but the bill would have come to as much as $4 million, a lot of money to justify to a sponsor.

Also, obtaining the right turbo engine had become more critical than ever. One definition was that it must have four cylinders for economy, and that it should be built either in-house or supplied by a major manufacturer giving the team first call on its engines. That narrowed the choice down to Ferrari or Brabham-BMW.

In any event, Ferrari designer Harvey Postlethwaite is no doubt right when he warns latecomers to the turbo race: 'Prodigious horsepower that is easy to produce on the dynamometer can evaporate on the track. And an engine that will run for twenty-four hours at full boost in Tokyo will melt down when it gets tyres, a gearbox and a Keke Rosberg attached to it.'

Also, there must be a lot of support for his view that, if the capacity limit for blown engines had been set lower, the sport would have been saved the complication and expense of the turbo-charged engine. 'I'm not complaining that it has ruined racing or that it creates the wrong sound, but only that it is irrelevant. It is an extravagant anomaly that racing can ill afford.

'It is a shame that we are developing these turbo engines that will serve the future only as museum pieces. For my bet is that not a single turbo-charged petrol engine will be offered by a series car manufacturer in five years time, though diesels, which we don't race, are an entirely different matter.'

Apologists, on the other hand, say there is more to it than engine makers seeking prestige through racing successes. And Formula 1 developments in electronics and materials certainly are relevant to the car enigines of the future.

At a more mundane level, turbo-charging has given an extended lease of life, relatively cheaply, to ageing road car engine designs that otherwise should have been pensioned off. For the motor industry, bludgeoned by fuel crisis, fierce rivalry and sales stuttering in world recession, anything to fend off capital investment is welcome.

Among the optimists is TAG. Not only may its engine be sold to other Formula 1 teams. But it is foreseen that variants of the V6 will find much wider markets, possibly powering road cars, helicopters and fixed-wing aircraft, all of which would benefit from its compactness, lightness and performance.

The point, as Christopher Columbus well knew, is that you don't know what's out there until you go looking.

7

TESTING TIMES

Long before the circus pitches camp at a circuit to begin a race weekend, the cars and drivers will have already clocked up thousands of kilometres testing there.

This is a measure of how complex and competitive the sport has become. Not only do individual teams rent circuits for private trials of a new chassis, engine or other changes, but, about four weeks before each grand prix, a two-day test session is run there, open to all the teams.

Here, the psyching-out begins in earnest because, essentially, each grand prix today consists of three races: first is to be quickest around the track during the public test session – a fair indicator of which cars and drivers may go well a month later. Second is to claim pole position by setting fastest time during official qualifying, one hour on each of the two days immediately preceding the big event. Third is to survive the race itself, and be first past the chequered flag.

For the public, these test periods have become the equivalent of a cinema trailer to a big movie: two days during which to enjoy those magic sights and sounds without being jostled by huge crowds. Perhaps 3000 to 5000 turn up. But, in motor-racing-crazy Italy, as many as 40,000 fans are said to crowd through the turnstiles, ready to hurl abuse – not to mention missiles – whenever the Ferraris or Alfa Romeos are bested.

For the media, there is the golden opportunity to glean the inside story, talking quietly with drivers, team managers and engineers, untroubled by all the hullabaloo and tension of a race weekend. Race promoters and circuit owners welcome the extra cash-flow from the punters who pay to watch this preview. Nervous as the day fast approaches when they will know whether or not their huge speculation in the race will pay off, they are also glad of any publicity the attendant media create to help swell takings at the gate.

Despite the apparent casualness in the pit road, the teams take the whole business very seriously, and plan for it carefully in advance. If not, the two days can so easily be a fiasco, a complete waste of time and money.

Even national politics have a bearing here. In the wake of a swing to the Left bringing President Mitterand's government to power in France came much stricter rules on working hours and time off. These make it impossible for even the most devoted of the Renault-Elf mechanics to attend every test and race meeting – the law says they must take a rest. So the team has to employ two crews of mechanics one for testing and the other for racing.

Unintentionally, this creates its own form of elitism. For only team manager Jean Sage and some of his engineers can be in attendance all the time. 'We don't have any timetable,' says Sage. 'For me it's no big problem. If you are an enthusiast, if you really like your job, you work without worrying about that. It's not a big effort for me because I have been passionate about motor racing since I was a little kid.'

To win a race, you first must finish. To win a world championship, you must finish consistently in the points. And there are no points for leading all the way to the penultimate lap and blowing up. So the quest for reliability, as well as pace, is relentless.

After the computer and the drawing board, the process continues in laboratories, destruction rigs, engine test beds and wind tunnels. And a string of heart-breaking failures may occur before a component is considered worth even trying out on a car. At Williams Grand Prix Engineering, for instance, design director Patrick Head makes the point by opening a cupboard to reveal dozens of expensively fabricated suspension wishbones, all design ideas discarded for not performing up to scratch in the lab.

Having sufficient sponsorship money to fund in-depth

research and testing plays a large part in the success of a team such as Williams. And this in turn makes it easier to continue attracting sponsors. The rich get richer, while teams without handsome backing find it hard to haul themselves up by their boot straps.

Getting a car to its optimum for a particular race is by no means as simple as calling up the mass of data a team will have from previous experience of that circuit. For one thing, the car will be new each season, in response to technological advances and changes in the rules. For another, a circuit can change from day to day, depending on factors such as weather, ambient temperature and how much rubber has been laid on the surface by recent use.

The testing process is therefore one of continuously fine tuning of all the elements of a car, progressing hopefully to a point where it is at its best for qualifying and the race.

With the end of the 1982 season came a ban on ground effect. From 1983 flat bottoms became mandatory in order to reduce what were considered to be dangerously high cornering speeds. Suddenly suspension mattered again.

To maintain ground effect, vertical movement of the car was virtually eliminated by use of very stiff springs, rated at around 725 kg. As there was hardly any suspension travel, the designer did not have to concern himself too much with camber changes affecting the interface between the tyre and the road. But now suspension is back in fashion, with spring rates of around 135 kg. Getting the geometry right is once more crucial in maintaining effective contact between tyre and track.

The Tyrrell Racing Organisation sees the change as a welcome opportunity to revive computerized testing techniques which Professor Karl Kempf began developing for the team in 1977. The upshot was that, in 1978, Tyrrell had probably the best suspension in the business. Patrick Depailler took the lead in the drivers' championship by winning the Monaco Grand Prix, and Tyrrell headed the constructors' championship jointly with Lotus.

For the next race, Lotus introduced the ground-effect John Player Special 79, and went on to trounce the opposition in both championships. Tyrrell shelved complex electronic equipment that had cost more than £100,000 to perfect, and only blew the dust off it for an intensive winter test programme towards the end of 1983.

The logic behind Tyrrell's project is that a racing car going round a circuit is a matter of physics, not magic. The problem was that the only measures of its performance were the stopwatch, tyre temperatures when it arrived in the pits, and what the driver had to say about the car's behaviour.

Nobody knew what the suspension was doing out on the circuit, what the camber changes and tyre temperatures were through a particular corner, and how these related to what the driver was experiencing, not to mention the ideas laid out on the drawing board.

However, the advent of micro-electronics meant that an on-board monitoring package could be put together, weighing only 5 kg and therefore light enough not to distort the fundamental characteristics of a car. But the equipment had to be able to function in the hostile environment of a Formula 1 car with its massive g-forces, vibration, magnetic fields and high temperatures. Hence a 32-channel 'black box' flight recorder, usually used in missile testing and costing £4000 – a normal recorder would destroy itself in about 30 seconds.

For suspension and tyre testing, the car is fitted with transducers that continuously monitor suspension movement, while infra-red sensors measure tyre temperatures all the way round the circuit. These data are recorded, and have provided some real eye-openers.

To function at its best the 'slick' tyre used on today's racing car must be kept in flat contact right across its width with the track, and the temperature of the tread compound must be within a consistent range.

The moment a car comes into the pits, tyre temperatures are taken and usually it is readily apparent if something is wrong with the choice of compound. This at least points the direction in which the engineers should try making changes.

On the other hand, everything may be apparently normal

when the car comes into the pits. Yet the driver is complaining about a handling problem that is costing him time out on the circuit. Intelligent assessment of what he has to say can lead to step-by-step changes that may or may not solve the problem. In any event, it is a time-consuming business.

By running their data through a computer, Maurice Phillippe and his design team at Tyrrell can get a much clearer picture of what is happening on the circuit and correlate this with what the driver has told them. The computer does not then spew out yards of paper with a cry of 'eureka' and an instruction to stiffen up the rear springs or change the front damper settings. But it does allow more meaningful assumptions to be made.

Using the suspension movement data, the computer can calculate the camber changes, relating these to tyre temperature fluctuations as the car moves round the circuit. In a corner where the driver has said the car was oversteering severely – poor rear wheel grip – the cause will be clear immediately. The cure required may only be a fine adjustment, or it may run to a fundamental re-design.

If it is the latter, twenty different ideas for suspension layouts that might fit the bill can be put through the computer. Within half an hour it provides a print-out of how each layout would behave round, say, Silverstone. The designer chooses the best, and has it fabricated. This is a lot less hit-and-miss than having to go straight from the drawing board to fabrication of a succession of layouts that each in turn may very well prove unsatisfactory on the circuit.

Other teams, such as Renault, have developed these techniques to include radio-telemetry, transmitting data from the car to the pits where it is recorded on equipment that gives an immediate print-out. Ferrari, with the giant Fiat group as a major shareholder, can afford to take the process much further. Just down the road from Maranello (near Modena) where the firm builds roadgoing supercars, is Fiorano, the base of Reparto Corse Ferrari, the racing team. It has 6000 square metres of workshop opening on to a 3-

km test track where new ideas can be tried in complete secrecy. There are fourteen corners to simulate a variety of real racing situations, even including a nasty bump on the way downhill into one bend to put whiplash into drive shafts.

Ten closed circuit television cameras allow a car's progress round the track to be followed in the control room, and the tape can later be played back during discussions between driver and engineers. Simultaneously, Longines timing equipment, fed by forty-five sensors around the track, records speeds through important sections. This provides immediate feedback on the effect of an adjustment to the car. A gain through one corner may coincide with a deterioration through another, and so the engineers are more quickly guided towards the best compromise.

Additionally, measurements of data – such as air pressure on wings and temperatures of tyres, engine coolant and oil – are recorded remotely by means of a transmitter on the car.

The needs of man as well as machine are looked after at Fiorano. There are changing rooms and sleeping accommodation for the drivers. And here also the formidable octogenarian, Ingeniere Enzo Ferrari, maintains a private office to which, habitually, his drivers are summoned after a test session or before a race.

All teams test throughout the year to a greater or lesser extent – an expensive pursuit when engine costs alone amount to £50 or more *per lap*. There is no let-up when the championship season finishes in October. Between then and the new season, teams engage in intensive winter test programmes, hoping to grab a head start from the first race.

The work is often shared between a team's two race drivers and the up-and-coming men who have been doing well in lesser formulae. The latter are only too glad to get their hands on Formula 1 machinery, even if it means drudging round, running in gearboxes for their superiors to use in a race.

As the teams are based either in Britain or on the Continent, poor weather during the off-season soon becomes a serious obstacle. The solution is to flee southwards in search of sunshine. Some favour the clement weather to be found in Florida or California, closer to Akron, Ohio, where Goodyear makes its racing tyres.

Despite almost manic secrecy, teams cannot go on developing their cars in private for ever, and must sooner or later come into the open to perform under the watchful gaze of their peers.

Prelude to the first race of the year is an 'open' tyre-testing session, now usually held in Brazil and prey to delay at Customs. In January it is high summer south of the Equator, and conditions are thus ideal for finding out how engines and tyres respond to the very high temperatures that are also likely to be encountered later on during the northern summer.

This Brazilian outing lasts for about a week, justifying the expense of getting there. During the rest of the season there will be around twenty such sessions, usually two days long – one in advance of each of the races on the permanent circuits, and a few more besides.

First aim is to find the right 'set-up' for the car – the best permutation of spring rates, damper settings, anti-roll bars, wing angles, even gear ratios. This process takes place using 'control' tyres – those with well-established compound and construction characteristics – and can be a very tricky business, taking up all of the two days.

Explains Renault's Jean Sage: 'Usually the drivers know the track. But almost every year, we have a new car, different from the previous one. So the set-up is not the same. And, very often, after two days we are still looking for the right thing. Especially at Brands Hatch it has always been very difficult for Renault. We have never been very quick at this track. We don't know why.'

This operation is doubly complicated because two different set-ups are usually sought for a car. One is to provide the best possible qualifying time – running light with hardly any fuel on board, the turbo boost 'wound up' to give an extra 150 to 200 bhp, and using short-lived super-sticky qualifying tyres. The other is for the race. Fuel load is much greater at the start, and obviously declines – so the balance of the car, and therefore its handling, alters continuously. And much harder tyre compounds must be used to go the distance.

A Formula 1 racing car, with suspension tuned for ultimate performance, is highly sensitive to fuel load. For 1983, the regulations allowed the minimum weight of a car to be 540 kg, while maximum fuel capacity was 250 litres. Filling up to the brim therefore added 188,75 kg – or 35 per cent – to the overall weight of the car, as well as varying the front-to-rear weight distribution. Reducing tank size to 220 litres in 1984 and 195 litres in 1985 is not going to alter this part of the equation all that radically. Whichever year you take, a full tank equates with putting two additional drivers on board.

Even the dramatic pit stops for mid-race re-fuelling, banned from the start of the 1984 season, did not necessarily mitigate this big weight change between full and empty tanks. During 1983, Tyrrell, then still using the less thirsty naturally aspirated Ford Cosworth engine, reckoned to start the average race with 150 litres, an advantage the team continued with in 1984. But the turbo cars, slurping petrol 40 to 60 per cent faster, often had to go to the line with tanks full. Now, with tanks reduced and a turbo monopoly, it is virtually certain that all cars, except the Cosworths, start full.

To get the best from testing it is essential to have an intelligent driver who has a good rapport with his engineers, will listen to their experienced advice, and can tell them fully what the car is doing.

Keke Rosberg's increasing maturity as a driver is a good case in point. He joined the Williams team in November 1981. By the time he started the first race of 1982, in January, he had already driven more miles testing than he had driven altogether throughout the whole of the previous season, including practices and races. One result was that he completed more racing miles during 1982 than any other driver, a consistency which won him the world championship. And he learned more in one year than he had in the previous five.

Now, says Williams design director Patrick Head, Rosberg is as useful in confronting problems on the car as previous champion Alan Jones was. From the outset of that first season with Williams, Rosberg avoided making mistakes during races.

However, his failing was that, during practice, his only interest was in attaining pole position, remembers Head. 'Therefore he only wanted to run the car light and on qualifying tyres. We could never get him to really seriously go out for fifteen hard laps in a row with forty gallons in the thing. But he now knows that, basically, is how a race is won.'

Before Rosberg, Williams had two drivers who were extremely precise and knowledgeable about their cars and complemented one another. Alan Jones retired on becoming world champion, and Carlos Reutemann, an Argentino, quit, not least because of foreboding that the Falklands War was about to occur.

Jones's knowledge was instinctive; he could tell Head exactly what the car was doing and what was preventing it from running quicker. If there were two or three problems, he would always explain the most important first. For instance, there might be a lot of understeer going into a corner and an enormous amount of oversteer coming out. Understeer bothers drivers because it makes a car slower. And, in a fast corner particularly, oversteer can be very disconcerting, especially if it happens suddenly.

In a racing car, if a driver feels understeer – a tendency to plough straight on instead of following the direction in which the front wheels are pointed – he may try applying some more power to counter it. In general, the car then swings into oversteer – the back wheels break away into a slide.

'The oversteer is only happening because the driver is trying to overcome the understeer,' explains Head. 'So, if you have a driver who comes in and tells you he has terrible oversteer exiting such-and-such a corner, but doesn't mention the understeer, then you can waste your time chasing completely the wrong thing.'

Seen from Frank Williams's vantage point, the ideal driver-designer symbiosis is between Nelson Piquet and Gordon Murray of Brabham. 'I admire Nelson – he has a good head and I'd go flat-out to hire him if we were to lose Keke. Nelson, for instance, will be sitting at home, thinking about testing the previous day at Brands Hatch and remembering that the car wasn't all that good turning into Clearways. He'll pick up the phone, and ask Gordon what is going to be done about it, pester him, suggest that the bump rubbers are too stiff.

'Most drivers maybe only call once a week between races, and come in three or four times a season – unless you drag them to the wretched factory. But Nelson has this brain that understands how to make a car a bit quicker. The evidence is there, and, for me, Nelson is the most complete driver.'

Not that Williams has a down on his own number one driver. Far from it. 'Keke is a very intelligent man, certainly at least as intelligent as Nelson – he speaks four languages, was a trained computer operator when he was younger, and is a clever guy. A shrewd, hard-working businessman.

'None the less he doesn't understand racing cars as well as Nelson. He makes up for it by being quicker as a driver. But the information doesn't come out of the cockpit unless Patrick bullies it out of him. What we have to do is get Keke and Patrick to be as great a team as Nelson and Gordon.'

Such a relationship is desirable because, the more intense the competition between the teams, the more marginal are the decisions that have to be made in chasing that extra advantage over everyone else.

'You are literally on the edge with everything the whole time. If your performance was miles better than the others', you could put on the extra-hard tyres, tilt the wings to maximum angle, and go out and win the race. But it isn't like that', says Head.

'Everybody is looking to see how little wing he can start with, just how soft a tyre will go the distance, just how much turbo boost he can get away with without running out of fuel.'

The best set-up for a car differs from one circuit to another. Equally, different set-ups may achieve the same fast lap time on one particular circuit because it is seldom as straightforward as it might first appear.

Although ground effect is now outlawed, external wings and upper body surfaces are still used extensively to create downforce to improve adhesion of the tyres. Increased downforce means faster cornering. But there is a trade-off. For creating the downforce intensifies aerodynamic drag.

Silverstone, currently the fastest of the grand prix circuits, can be tackled in two ways, broadly speaking, with equal success. One is to run the car with low wing angles, minimizing drag. It will be slower through the corners, but will make up for this with more rapid acceleration to very high terminal speeds at the ends of straights. The other is to adjust the wings to their maximum angles. The greater downforce will allow the car to be driven flat-out almost all the way round Silverstone, blindingly quick through the corners. But acceleration and terminal speeds will be reduced.

In the days when the Williams cars were still Ford Cosworth-powered, Jonathan Palmer tested two types of wing 'back to back' at Silverstone. One produced a lot of download for use, typically, at more tortuous circuits such as Monaco and Brands Hatch. The other was a low-drag set-up.

Using the same tyres, lap times were within one-tenth of a second. With the high download wings, the car would pull a maximum of 275 km/h. With the lower drag, it was attaining 294 km/h.

The latter would probably be better for the race. In general, it is difficult to overtake going round corners. Tyre wear is so high that the driver must follow a clean line – off it, there is loose rubber all over the surface and the car will slither about. And, if a car is slow along the straights, it cannot catch up with the car in front, close enough for outbraking on the way into the next corner.

The exception to the rule, however, may be the driver on pole position. If he can get a clear run into the first few corners, using maximum downforce, he should be able to open up a gap between himself and his rivals. And, as he can go into and come out of corners really quickly, he is less likely to be overtaken by another driver outbraking him.

Patrick Head points out that, when a Williams won at Silverstone, it was with the same maximum wing angles as at Monaco. And, with the demise of ground effect, designers seek a much bigger proportion of downforce from front and rear wings today, exaggerating the difference between the effects of maximum and minimum wing.

High download may be quite satisfactory when running with the harder rubber to be used for the race. But this will not necessarily be true when the soft qualifying tyres are fitted.

'During practice, you quite often find you run a lower download set-up with qualifying tyres because of their better grip,' Head explains. 'You gain on the straights, and the softest tyres will compensate on the corners. But you just can't run that little download with race rubber. The car is just too slidy altogether. And the driver says: "Look – in the race, it's going to get away from me." '

Each team turns up for a test session equipped with a range of springs, from the hardest to the softest, and a variety of anti-roll bars, as well as, possibly, a number of front and rear wings.

It is not always possible to bring a car for each of the drivers because the others are being rebuilt in preparation for the next race, or being repaired after a recent crash.

Where this is the case, one driver may spend the first day arriving at the best set-up, using identical tyres throughout while the other has to sit around twiddling his thumbs. Says Nigel Mansell: 'You just have to put your brain in neutral, basically de-tune yourself. You watch what goes on, learn how the car is made to go quicker, think about motor racing, and perhaps some improvements you might make the following day.'

Once JPS team mate Elio De Angelis had done his stint, the seat, pedals and steering wheel will be altered to suit Mansell. But the chassis set-up will remain largely unchanged. Explains Mansell: 'We both like fast cars. And whatever suspension set-up is fast we like.'

During Mansell's second-day session, the set-up arrived at by De Angelis will be retained. 'All they do then is throw different types of tyre at the car, see how this alters the balance, and how fast it can be made to go.'

Subterfuges are often brought into play during these tests to prevent other teams comprehending just how quick a particular car-driver combination really is. For instance, Keke Rosberg qualified his naturally aspirated Williams on pole position for the Brazilian Grand Prix, first of the 1983 season. Yet, during the tyre tests at Rio de Janeiro, nobody had paid much attention to the performance of the Williams cars which appeared relatively slow in terms of the times registered at the start-finish line. The drivers had been briefed to ease up when crossing the line – they were being timed from a different place.

'We didn't want to show the turbo teams how quickly we could go because that would have told them how dangerous they must get with their boosts,' confides Patrick Head. 'Then, if they saw us set a really fast time, they would know that was our limit – we didn't have a knob on the car to screw more power out of it – whereas they could run 700 to 740 horsepower, but only for a very short time.'

That, generally speaking, entails the use of 'trick' fuel additives such as acetone – and the risk of disqualification, should the fuel be checked – in order to make the engine survive long enough during those few crucial qualifying laps.

Tipping a vital glass of acetone into the fuel has been a source of some amusement. One team even teases by raising the glass in a mock toast. You might expect someone to blow the whistle on this practice, but let he who casts the first stone. . . .

Generally speaking, Williams doesn't run on qualifying rubber during tyre tests – the team thinks it more important to do its homework for the race than to throw down the gauntlet in this kind of spectacular way. But then it is not under the same pressure to grab a share of the publicity in the national press as the teams from France and Italy.

Unless they have been particularly slow, someone from the *grande marque* teams – Alfa Romeo, Ferrari and Renault – gets on the phone at the end of the day to ensure that the story appears in next morning's papers at home. So, for example, at an Imola test session, Ferrari fitted qualifying tyres, wound the boost off the clock, and scorched round in 1 minute 33,9 seconds, whereas its cars had previously been lapping in about 1 minute 37 seconds. Meanwhile Williams was content to be circulating in 1 minute 36 seconds on ordinary race tyres and with 70 to 90 litres in the tank.

Nonetheless, considerable pressure on any designer is always there. Among his tasks are to bring today's car to race-winning pitch for tomorrow, dream up and test even better 'demon tweaks' for the race after next, and be ready with an all-new state-of-the-art concept to pulverize the opposition next season.

So, as early as the Imola tests in April 1983, Williams was trying out redesigned front suspension – with new uprights and hub spindles. The aim was to reduce weight as well as stopping a turbo car from 340 km/h, as opposed to the 290 km/h of a Cosworth car. This was in anticipation of the Williams Honda, given its first trial in September and its racing debut at Kyalami in mid-October.

If everything goes fairly smoothly during the two days of testing, it is not uncommon for a car to clock up 1000 km in pursuit of the perfection essential to a good showing during race weekend. Then, there will be scant time to prepare. During each of the two days preceding the race there are only one and a half hours of untimed practice in the morning, followed by one hour of timed qualifying. During the latter, with only two sets of qualifying tyres

141

allowed per car, there are only few minutes in which to do anything worthwhile.

'If you turn up, and the handling of your car is all at sea, you're in trouble,' asserts Patrick Head. Small wonder he is such a firm believer in homework.

8
TYRE WARS

Watching the start of a grand prix for the first time, from outside the first corner, is an awesome spectacle, vividly remembered. The cars thunder towards you, jockeying for advantage. And you can hardly believe your eyes if, impossibly, they manage to elbow their way through the corner unscathed.

In the 1960s, during the brief quiet that followed, flakes of over-sized 'dandruff' would begin falling on the hair and shoulders of onlookers. It was a great cloud of rubber ash, created by the close-packed bunch of cars, scrabbling for grip on narrow, treaded tyres. The racing tyre used then looked much like a road tyre, and would be laughed out of court today, if only for its comical appearance.

Now, if you are in the danger zone close to the track, you may be bombarded by the odd sliver of sticky rubber, kicked up by a passing car. It has the consistency of recently spat-out warm chewing gum. If it lands on your head, cooling fast and matting strands of hair together, only drastic action with a pair of scissors will get rid of it.

Achieving the right consistency mix of the rubber – compound – is a black art, jealously guarded by the chemists and engineers who practise it, and little understood outside a small circle of specialists. Even chassis designers, despite having to work closely with the tyre makers, confess to being kept in the dark. The mix has twenty five to thirty constituents – synthetic and natural rubbers, oils, waxes, carbon black among them.

As they are the only points of contact between car and track, tyres are crucial to performance and safety. And, when a car fails to run competitively, it is the tyres that are blamed as often as not. This is a sensitive issue with the tyre men. They point out that while it's their role to provide effective rubber, it is just as important that the designer comes up with a chassis to make best use of the tyres.

Like other elements of the car, tyres are a compromise, though far less so than for a roadgoing vehicle. Lightness is important – to keep down the overall weight of the car, as well as to minimize un-sprung weight so that the suspension has less work to do. Yet the tyres must be durable and strong enough to withstand immense loads: acceleration, cornering and braking of up to three times the force of gravity have to be contained within the small contact patch between tyre and track.

Increasing the area of contact improves grip, and this can be done by making the tyre wider. However, this means greater aerodynamic drag and rolling resistance. So, here again, the designer must consider the trade-off between a gain in cornering speed and extra drag slowing the car on the straight.

From the inception of the world championship in 1950, Pirelli enjoyed four years of complete dominance, but it was progressively overtaken by Continental and then Englebert before returning to the top of the heap in 1957 – when it pulled out of racing. In 1958, Dunlop came to the fore, and won all the races until the mid-1960s when Goodyear and Firestone came into the arena. Then the tyre war began in earnest.

The three companies fought it out for six seasons, each winning the drivers' and constructors' championships twice. Then Dunlop withdrew from Formula 1 at the end of 1970, and left the two American companies to slug it out.

Goodyear won three of the four following championships before Firestone retired, leaving Goodyear a three-year monopoly. This was challenged only when Michelin began supplying its radial tyres, then a novelty in Formula 1 for Renault's debut in 1977, and to Ferrari the following year.

Since then the sharing of results between the two has been quirky. Michelin beat Goodyear fair and square only in

1979, taking both championships. In 1981, the two makes shared both honours – Goodyear tyres were withheld for the first half of the season as a political lever. And, in 1983, Michelin was able to claim the world champion driver, Nelson Piquet, while the champion constructor, Ferrari, was Goodyear's.

Pirelli returned to Formula 1 in 1981, supplying Toleman first, with additional teams in 1982, and then concentrating on Toleman and Lotus in 1983. Race results from those first three seasons were not much to write home about, but there were encouraging signs.

Avon took a stab at the sport for fourteen months in 1981–82, supplying some of the lesser teams. The firm was charging £500 for a set of four tyres, and said it would not continue unless it could make a profit – a prospect that dimmed with Goodyear's return.

As with the cars themselves. competition has forced considerable innovation in tyres. When Goodyear came into Formula 1 in 1965 these were only 127 mm wide and had tread pattern. Now the width is restricted to 457 mm.

An important step along the way was to dispense with the tread pattern, greatly increasing the area of the face of the tyre directly in contact with the track, and providing much more grip. This idea was taken from drag racing, and these 'slick' tyres were first used in a grand prix in 1971. However, the absence of a pattern means there are no channels cut in the contact patch, and through which track surface water can be dispersed, allowing tread blocks to maintain contact with the road. In wet weather, a 'bow wave' builds up in front of the slick, and it rides along on top of the water, unable to penetrate it. All grip is lost, the front wheels will not steer, the back wheels spin uselessly, and the car becomes immediately uncontrollable.

Another sort of tyre is held in readiness for rain. These 'wets' have hand-cut or moulded-in grooves to disperse the surface water, and a super-sticky compound to maximize the grip of the parts still in contact with the road. This compound is formulated on the assumption that it will be cooled by the rainwater while reaching an effective working

145

temperature. If the circuit dries out, the wet tyre quickly overheats, losing its grip and wearing fast. Doubtful weather before the start of a race can make the choice of tyre a very tricky decision for the driver and team manager.

Next to be taken over from drag racing, introduced by Goodyear to Formula 1 at the end of 1972, was the soft 'wrinkle-wall' tyre which had a carcass constructed to wind up like a spring in slow corners and 'catapult' the car away up the straight.

As power outputs went up, so the size of the rear tyres was increased much more than those at the front to improve traction, putting more power down on the road, instead of wasting it and losing time while the wheels spun as the driver accelerated away from a corner.

As the car speeds up, the tyres tend to 'grow'. At 320 km/h a rear tyre with 660 mm diameter, the maximum allowed, is revolving at almost 2600 rpm and this subjects the face of the tyre to centrifugal acceleration of 2440 times the force of gravity.

In the days of ground effect, about 2700 kg – the weight of a Rolls-Royce – of aerodynamic downforce was created at speed, adding to the static weight of a car with fuel and driver aboard by nearly three and a half times. Even with today's flat-bottomed cars, aerodynamics – most visibly in the form of large and complex wings – are used to more than double a car's static weight. Each of the rear tyres must be able to support a load of 480 kg, passing this to the track through a contact patch little bigger than a man's footprint, while also handling its share of 700 to 800 bhp.

This is only when running in a straight line. When the car is cornering, 2 g lateral acceleration transfers much of the car's weight to the wheels on the outer side – opposite to the direction in which it is turning – and this can load up the outer tyres by almost double.

Temperatures are a major preoccupation of the racing tyre specialist. Ambient temperature influences the chill – cooling – effect on the tyre as it rushes through the air. Track surface temperature affects the amount of heat built up by friction at the instant a portion of the tyre is in contact with the road. Friction is also taking place within the structure of the tyre, creating heat, as it works, or flexes, in response to the twisting and lateral loads applied to it.

The amount of grip provided by a tyre is, for the most part, a direct result of the stickiness of the compound which, in turn requires that the right working temperature – neither too cool, nor too hot – be attained out on the circuit. Depending on the precise compound, the ideal working temperature is between 60° and 100° C. Tyres are inflated to about 0,9 bar (13 lbs per sq in) cold which increases by one-third to 1,2 bar when warm.

The need to warm up the tyres to get grip explains why the cars weave about, generating extra friction, as they roll slowly round the circuit, coming to the grid immediately before the start. For the same reason wheels, waiting to be fitted to the cars during mid-race pit-stops, are pre-heated.

During testing and practice sessions, every time a car comes into the pits, temperatures at three points across each tyre are recorded, along with ambient and track temperatures. And these can later be correlated with lap times. Since it was realized that tyres may cool off between a 'hot' section of the circuit and the pits, thus not giving an entirely clear picture, infra-red sensors are used to record temperature fluctuations as the car proceeds round the track.

The wear rate of each tyre is also noted, so as to check whether it is likely to last the distance during the race. On a circuit where, for instance, right-hand bends predominate, it will be the left-hand tyres that do most work, and therefore tend to run hotter and wear faster. Oddly enough, however, it is not always the heavily loaded outer portion of the contact patch that reaches the highest temperature. The middle or inner sections may be hottest because of the way the compound tends to 'squirm' or distort, in the direction of the car's centre when subjected to a high cornering force.

A major factor in the choice of tyres is the abrasiveness of the track surface. It affects working temperature, grip and wear rates. And it can change hour by hour – certainly from day to day – depending on ambient temperature, the amount of sunshine, and how many cars have been running on the circuit, laying a line of rubber and oil.

So critical are all these elements that the best combination of tyres may well be one that uses a different compound at each corner. Some tyres are even produced with two different compounds, half and half across the contact patch. And, quite possibly, a car, set up with the optimum permutation of tyres and suspension and wings-angles to lap a circuit quickly on day one, will be rubbish on day two because of a change in conditions.

The transition from full ground effect to flat bottoms at the beginning of 1983 highlighted the difficulties in matching chassis to tyres.

To cope with the increasingly extreme loadings that resulted from ground effect, tyre construction had become steadily more rigid. And adequate traction could be obtained without using rear tyres of the full permissible width. Relieved of ground effect, the tyre and chassis engineers had to relearn design of more supple tyres that would respond to less brutish treatment and suspension capable of keeping the tyres flush with the track and warming them up sufficiently.

Even the best of them had trouble coping and there was a lot of experimentation. At Las Vegas, early in the season, Niki Lauda and John Watson managed only to qualify near the back of the grid. But during the race, these two picked their way through the field. Watson swanned into the lead two-thirds of the way through, and won by 28 seconds from Lauda who in turn was nearly 46 seconds ahead of René Arnoux's third-placed Ferrari.

The Monaco Grand Prix, seven weeks later, was a disaster for McLaren. Neither of its cars qualified for a place on the twenty-car grid, thus restricted because the circuit is so cramped.

Seen from the viewpoint of the Michelin technician who

looks after McLaren, John Redford: 'They were lost for three or four races early on in the year, and were sliding all over the place. They did everything to the cars, but they couldn't get rid of the problem. Then, over a period of time, they came back again – there was temperature and grip once more.'

McLaren's John Barnard explains: 'With the change of rules we were suddenly running with only thirty per cent of the downforce we had in 1982. In addition, the weight limit was reduced by forty kilograms, and we were right down to the new five hundred and forty kilogram limit. At that period, also, we were still only using the Cosworth engine.

'Renault, on the other hand, also running on Michelins, probably had less downforce than us during the previous year. The extra power of their turbo engines meant they could afford to bolt some pretty huge wings to their cars and compensate more for the loss of ground effect. So they maybe had forty to forty five per cent of the downforce they were generating the year before. That's why they could make the tyres work where we couldn't.'

The answer to McLaren's problem came first in the form of tyres with a more pliant construction. This had two effects: the contact patch increased, and the compound, being attached to a more flexible base, was able to 'work' better and heat up further. Then the team began running the TAG Porsche turbo engine with the power to pull more wing.

That 1983 Monaco race was also a good example of how the right tyre choice makes winners. As the time to begin approached, the track was damp, and it was drizzling. The pessimistic decision was to start on wets – but the Williams camp disagreed.

Calculating that a dry line would soon be cleared around the circuit, Rosberg made a hard-charging start on dry tyres from his fifth place on the grid, and was second before the first corner. Exercising his renowned car control, he took the lead on the second lap and began pulling away. Never really challenged, except by team-mate Jacques Laffite, he got on with winning while the rest were in disarray, swapping wets for dry tyres.

Explains Frank Williams: 'If the track is damp and more than half the field starts on wet tyres, it is a 'wet' race. If it then really rains, they don't stop the race. So, if you're one of the forty-nine per cent on dry tyres, tough shit, mate – you've got to stop and change tyres. But, if it's a 'dry' start and then it rains, they do stop the race.

'The logic was that it was drizzling, but there was no standing water. During practice, we had found that the Goodyear wets would have given us no advantage over their dry tyres. And we thought that, with twenty cars piling round Monte Carlo, there would soon be a dryish line.

'We were reasonably satisfied with our decision. Our only gamble was that it wouldn't piss with rain for the first ten or fifteen minutes of the race. Keke was three or four seconds a lap faster than the rest of them. So, if it had rained but he had pulled out a thirty-five seconds lead by then, he could still have changed to wet tyres without losing his place at the front. But you don't always get it right – next time, the tyre choice could easily be wrong.'

Tyres that give so much in terms of immense grip and ultimate performance also demand a lot from the driver. To begin with – even though this may not seem compatible with straight-line speeds of 320 km/h plus and cornering at 260 km/h – the driver must control the car very smoothly, almost delicately, all the time. Neatness is the watchword.

Two main reasons for this are that the car is, for the most part, very finely balanced at its limits, and there is no room left for violent unpremeditated action; and the tyres are extremely sensitive to abuse – this can lead to a serious deterioration in performance.

Particularly when attempting to pass another car on the way into a corner, the driver leaves braking until the very last possible instant. But he cannot just slam his foot on the pedal and grit his teeth – he must feel his way up to maximum braking effort, and be sensitive to any tendency of the wheels to lock.

If one or more do lock, the car will not slow as quickly

and may go off line. Flat spots will be worn in the compound, causing the wheel to go out of balance, and the affected area will overheat and lose grip. A severe case can entail time wasted in a stop for fresh tyres.

Cornering grip is created by virtue of the 'slip angle' – that is to say the difference between the direction in which the tyre is pointing and the direction in which it is actually travelling. In a modern grand prix car, the slip angle is generally very small – about 4° – as this is sufficient for today's racing slick to achieve maximum grip in its wide footprint.

If slip angles consistently go much above 4° (understeer at the front wheels or oversteer at the back) – the car is unbalanced, difficult to drive quickly, and tyre performance is below par. It may be just that the compound runs too hot, and grip is reduced.

A more severe symptom is blistering – when patches of the compound part company with the tyre. The outside – the top – of the tyre benefits from being cooled very rapidly as it rotates at speed in the air. However, flexing of the internal construction creates heat, and this is increased by running at a high slip angle.

Heat build-up within the structure can cause chemicals in the compound mix to vaporize, creating pockets of gas. When these burst, chunks of rubber break away from the crown, and the contact patch is diminished. Here again a balance must be found. For the quickest way through a corner is to slide, or drift, the car, but not too sideways. That may please the spectators. But, as well as threatening tyre performance, it creates extra drag that makes the car slower.

The technique, then, is to be very careful turning into a corner, so as not to get the car out of shape. If it does, the driver will feel a grating sensation as the tyres scrub across the track, and then the grip going off.

Some tyres will recover rapidly in response to slackened pace, and allow the driver to corner fast once more. Others will never come back.

Another pitfall to be avoided is running off the established racing line on to areas covered in dirt and slivers of rubber. Not for nothing is this likened to driving on marbles. Not only is grip diminished at that instant, but as sticky tyres pick up debris very easily, it may continue to be lost, making the car almost undriveable for a lap.

Racing tyres don't wear out in the same way their road-going counterparts do. During the first ten laps or so of a grand prix, tyre diameter reduces as soft compound is worn off on to the track. But then compound depth on the crown tends to stabilize at 4 to 5 mm as the tyre in effect begins to pick up as much rubber from the track as it is losing.

During the course of the race, then, conditions are in a continual state of flux. Lap by lap, the weight of the car declines by as much as 154 kg between start and finish as fuel is burned. That affects the amount of weight applied to each tyre, making it work and grip. However, a centrally positioned fuel tank means that weight distribution, as such, is not radically altered.

But the state of the track surface is changing all the time, and so are the sensitive tyres. To help the driver maintain the equilibrium of the car, he is provided with cockpit controls to adjust the stiffness of the anti-roll bars and the balance between the hydraulic pressures applied to the front and rear brakes.

Race-winning performance is so susceptible to the fickleness of tyre behaviour that competition between the tyre companies is quite as fierce as it is between the teams. And the pace of development demands at least twenty major tyre testing sessions a year. Add those to the grands prix themselves, and key tyre personnel have to be away from home for thirty-eight weeks a year – a tough sport for even the most devoted enthusiasts.

Typically, during a two-day testing session, Michelin will bring along fifteen new types of tyre for a team to try – maybe five varieties of race rubber, two kinds of qualifying tyres, and three wets, the balance being made up of new carcass constructions that have to be proved.

'Control' tyres – of a type used previously and thus having known performance parameters – are used during the first day while the car is set up to suit the circuit. Then step-by-step trials of the new tyres begin, fitting a set to the front first, then the rear, and then trying them in combination with other types with the aim of arriving at the best 'package'.

Says Michelin's John Redford: 'It's all as big a race for us as it is for the car makers. We're looking two – or sometimes only one – races ahead to try to find the best tyres. The only way to do this is to actually go to the circuit in question, and do this testing. And then we have a pretty good idea of what's going to happen in that race.'

All the information thus gleaned is passed quickly back to headquarters where much of it is computerized, and some 'goes straight on to the drawing board'. Nothing is thrown away. Every Michelin tyre that has been run on a circuit is taken back to the factory where it is carefully stored, ready to be located by computer, should the engineers need to make an inspection.

As the weather is never entirely predictable, even in countries with a record of non-stop sunshine for months on end, deciding how many tyres and of which type to take to a race is tricky, test sessions notwithstanding.

Assuming it doesn't rain, a two-car team will probably get through twenty sets of tyres during a grand prix weekend. A company supplying five teams can therefore expect 400 to 500 of its tyres to be used. However, to cover eventualities such as rain and cooler or warmer weather than usual in that part of the world, it is necessary to bring as many as 1500 tyres.

'It's very difficult in this game', says Redford, 'because we could make a thousand of a particular type of tyre, then discover we're going in totally the wrong direction, and we'll have wasted six hundred. So we try to make them in quite small batches. Then, occasionally, if a particular type of tyre works well, we have to be very careful how many sets we release so that they last long enough. Then again,

153

we could have a lot of that type left over because changes on the day decide what tyre works best.

'A lot of it is very much long-range weather forecasting where you have to predict ambient temperature and circuit conditions. Nine times out of ten, we're right.'

Providing a service at this level costs a minimum of $1 million per team for a season, but there are few hard and fast rules as to the financial relationship between tyre-maker and team.

Favoured top-line teams certainly get their tyres at no cost. In addition – as is the case in Goodyear's relationship with Williams and Ferrari – some also have contracts to undertake extra testing, for which their expenses are reimbursed.

A company wanting to break in will have to offer more than just free tyres if it is to establish ties early with a leading team. So, for instance, Pirelli, a relative newcomer to the contemporary scene, was thought to contribute $750,000 to Lotus, with which it had a three-year contract from the start of the 1983 season. However, the team reverted to Goodyear for 1984.

No doubt Pirelli anticipates that the day will come when it has established a reputation for making race-winning tyres, and then the boot will be on the other foot.

Michelin announced that it would concentrate on Brabham, McLaren and Renault during 1984, and would not renew contracts with Alfa Romeo and Ligier. 'The decision was based on the major investment necessary to support a large number of teams in Formula 1 and, for economical reasons, we cannot support more than three teams,' explained Pierre Dupasquier, Michelin's director of racing. 'Our objective is not simply to win races and score points, but to learn, take the knowledge gained in racing, and utilize it in all our radial tyres.'

The point behind this move is not so much the cost of making enough tyres for additional teams, or even the capacity to do so. It is really much more to do with the sheer expense of development and testing necessary to tailor tyres to the individual requirements of teams. For those not among the chosen few, it would be a matter of a truck arriving, the doors being opened with the call: 'Okay, guys. Go get your tyres.' Less personal service, and no guarantee that those tyres will be the very latest available.

In any event, Dupasquier did not slam the door in the faces of other teams, but said Michelin would consider providing them with tyres and technical help 'on a paying service basis'. That is a euphemism for $600,000 for a two-car team for the season, without the benefit of the very best qualifying tyres supplied to favoured teams.

It was Michelin that brought the radial-ply tyre challenge to Formula 1 – at the time of Renault's debut in mid-1977 – and then cracked the Goodyear monopoly by winning four races with Ferrari the following year. Goodyear responded promptly with experimental radials in addition to the cross-plies on which its successes were founded.

The first time Goodyear radials were raced was on Patrick Tambay's McLaren M26 at the British Grand Prix in 1978 when he finished sixth. However, only towards the end of the 1983 season did the company announce that it was to invest $3.5 million on developing radial tyres. And that is only the tip of the iceberg.

Goodyear makes all its Formula 1 tyres at a $100 million technical centre, employing 575 people, at Akron, Ohio. Experimental radial tyres are made one at a time by hand on a machine costing $4.5 million. Meanwhile, twenty other costly machines – including those that make carcasses fully automatically – are engaged in producing the firm's main-stream cross-ply racing tyres.

To make a switch fully to radial tyres would involve spending $30 million on new equipment. This is a step to be taken only when Goodyear has conclusively satisfied itself that it can make fully competitive radials.

In racing, a major advantage of radial construction is that it includes a circumferential belt, made of materials such as Kevlar, rayon and steel, in the crown of the tyre. This allows a wider contact patch, increasing potential grip. Also, it helps maintain this footprint flat on the road by containing the tendency of the tyre to 'grow' – which makes the crown convex instead of level under the influence of very high centrifugal force – when revolving at speed.

Special tyres for qualifying are one of the more controversial aspects of the sport. At one stage during the Goodyear monopoly, they were not made available. However, competition now between a number of suppliers makes the practice difficult to stop because each, quite naturally, wants to give its teams the best chance of high placings on the starting grid.

Also, it is virtually impossible for the authorities to define what is a qualifying tyre and what is not, such is the secrecy that surrounds compounds and constructions.

Qualifying compounds are extremely soft so that, when they reach working temperature they are much stickier and have far more grip than those used for the race. Lap times, therefore, in the battle for pole position are much lower than during the race. For instance, Patrick Tambay's Ferrari was quickest in qualifying for the 1983 Austrian Grand Prix with a lap of 1 minute 29,871 seconds. But the fastest race lap set by Alain Prost's Renault – 1 minute 33,961 seconds – was more than 4 seconds slower.

In becoming involved in grand prix racing, a tyre manufacturer is very much putting its reputation on the line. One of its major motives of course, is to establish a reputation for its products and technology in, it hopes, the full glare of publicity attendant on a championship win.

Another main reason, expressed differently by each of the companies, is to expose its managers, technicians, engineers and scientists to the full blast of the concentrated competition unique to the sport. In this way, the rate and range of their learning is vastly increased, and there is a tremendous incentive to organize better.

But none of this is without risk. Tyres, much misunderstood, are often blamed where they are not blameworthy. And when they do fail, this happens very visibly, even though the cause may have little or no connection with the quality of the tyres. It could be that a sharp stone has

156

impaled itself in the tyre and worked itself into the carcass. At best, this may start a slow puncture that reduces speed and forces a car into the pits for fresh tyres. Or it can cause a sudden, quite unexpected blow-out at high speed, rendering the car instantly uncontrollable and letting it fly off the track.

In the hope of leaving the driver with some degree of control at such a time, wheels are fitted with safety bolts. These serve to prevent a tyre slipping off the rim if it deflates. For, if it starts to flail about as it parts company with the wheel, it can completely destabilize the car. And then the trouble really starts.

9

POWER PLAY

The grand prix circus has achieved a certain notoriety for being volatile – though, if it weren't, it would atrophy fast. Inherently, it has a much higher profile than most businesses. And it is an immensely complex mechanism in which are resolved the often conflicting influences of circuit operators, sponsors, teams, drivers, technical regulations, the governing body, the media and even, God bless 'em, the paying public.

The sport has certainly been through some very turbulent times which many feared could destroy it. Important protagonists in these recurring battles of will have been Bernie Ecclestone, president of the Formula One Constructors Association – FOCA – and Jean-Marie Balestre, president of the *Fédération Internationale du Sport Automobile* – FISA – the motor sport arm of the *Fédération Internationale de l'Automobile*, the world forum for national motoring clubs or associations, such as the Royal Automobile Club.

Ecclestone is a clever millionaire businessman, long interested in motor sport. He came into the present grand prix scene in late 1971 when he bought the Brabham team. During the twenty-odd years before that, he had raced himself, then run cars for other drivers, and had developed successful interests in car and motorcycle sales as well as property.

He formed the view that grand prix racing could either be allowed to trundle along as it had always done and thus degenerate, or be commercialized and given a healthy future.

Traditionally, individual teams had negotiated their starting money with race promoters in a catch-as-catch-can manner which meant hassles and uncertainty for both sides. Out of this grew the present *modus operandum* whereby the Formula 1 constructors banded together to offer promoters a package deal with a guaranteed minimum number of cars to start each race in return for a single overall fee or prize fund.

The attraction for the promoter was that he only had to negotiate with one party, after which he could be sure of staging a race with a respectable entry that would attract the fans and give them their money's worth. From the constructors' point of view, it was more satisfactory because they had steadier incomes, greater clout from negotiating collectively, and an increasing say in ordering their own affairs.

By 1978, the race prize fund commanded was $350,000 and the sport was attracting extensive television coverage. That same year FOCA first ventured seriously into race promotion, something Ecclestone now undertakes for maybe seven grands prix each season. Previously, in response to complaints from some promoters that that package was overpriced, FOCA had agreed on occasions to race for a reduced fee, taking instead a share of the profits. So to underwrite the German Grand Prix, completely, taking all of the profit or loss, was a logical step.

However, ahead of this businesslike advance lay a cloud on the horizon – in the form of the presidential election to motor sport's international governing body, then called the *Commission Sportive Internationale*, subsequently to be known as FISA. Frenchman Jean-Marie Balestre campaigned on a reformist ticket, and won.

Among the new president's early pronouncements, apparently motivated from behind the scenes by Ecclestone, were rule changes for Formula 1. Teams would have to undertake to race in every world championship grand prix, using the same previously nominated drivers throughout. And licensing of drivers would be tightened up.

However, it soon became plain that Balestre intended to be his own man and put control of motor racing's premier category, Formula 1, back where he thought it belonged –

in the hands of the world governing body. The battle lines began to be drawn when he incensed the circus by high-handedly fining John Watson 10,000 Swiss francs for his involvement in a first-lap accident during the 1979 Argentine Grand Prix.

That happened in February. Within a month, FOCA had unanimously decided to ask for autonomy in running the Formula 1 World Championship. Balestre's response was that within the CSI 'all the sporting structures exist for reconciling the interests of the parties involved.' In a word – no.

The conflict soon took on a somewhat nationalistic hue. Ecclestone was, after all, an Englishman, and eleven of the teams were British-based. Balestre was French and operated from Paris. Was it any coincidence that Britain's RAC Motor Sports Association abetted FOCA, saying that the four-year contract to stage the British Grand Prix would be adhered to whatever the outcome of the argument?

Even the senior man of the sport, Enzo Ferrari, sided with the Ecclestone camp. Yet Balestre stuck to his guns, and the stand-off continued for much of the year. Relative calm, however, appeared to have been restored when Ecclestone joined the Formula One Commission, newly formed to control the sport. At about the same time, moves were afoot to stave off the expense of having to follow Renault into turbo-charging, and some form of fuel-saving rule was suggested.

Meanwhile, the drivers had been becoming restive again about safety, and had re-formed the Grand Prix Drivers' Association to put forward their case. Their leader, new world champion Jody Scheckter, agitated hard for improvements to circuit safety, then for measures to slow the cars by dispensing with ground effect. Matters came to a head at the Brazilian Grand Prix, second race of 1980, when the drivers voted only narrowly not to blackball the event.

FISA responded by announcing that the sliding side skirts, vital to creating ground effect, would be outlawed from the following year. And the proposal was met with disdain from FOCA.

Hostilities between the two camps flared up once more in June at the Spanish Grand Prix. The Cosworth-powered teams were protesting the impending ban on skirts that would snatch away their chances of remaining competitive with the turbo cars. The upshot was that the race was to be staged, but not under the aegis of FISA. In other words, to start implied support for the FOCA cause. Renault, at the root of the conflict in the first place, was in a dilemma.

It disliked the skirt ban because it saw no point in winning races against uncompetitive rivals, and it wanted to race in Spain. But it believed the sport could only be conducted in an orderly fashion if the international authority was respected. As it turned out, the FOCA 'kit car' constructors – the *garagistes* using Cosworth power – put on a race, while the *grandes marques* – the manufacturers' teams, Renault, Ferrari and Alfa Romeo – sided with FISA, and declined to participate.

FOCA's response was to feint with a threat not to appear at the French Grand Prix. This, leaving only half a dozen of the *grande marque* cars on the starting grid, would have made Balestre look pretty silly on his home ground. However a proper race was run, FOCA hoping to keep things together and reach a *rapprochement* with Balestre. He responded with his usual tact by announcing after the finish that all the participants in the Spanish event were to be fined.

The rift continued. Balestre waved the big stick, declaring that entrants in the 1981 'official' world championship would have to sign an undertaking to adhere to the FISA rules which, of course, included that skirt ban. FOCA, meanwhile, was working hard to set up its own 'pirate' World Federation of Motor Sport Championship. And the world was treated to claim and counter-claim about which of the opponents had stitched up which of the races. It was a time for strong nerves, particularly as sponsors were becoming decidedly twitchy about the affair.

A glimmer of sanity came in November with Balestre's

nomination of Renault team manager Jean Sage as mediator. Another Frenchman, yes, but a believer in skirts as well as law and order. Nevertheless, events began to assume the dimensions of the Napoleonic Wars. A FOCA broadside declared that Balestre would be unable to stage grands prix – he didn't have the cars or the structure to do the job. Balestre's riposte was that FOCA was dead – a non-organization.

By the end of January 1981 they had slugged themselves to a standstill. Maybe they were beginning to realize that there are no winners in all-out war. In any event, the time was coming to shut up and get on with the new season's racing, essential to keeping the money-go-round turning. At least that was achieved, even if FOCA had apparently conceded on the skirts issue in return for being allowed financial control, while FISA's – pretty inept – grip tightened on technicalities.

In early March, the South African Grand Prix was run as a non-championship event with FOCA cars only. A week later, the full circus turned up at Long Beach, California, 15,000 km away, for the first round of the championship proper.

Though the so-called Concorde Agreement, arrived at earlier in the year, had attempted, among other things, to render skirts ineffective by calling for minimum ground clearance of 6 cm, a coach and horses was soon driven through this. It was quickly realized that there was nothing in the wording about what the gap had to be when a car was running. Soon fixed but flexible skirts combined with hydraulic devices – to lower the car into contact with the track, then raise it again upon entry to the pits – were all the rage. Ground effect was still in business.

Much of the counter-attack centred on the Lotus 88 'twin-chassis' car, described in Chapter 1. This was first declared illegal by the Long Beach scrutineers but, too late for the race, the ruling was overturned on appeal. In the legal wrangle that ensued, the car became a political football. Though, in advance of the British Grand Prix, the RAC Technical Commission decided that a modified version

Right: One up the chuff – Lotus air starter

Below: Handful of heat – Renault's turbo plumbing

Above: Rubber freaks – just pick a tyre, any tyre

Left: Temperature check – essential to the tyre maker's black art

Right: Limbering up for the 155th Cosworth win – Michele Alboreto's Tyrrell on grooved wet tyres during practice in Detroit

Above: Piquet's oversteer leads Prost's neat turn-in at Zandvoort. One lap later, an attempt to reverse the order had blown it for both of them

Below: Leaping at Long Beach – René Arnoux's Ferrari takes a bashing

Above: At 250 km/h, 1 metre off the barrier, Mansell, with blistering tyres, is pursued by Cheever out of Osterreichring's Boschkurve

Left: Carbon fibre brake discs (seen here on the front of a Brabham) save weight but are frighteningly expensive, though, one day, they may be commonplace on family cars. Note lightweight scoop drawing cooling air to the brake, temperature indicator strips on the caliper, and slender construction of the suspension

Above: Italian *tifosi* – fans – gather strength to cheer the Ferraris – even if they are driven by foreigners

Facing page:
Above: Presidents both – Bernie Ecclestone (centre), businessman from the Formula One Constructors Association, with Jean-Marie Balestre, politician from the *Fédération Internationale du Sport Automobile.* Après la guerre, an entente reasonably cordiale

Below: Murray Walker keeps the chat going nineteen to the dozen with the aid of lap charts by journalist Mike Doodson (centre) and inter-round summaries from articulate former Champion James Hunt who knows how it really is out there.

Left: Fast fill and four new tyres in about 9 seconds — thanks to on-board air jacks and slick Brabham pit crew drill

Below left: Split-second accuracy brought to your screens by Longines and Olivetti

Below: Laying it on the start line — metallic tape to feed coded impulses from the cars to the timing computer

Left: Television takes an overview during the 1983 Grand Prix of Europe at Brands Hatch as cars rush up the hill out of Surtees and over the crest to Pilgrims Drop

Above: Hands up who's finished – spirited work to get the boy back on the track fast

Right: Damn close-run but no dispute. De Angelis pips Rosberg in Austria, recorded at 100 frames per second

A lot of money, but worth every centime. Renault Sport's team manager Jean Sage and director general Gerard Larrousse salute

A shameful waste of good fizz, but an established part of victory ritual

of the car was eligible to race, FISA would have none of it. Litigation continued throughout the year, and the car never raced.

In May, during practice for the Belgian Grand Prix, a mechanic was killed in the pits when he fell backwards into the path of Carlos Reutemann's Williams. Drivers gave vent to their anxieties once more by staging a strike on the starting grid. In the shambles that ensued, Riccardo Patrese was waving his arms to signal that his engine had stalled. A mechanic leaped to his aid with an air starter line; then the race was started, and he was mown down by a back-marker.

As the season progressed, Balestre became uncannily silent, no doubt preoccupied with behind-the-scenes lobbying to ensure his re-election at the end of his first three-year term as FISA president.

Stirred by what it considered to be the Frenchman's autocratic behaviour, the RAC Motor Sports Association nominated its managing director, Basil Tye, for the job, saying: 'We have been increasingly concerned about recent developments in international motor sport which have detracted from its image, and believe that this can only work to the detriment of national sporting authorities and the millions of motor sporting enthusiasts around the world.'

Balestre was returned by thirty-three votes to seventeen. Tye, disappointed because he had been led to expect support from half the voters, was at least able to claim that his share of the poll showed there was 'a not inconsiderable number of people who are not totally satisfied'.

Reflecting those words, at the start of the 1982 season, the organizers of the South African Grand Prix were confronted with the bewildering sight of the drivers barricading themselves in a hotel ballroom, dossing down on mattresses, and refusing to talk to anybody. Their concern, yet again, was that they were not getting a fair crack of the whip on issues such as safety. The trigger was the move to make them sign 'super licence' undertakings that they would not break contracts with teams while, they felt, not getting any concessions in return.

Negotiations were carried out by drivers' representative Didier Pironi, who shuttled back and forth between hotel and circuit every half hour by helicopter, and FISA's Balestre. FOCA's Ecclestone kept mum, leaving Balestre to sort it out. Fines of $5000 were imposed. But the drivers did eventually extract a promise that they would be consulted on the formulation of new regulations.

Next it was the turn of the teams to have a go at one another. After the Brazilian Grand Prix, Ferrari and Renault joined in protesting that Brabham and Williams were running under the weight limit, the grounds being that the 30 to 40 litres of water being poured into 'brake cooling tanks' after the race went way beyond replenishment of 'essential fluids' allowed by the rules.

Ken Tyrrell countered with a protest that Pironi's refuelling stop had broken the rules because a mechanic had opened a vent to speed the fill.

The protest against Brabham and Williams was at first turned down, but was upheld on appeal. This was taken by the British to mean an abrupt change in the rules which was not allowed under the Concord Agreement. FOCA declared that the decision disqualified all its cars from racing in grands prix. Also, races staged under the changed rules could not be regarded as valid world championship events.

The upshot was that only fourteen cars came to the line to start the San Marino Grand Prix in April; the FOCA teams mostly stayed away. And, once more, there was talk of the two factions going their separate ways.

After the race, Ken Tyrrell, fighting the Cosworth corner, put in a protest that the turbo-charged cars broke the rules because turbo-chargers were turbines which had been prohibited from the sport. This was turned down, both initially and on appeal.

That season the drivers' concern about safety was once more brought into focus, first by the deaths of Gilles Villeneuve in Belgium and Ricardo Paletti in Canada, then by Didier Pironi's major accident in Germany. It was this '*force majeur*' that gave Balestre just the leverage he needed to precipitate the rule change to ban ground effect properly this time.

Controversies continued from the first race of 1983. But the litigation somehow seems to have less acrimony, the appellants perhaps being more concerned with getting clarification on rules than scoring political points.

For being push started after a mid-race pit stop fire, Keke Rosberg was disqualified from his second place in the Brazilian Grand Prix. But many were confident that the appeal against this decision would succeed on the grounds that the mechanics doing the pushing constituted a legitimate 'external power source' allowed by the rules. However, the plea failed, and Rosberg was denied important championship points that many felt he was quite entitled to.

The Belgian Grand Prix brought more protests. Frank Williams objected that, after the false start, Renault and Ferrari topped up their tanks illegally before the restart. Renault was fined $5000 for having fuel churns on the grid, but Williams withdrew the protest against Ferrari after being assured that the mechanics who were about to add fuel had been stopped just in time.

Brabham designer Gordon Murray protested that the pipes on the Renault exhaust system were arranged so that the departing gases helped reduce aerodynamic turbulence around the tail of the car. Renault said the set-up was to keep heat away from the rear tyres, but Murray felt it was in fact a contravention of a ban on 'moveable aerodynamics devices'. If the ruling went against him, he would take advantage of a similar layout. The argument went in Renault's favour, but the team quietly dropped the idea, rather than precipitate a scramble in that direction. And, anyway, it was felt to have a detrimental effect on throttle response.

However, with the introduction of a new engine for 1984, the arrangement reappeared, both on Renault's and Lotus's cars.

After the start of the 1983 British Grand Prix, Ken

Tyrrell challenged the eligibility of the Renaults and the Ferraris on the grounds that their use of water injection broke the rules. He said he thought it wrong to have to make a protest on a matter which ought to be sorted out behind the scenes, and he had no desire to see those drivers disqualified.

At the German Grand Prix, Frank Williams joined Tyrrell in a second similar protest. One of Williams's motives was to get clarification for his new engine supplier, Honda, so it would know whether or not to go ahead with water injection which, as it turned out, was declared OK.

The sport may be something of a lawyer's paradise but Ken Tyrrell, for one, makes the point that he is not litigious for the fun of it. 'I don't do it for devilment. There's too much bloody work involved, and protesting and appealing the Ferrari and Renault water injection cost about eight thousand pounds. But I don't know how else you can get the rules interpreted. It would be much better if you didn't have to go to the International Court of Appeal (where there are five judges appointed, none of them of the same nationalities as the parties involved).

'I would rather be able to go to the FISA, and hear them say: 'Yes, there is an anomaly in that regulation, and this is the way it will be'. Then you would know where you were. But the rules governing motor racing don't permit that. The only way you can sort something out is to protest at a race meeting, and then take it to appeal.

'All rules can always be better written. Everyone knows what a rule is intended to do, but there are always anomalies creeping in. Different interpretations can be put on it, depending on how the development of a car goes. And, because of that, everyone wants to use it to his advantage. Let's face it, the laws of the land are being interpreted all the time by judges, and their rulings are used as precedents. But it's a pity we have to do it after a race.'

The sums spent on such litigation are peanuts in relation to the huge sums spent in the sport. The FOCA prize fund that has to be put up by the promoter of each race now ranges from $55,000 to $850,000. This is distributed among the teams in accordance with a series of complex sliding scales.

Twenty per cent is split among the fastest twenty qualifiers on a scale ranging from 2 per cent for pole position to 0,4 per cent for the slowest.

Forty-five per cent is divided up in line with the first twenty positions during the race at a quarter, half and three-quarters distance, and at the finish. A car leading from start to finish would warrant 13,94 per cent, while one running all the way in twentieth place would get 0,3 per cent.

Thirty-five per cent is handed out as 'fixed compensation' in two equal parts of 17,5 per cent. The first of these is divided equally among the top twenty cars in the two previous world championship half-seasons. The second is divided in proportion to the number of championship points gained in the two previous half-seasons.

If a team scooped the pool and got its two cars on the front row of the grid, it would collect $31,875. If those cars led the race from start to finish, that would be worth $72,250. One-tenth of the 17,5 per cent fixed compensation would add a further $14,875. And, taking Brabham's championship placings at the end of 1983, its share of the other 17,5 per cent would amount to £29,024. That adds up to a 'best case' prize fund share of $148,024.

This hardly matches the cost of going racing competitively. Assuming every promoter pays the full rate during a sixteen-race season, prize monies would amount to $13.6 million, but that is less than one-tenth of the teams' collective income.

10

THE ARENA

At the top of Paddock Hill stands an unassuming single-storey building that faces out across a green field. Inside a telex chatters, and telephones ring in offices off a long corridor. Decor is strictly utilitarian – no smoked glass, cork walls or shag-pile carpeting. It looks more like the spartan admin block of a light-engineering firm, rather than a nerve centre of one of the world's major glamour industries.

The only indications that this may be somewhere out of the ordinary are grand prix posters pinned up in the reception area and the distant roar of unseen racing cars in mid-week practice session.

In an adjacent bungalow, there is a modest pine-panelled boardroom. Eight chairs, upholstered with a bright green tweed, are drawn up to the table. At the far end sits a slim man in a dark grey suit. His greeting is cordial, but low-key.

This is John Webb, managing director of Motor Circuit Developments Ltd and one of motor racing's most influential and enterprising figures, in his inner sanctum at Brands Hatch.

The telephone rings. 'Hello, Bernie. Yes. I'll see you this evening.' Webb agrees a rendezvous with Bernard Ecclestone, president of FOCA. For some time the two have been meaning to have a general natter over a quiet dinner. But, confides Webb, he now has a specific topic to raise with Ecclestone – money.

At best, staging any motor race, let alone a top event such as a grand prix, is a high-risk business. Shrewd management can do much to ensure survival, but it cannot control every factor.

Brands Hatch is the venue for the British Grand Prix every two years. On alternate years, when the race is run at Silverstone, Brands puts on the 'Race of Champions'. This is not a round of the world championship, but it gives fans the chance to see some of the best cars and drivers racing in Europe for the first time in the season.

Attractions in 1983 included World Champions Keke Rosberg and Alan Jones, as well as British stars John Watson and Nigel Mansell. However, with such a tight championship calendar, it was inevitable that the field would be about half the usual number. Vital tyre-testing at the Paul Ricard Circuit, in preparation for the following weekend's French Grand Prix, was one reason.

As it turned out, a hard core of only 13,000 enthusiasts braved the elements to watch the Race of Champions, and got great value for their trouble. Foul weather kept many others at home, and Brands Hatch lost £113,000 on the event.

Webb considers himself fortunate because he has the backing to stand a knock of that magnitude. Motor Circuit Developments is owned by Grovewood Securities, a £20 million-a-year company that, in turn, is now part of Eagle Star, the large insurance group.

Grovewood is a property company. Its investment in racing circuits – Snetterton and Oulton Park, as well as Brands Hatch – was never expected to provide a huge return. Rather, the company sought a high-profile public face. And, in any event, it can look forward to a Grand Prix bonanza at Brands Hatch every other year.

This should provide a welcome £500,000 contribution to the circuit's fixed overheads, which run at £20,000 per week, and thus help keep it in business. However, this can only happen if the public continues to turn out in force to support the grand prix. And the level of ticket pricing that might make people stay away is a matter of fine judgement. Webb is concerned that rebellion may not be far away.

Yet he must reconcile this with the ever-rising costs of

staging the big race. Of the 22,000 grandstand seats, 17,000 are put up temporarily. The scaffolding firms wanted £145,000 to do the job for the 1984 Grand Prix. That was 33 per cent more than the 1982 price, but there was still time to haggle.

In 1981, it was known what FOCA would require as a British prize fund, in effect a fee for putting on the show, for the subsequent four years. If these projections were adhered to, Webb would have to find £560,000 for the 1984 GP – about 40 per cent more than in 1982.

If he is to get the same return as in 1982 in face of such increases, Webb reckons that he has little choice but to raise the price of circuit admission, bought on the day, by 25 per cent to £12.50. Yet, with UK inflation now below 5 per cent, the public may not be all that understanding. And neither Webb nor Ecclestone wants to kill the goose that lays the golden egg.

Even so, ticket prices for the British Grand Prix look reasonable when compared with those in some other countries. At the 1983 French Grand Prix, for instance, it cost £15 to get in, plus £15 for a transfer to a paddock where you couldn't see the Formula 1 cars close-up anyway, plus £15 for a grandstand seat.

In any event, Webb feels he and Ecclestone still have room to manoeuvre: with the top teams running on $10 million budgets provided by their sponsors, the odd $100,000 either way on the prize fund for one of sixteen world championship races won't make all that much difference to them.

All these 'telephone numbers' are a far cry from when Webb was first attracted to the sport. He got the bug in 1953 when he rode his Vespa motor scooter to watch car racing on the airfield circuit at Goodwood, long since closed. In those days, young men such as Stirling Moss and Mike Hawthorne were starting to make their way in the sport.

Webb started a publicity consultancy firm. Early clients were Silver City Airways, which ferried cars and passengers across the English Channel, and Connaught Engineering. With Tony Brooks driving at Syracuse in 1955, the team achieved the first major grand prix victory by the British in thirty years.

This prompted Webb to hire a Dakota aircraft to fly drivers and supporters to Syracuse for the 1956 race, and led to the formation of a charter company specializing in such trips, which he ran until 1964.

On that first journey, the airport bus blew its radiator, and budding world champions had to form a bucket chain down the Sicilian mountainside to fetch more water. But what else could they expect for the money? The return fare was only £35 a head, and air-freighting a racing car cost £150.

A year later, Webb bought a second-hand Jensen which he drove to work every weekday. On Fridays, he would clean the spark plugs and top up the engine oil, and race the car at weekends. In twenty-seven events he won twenty-four times, occasionally beating off opposition from such as Innes Ireland and Jack Sears. He continued racing on and off until 1975 – 'when my wife beat me' – but business was taking up more and more of his time.

Until 1961, Webb also handled publicity for Brands Hatch. That year he was called in by the then managing director, John Hall, to discuss ways of securing the long-term prosperity of the circuit. The underlying problem was that it had evolved willy nilly. There were 55 shareholders, most of them enthusiasts and none of whom held more than 8 per cent.

The story had begun in 1926 when cycling devotees discovered a natural amphitheatre set in rolling farmland about 30 km out of London on the road to Maidstone. The farmer agreed to their racing here and, two years later, motor-cyclists also appeared.

During the war, the army used the grass track and surrounding area for training. But, by 1947, motorcycle racing was back. It proved so popular that £17,000 was found to lay a 1,6 km kidney-shaped tarmac track on which car racing began in 1950, running anti-clockwise. Mostly the cars conformed with what became the Formula 3 of the time, and were powered by 500 cc single-cylinder JAP or Norton motorcycle engines.

When a nearby horse racecourse was sold as a housing development the car and motorcycle racers bought the grandstand for next to nothing, dismantled it, and re-erected it next to what is now the Brabham Straight at Brands. The circuit was extended to 2 km with the addition of the Druids Hairpin in 1954, and the direction of travel was switched to clockwise. All classes of racing cars could now run there, and Brands was well on its way to becoming established as one of the magic names in motor sport.

During the 1959–60 winter, further track was laid, creating a 4,2 km circuit. From the outset, it was the scene of major Formula 1 races, the first of which was won by Jack Brabham. But getting full grand prix status, to draw bigger crowds and justify the investment, was a problem. However, circumstances began to conspire to provide a solution.

From 1948 to 1954, the British Grand Prix had been run every year by the British Racing Drivers Club at Silverstone, mid-way between London and Birmingham, and now the world's fastest grand prix circuit. Silverstone's great success in attracting the public had not been lost on the management of Aintree, home of horse racing's great classic, the Grand National. It made sense to build a car racing circuit parallel to the steeplechase course, to make double usage of the extensive grandstands and other spectator facilities.

Aintree thus came to host its first British Grand Prix in 1955, the year Stirling Moss became the first Briton to win his home grand prix, albeit in a Mercedes-Benz. Silverstone and Aintree then shared the race turn-and-turnabout until 1961. In similar fashion, the BRDC and the British Automobile Racing Club shared the prerogative of organizing the event. In honour of the BARC's fiftieth anniversary, Aintree staged the grand prix for a second year running in 1962. But this was to be the last time it was held there because of doubts about the circuit's future.

Meanwhile Brands Hatch had nearly been sold to

Lombank, a large finance house with strong motoring ties. But restrictions on car hire purchase put paid to a bright idea which would have given the circuit strong financial backing, as well as providing Lombank with a very effective promotional platform. However, Grovewood Securities emerged as a firm buyer in 1961. The price was £112,000.

At the time, only sixteen race meetings a year were held at Brands Hatch. Grovewood's chairman John Danny realized from the outset that the success of his new acquisition depended on maximum utilization. To help provide the necessary promotional impetus, John Webb was appointed a director, part-time at first, and then managing director in 1964.

This was the year everything fell into place. The grand prix had reverted to Silverstone in 1963. However, the precedent was well established that the race should be shared with another circuit. Yet Aintree was no longer an alternative. Brands Hatch was waiting in the wings, and it now had the financial muscle to hit the big time.

Auspiciously for Brands Hatch's first grand prix, interest in Britain was high. Britons – Graham Hill and Jim Clark – had won the world championships of the two previous years. Ten of the twenty-three drivers on the starting grid were British, four were from the Commonwealth, and four from the United States. Only two of the cars – the Ferraris – were not made in Britain.

Clark and Hill did not disappoint their home crowd. Clark took pole position with a lap time of 1 minute 38,1 seconds (an average of 156,49 km/h), set fastest race lap, and led from start to finish although hounded all the way by Hill.

During the subsequent twenty years the scene has changed a great deal. In 1982, Keke Rosberg took pole position with a time of 1 minute 9,540 seconds – 217,747 km/h. That was the last season of 'ground effect' cars. Their abolition greatly reduced cornering speeds, so much so that Rosberg's pole position time in the 1983 Race of Champions was 1 minute 15,766 seconds – 199,854 km/h.

Among the twenty-six drivers on the grid for the 1984

British Grand Prix, the likely line up is six Italians, six Frenchmen, three Brazilians, three Britons, two Americans, and one each from Austria, Australia, Colombia, Finland, Switzerland and Venezuela. Remarkably, however, British-based teams still predominate – there are ten, against two from France and three from Italy.

At a practical level, this far wider diversity of drivers' nationalities means that Brands Hatch, like all other grand prix circuits, has had to buy many more flags to fly over the pits, as well as making sure the band can play all those national anthems – just in case.

More profoundly, increasing average speeds by two-fifths has necessitated drastic changes around the circuit to protect spectators and drivers. For most of the reduction in lap times has come from increased speeds through corners rather than along straights.

Twenty years ago, the limit through Paddock Hill Bend, a steep downhill right-hander, was reckoned to be about 145 km/h. Today, Formula 1 cars take it at 210 km/h. Maximum speed through the Druids hairpin was 70 km/h; now it is nearly 110 km/h.

This points up driver skill and the progress of technical ingenuity, the very stuff of which motor racing's great appeal is made. But it is a development that has sparked many rows over safety and interpretation of the rules. For incontrovertible laws of physics are at work here.

Cornering forces rise in proportion to the *square* of a car's speed. Thus, if cornering speed rises by one quarter from, say 160 km/h to 200 km/h the force with which the car will crash goes up by more than half. Cornering speed need only increase by less than half – from 160 km/h to 228 km/h to more than double the potential impact.

So, what ten or twenty years ago may have been a splendid vantage point for spectators is often distinctly perilous today. The implications for the drivers are similar. What may have once been a quite adequate run-off area is now absurdly risky. Where there was room for a car to spin off harmlessly, now it would hit a wall with great force, possibly cartwheeling into the spectator area.

As a result, the faces of circuits now in use have changed dramatically; some have been closed for considerable periods to allow drastic modification; others have not re-opened because the changes proved too expensive to make.

One ruled out was Spa-Francorchamps, then fastest of the grand prix road circuits, and set in Belgium's imposing Ardennes mountains, Battle of the Bulge country. Characterized by long straights and flat-out corners, it had a lap distance of 14,1 km.

In 1969, the increasingly influential Grand Prix Drivers Association protested at the dangers of racing at Spa, and the Belgian Grand Prix was not run that year. The race took place once more in 1970, but for the last time, when New Zealander Chris Amon left his mark with a fastest race lap at an average of 244,7 km/h. Although other forms of racing continued there, the grand prix moved to another circuit, and meanwhile £1.8 million was spent on bringing Spa up to standard. Much of the original circuit remains, but the lap distance was reduced to 6,94 km. And so the Belgian Grand Prix was once again run there in 1983.

Increasingly, during the late 1960s and 1970s, circuit owners found themselves confronted by grand prix drivers who demanded safety improvements – or else. This added to the expense and uncertainty involved in promoting a grand prix. But these matters have since been put on a much more stable footing.

International motor sport's bible, the *Annuaire du Sport Automobile* of the FIA now contains sixty-nine pages on circuit safety criteria and inspection procedures. Full-time inspectors fly the world, checking that circuits are up to standard and giving advice; racing is banned where they have not issued a course licence.

Minimum track width allowed is 9 metres. This is increased to 10 metres where cars travel at 200 to 250 km/h (124–155 mph); to 11 metres for 250 to 300 km/h; and to 12 metres for more than 300 km/h. So that drivers don't 'get lost', maximum width is 15 metres.

Maximum gradients are 10% (1 in 10) downwards and 20% (1 in 5) upwards. And, from any point, the driver of

175

the quickest car should be able to see along the circuit as far as his braking distance.

The shortest circuit length on which a grand prix is allowed is 3,5 km. It is even specified how the starting grid shall be laid out, depending on track width and distance to the first corner. Whatever layout the guidelines come up with for the starting grid at a given circuit, grands prix are always started in two lanes, staggered so that there is 14 metres of lane per car. Drivers can see past the cars immediately ahead and have some room to manoeuvre in the mêlée of the start.

If the track needs to be resurfaced, it must be done at least sixty days before the event to prevent the danger of cars sliding about and showering one another with loose chippings. The surface should be smooth and porous to help dispersal of water or oil. Silverstone, for example, is surfaced with Delugrip, an anti-skid material developed for braking areas on the approaches to pedestrian crossings and other potential road hazards.

The grand prix circus is pretty fussy about its working conditions. Each team bringing three cars, two for the race and one spare, requires a pit allocation of at least 15 metres along its frontage and 8 metres deep. And there must be at least 21 metres of space behind the pit for the team to park its transporter. Total length of the pits must be between 184 metres and 230 metres, and the pit road must be at least 10 metres wide, with a signalling platform built between it and the track.

If you can't lick 'em, join 'em was John Webb's philosophy when it came to rebuilding the pits at Brands Hatch. He gave FOCA *carte blanche* to come up with its own design – this was done largely by team proprietor Ken Tyrrell. The work was undertaken in 1976 at a cost of £500,000. And, if FOCA members were unhappy with their new accommodation, they had only themselves to blame.

Out on the circuit details are defined for verges on the straights, kerbs around the corners and run-off areas. Where potential impacts are likely to be oblique, walls or double or treble steel guardrails, backed up by mesh fences, are recommended. Walls should be able to withstand a 7000 kg thrust, yet grand prix cars weight not all that much more than 540 kg.

Where space permits, catch-fences are used for protection around the outside of a corner. The aim is to bring an out-of-control car to a halt, rapidly but progressively, before impact with anything solid. You can get an idea of the likely speeds involved from the number of fences; 100 km/h – two fences; 100 to 150 km/h – three fences; 150–200 km/h four fences; 200 km/h plus – five fences.

To be effective the fences must be at 3 to 5 metre intervals and at least 15 metres long with posts every 3 metres or so to support the wire mesh. The posts are slotted into sockets set in the ground. This allows prefabricated lengths of fencing to be quickly installed to replace any knocked down by a car going off, so that delay to the racing programme is minimized.

Gravel or sand may also be used, on the same principle as escape roads placed to stop runaway trucks on steep hills, and then to soften the bump, there may be a barrier of tyres, at least 75 cm high and as many as three deep. They must be strapped together tightly, enclosed with wire netting, and stacked either in uniform piles or diagonally interlocked. Behind these protective devices, there must be further fences to keep spectators at a distance, and shield them from debris such as runaway wheels. Height and strength are determined according to likely speeds in the area.

It is also obviously important that run-off areas are free of obstructions or gradients likely to launch a car into the air. At many existing circuits banks have been reshaped and moved back to give spinning cars more space.

This does tend to alter the spectator's perspective, making it harder to judge speeds. But you can get help from the distance marker boards, placed at 100-metre intervals from before the braking point on approaches to corners. The more marker boards, the greater the approach speed.

Despite all the progress that has been made in mitigating impacts with the scenery during accidents, tragic experience has shown that rapid intervention is a very necessary second-line precaution. To this end, there must be access points at least every 300 metres for ambulances and rescue/firefighting vehicles, as well as for the removal of race cars that have been immobilized.

Also, every part of the circuit must be visible from one of the marshals' observation posts, properly protected and placed at maximum intervals of 500 metres. Each post must be able to communicate, by field telephone or radio, with the central race control. So, if the worst happens, a decision can quickly be made to slow or stop the race, and activate emergency procedures.

The posts are equipped with signalling flags to warn drivers, containers of cement powder to put on the track to absorb spilled oil, shovels and stiff brooms, and fire extinguishers. Portable extinguishers, with trained operators, have to be at 300-metre intervals along each side of the track (every 150 metres, if it is only safe for them to be on one side) and there must be extinguishers every 50 metres.

The medical centre at Brands Hatch can accommodate two major operations simultaneously. And, in excess of grand prix regulations, three helicopters are on stand-by to whisk the injured driver to nearby hospitals – the Queen Elizabeth Military Hospital, in Woolwich for burns; the Brook, in Woolwich, for head injuries; or Queen Mary's, Sidcup, for others.

The focus on safety precautions at Brands Hatch is by no means entirely on whatever dramas may occur out on the circuit. There is even a 'total disaster plan', under which the police would take complete charge, setting in motion a massive rescue effort to cope, for example, with the collapse of a crowded grandstand, an air crash, or with a race car ploughing into a spectator area despite the debris fence.

At a much more everyday level, human existence is seldom without incident. To contend with this, seventy members of the St John Ambulance Service, fifty doctors and twenty ambulances are on hand. On grand prix day, they can expect to book six hundred incidents among the spectators, ranging from cut fingers and bee stings to diabetics in urgent need of insulin and mothers going into labour. So far as is known, however, no baby has yet achieved the distinction of being born at the trackside during the big race.

The grands prix run in Britain are probably the most commercially successful of all. Unlike some others, they receive no hidden state or tourist promotion authority subsidy. Yet they attract sufficient revenue to cover the large cost of staging the event and of keeping the Brands Hatch and Silverstone circuits in business over the two-year periods between grands prix. Such has been this success, and encouraged by the UK's second – European – grand prix in 1983, it is expected that, by 1987, there will regularly be two grands prix a year in Britain.

A British Grand Prix attracts 20,000 fans from abroad, and they bring at least £2 million worth of foreign currency into the country. Similarly, the municipality of Zandvoort, a seaside town of only 16,000 people which owns the Dutch Grand Prix circuit, receives 600,000 guilders (£140,000) each time the race takes place, while the spectators are reckoned to spend 5 million guilders in the locality.

Donington Park near Derby opened in 1931 as England's first true road racing circuit, and was the scene of grands prix before the war. Subsequent attempts to revive racing there failed. Then, in 1971, it was bought by millionaire builder and car enthusiast Tom Wheatcroft. He has since carried out an ambitious scheme to bring it up to international standards, and has provided some of the finest facilities available.

Understandable reluctance on the part of Brands Hatch and Silverstone to let Donington in on a third share of their valuable cake has since given way to more positive thinking. If this wins the day, each of the circuits will stage a grand prix twice in three years. It would have been churlish to refuse Donington after all Tom Wheatcroft's expenditure of enthusiasm and money. As one motor sport supremo said of him: 'That man is incredible – he seems to have this insatiable urge to go on putting one brick on top of another.' Be that as it may, the newcomer to this exclusive club will also have to rely on getting his sums right and on putting on a great day's entertainment to get 'bums on seats' in sufficient numbers.

The twenty-four month cycle of promoting and organising a Brands Hatch Grand Prix begins with the previous one. The programme contains an invitation to secure a seat with a £10 deposit and by January 1983 all of the 22,000 seats for the 1984 race – except for 2000 to 3000 retained for sale on the day – were taken at prices ranging from £17.50 for an uncovered grandstand to £40 for a covered seat.

The race is watched by about 65,000 adult paying customers, of whom 37,000 buy their tickets in advance while the rest pay at the gate, and 10,000 children. In addition, 18,000 free tickets are issued to people such as the press, radio and television (1500) race marshals and other officials (2000), ticket and programme sellers, catering and security staff. Including the two practice days, it is reckoned there are 150,000 individual ticket usages, representing 90,000 individuals.

They consume 65,000 hamburgers and 100,000 half pints of beer. At the other end of the cycle, 900,000 litres of water are needed to flush the lavatories.

Of those present on race day, 20 per cent are company guests, there to maintain business contacts and buy or sell more widgets. They may not be dyed-in-the-wool enthusiasts but – as with Derby Day or Royal Ascot – they will get a great kick out of telling friends and colleagues: 'I was there.' Expensively too. For to entertain on this scale, providing a good grandstand seat, lunch with plenty to drink in one of the forty-seven company hospitality marquees, private trackside suites or mobile units, and a two-way helicopter flight, costs £100 to £150 a head.

However, 1500 helicopter movements on race day show there is no shortage of demand for the full treatment. It really is grand to be whisked over the 40,000 cars jamming the roads towards the circuit, and be back on the ground, a cold drink in your hand, within twenty minutes of take-off.

Others – 10,000 of them – beat the traffic by spending the night under canvas or in caravans at camping sites dotted about Brands Hatch's 180 hectare spread.

And, when it's all over, it takes three weeks to clear up the 200 tons of litter strewn about the place – not a pretty sight.

Focus of the whole great occasion is the grand prix itself, lasting less than two hours. If only it were as simple as that: stage the big race, and pay FOCA for the package deal on the morning after the race. But there are supporting races, involving a further 170 cars, to be run. Space has to be found for them in the paddock, and time allocated to practice sessions.

But there's more. To allow the paying customers a closer look at the grand prix machinery, there is a 'Pits Walkabout', and the contract states that cars must be visible. And there is a packed display programme, just in case anyone gets bored while eating lunch.

Any grand prix is a great international showcase. Never was this more true than at Brands Hatch in 1982. In the wake of the Falklands War, here was a popular opportunity to pay tribute to the British forces who had fought there. An RAF Harrier did its amazing hovering tricks, the Red Arrows roared through their breathtaking routine, often streaking low over the grandstands, a Royal Navy helicopter went through its paces, and the Royal Artillery Band played stirring tunes. The daredevil Marlboro aerobatic team tumbled about in the sky, trailing multi-coloured smoke. And a British Airways Concorde loomed overhead at minimum height.

None of this was organized at the drop of a hat. Harriers were in short supply, and top brass in Whitehall were asked to help. British Airways, surprisingly, seemed less than enthusiastic about this chance to show off the pride of its fleet – for money. Civil and military air traffic control had to be persuaded to talk to one another to co-ordinate the split-second timing in that busy air space.

The success of the event depends on pleasing the 'punters' on the one hand, and persuading companies that here is an unrivalled promotional opportunity. Without the revenue from all those sponsors and advertisers, the show would be prohibitively expensive to put on – at least on its present scale.

Some of these spenders do not really care how many people actually pay to come through the gates – they are far more interested in the worldwide television audience that pulls the sponsors.

Large trackside hoardings, the grand prix cars, even the helmets and overalls of the drivers, represent valuable space from which to get their messages on to television screens around the world. The sum of the parts may well be greater than the whole. And, however fabulous the sums of money spent, the fact is that even the main sponsor for the event – whose name is so much in evidence on banners, programmes and tickets – only accounts for 6 per cent of the turnover at the event.

Others, albeit less ambitious in the scope of their endeavours, pay considerable sums for a presence, either advertising or selling wares, from books and films to T-shirts and anoraks, to a captive audience.

The run-up to the big day involves a massive amount of in-depth staff work while, at the same time, major interests jockey for advantage with increasing pushiness as time runs out.

For the two years that this builds up, it has to be work as usual for Brands Hatch and its seventy full-time staff. For, to stay in business, the circuit and its facilities must be in use at least 350 days a year. In addition to a full calendar of car and motorcycle racing, there are practice/test days, a racing school, sales conventions and even bicycle races.

Through the lottery of history, motor sport got to Brands Hatch early, and so a precedent was set for its continued use. And a location in the Green Belt around London means that few houses – for 5000 people – have been built in the vicinity.

Maintaining a good relationship with the local community is essential to the circuit's well-being. But it is largely a two-way trade. For Brands Hatch provides its close neighbours with free tickets, not to mention work opportunities.

And, beyond the wildest dreams of those original founding bicyclists, it is becoming increasingly accessible from all parts of the country. What was once quite a slog from London or the Home Counties is being brought within easier reach – no more than two hour's drive – of 15 million people, thanks to roadbuilding such as the M25 London orbital motorway, the Dartford Tunnel under the Thames, the M2 towards Dover and the M20 to Folkestone.

Once the decisions have been made that set the juggernaut in motion, John Webb claims to take a back seat, and leaves the real work (down to details such as how many press telephones and telexes to order from British Telecom) to his wife Angela and the rest of the team. 'They are much better at this sort of thing than me, anyway,' he says.

No matter. Disaster can strike with breathtaking speed. On race morning in 1982, a helicopter on its way to land put its tail rotor through the mains electricity line supplying the whole of Brands Hatch. The water pumps to the lavatories stopped. Telephones and public address ceased. The organizers' hearts skipped more than a beat, for it would have been impossible to run the meeting. Then it was remembered that there was an emergency generator to hand.

Two years earlier, at dawn on race day it was discovered that gangs of thugs had got in without paying by cutting their way through perimeter fences overnight. Not only did this cost Brands a lot of money, but it was reckoned to account for much of the deliberate vandalism to lavatories and other facilities.

That has since largely been put to an end by an intimidating presence of security guards, many with dogs. Most likely, however, anyone trying to cut his way in will be caught in the act and 'taken prisoner as a spy' by Territorial Army units who just happen to be undergoing counter-insurgency training in the area.

Another important safeguard against the day being ruined for everyone is an 'abandonment insurance', premium £25,000 in case, for instance, the drivers go on strike, or a major public figure dies. Should the worst happen, everyone who is owed can be paid, the public gets its money back, and Brands Hatch still makes some of the profit it had been budgeting for.

As two years of blood, sweat and tears come to a climax for John Webb and his team, they exercise so much self-control under pressure as to be virtually in a trance. There's certainly no going back. Spectators arrive in a state of high anticipation of a supreme sporting spectacle. As they go home, sated by the experience, life turns uncannily quiet for the organisers who sink into 'a most depressing state of anticlimax', almost too exhausted to count the money.

There's only one thing for it. Have a good night's sleep, and start all over again in preparation for the next one.

11

SPLITTING SECONDS

With so much ego and money at stake, it is inevitable that this highly competitive circus is fraught with passion and power-play. Teams vie with each other for the slightest advantage and watch one another like hawks, hoping to catch rivals overstepping the mark. For there is gain, too, in having them penalized.

A protest by one team, alleging that another has broken the rules – unwittingly or not – is as much a part of every-day life of the grand prix circus as are the barbed insults bandied about the House of Commons by MPs who are often quite good friends behind the scenes, despite party rivalries.

One aspect of grand prix racing where the protest has become redundant, however, is timing – that slender thread on which the whole thing hangs. It took the patient endeav-ours of the Swiss, a painstaking and neutral people, to achieve this unusual patch of calm in a generally stormy sea.

In the good old days, grand prix qualifying sessions were timed manually, just like other forms of racing. Dedicated amateur timekeepers sat in deep concentration, clicking stopwatches and keeping detailed records. It was – and still is for other racing – an operation of mind-boggling complexity with no room for lapsed attention or slip-ups.

Down in the pits, the teams' timekeepers, wielding clip-boards with batteries of watches, kept tabs on their own cars and on rivals as well.

Once a qualifying session was finished, an agonizing wait of an hour or more would follow while official timekeepers checked and double-checked their records. Publication of the starting grid was often the signal for heated dispute as team managers, jockeying for advantage, rejected what had been handed down from the timekeepers' box.

All too often, the teams were right. They had the experience and accuracy which comes with being in the thick of every race in the world championship season. As likely as not, the official timekeepers undertook this particular task only once a year. The racers were usually better clued-up, but lacked impartiality.

If it is possible to put a date on it, this particular controversy came to a head at the US Grand Prix West at Long Beach, California in April 1978. Official timekeeping got into such a mess that experts from the Ligier, Ferrari and Renault teams had to move in to unscramble it, and finally produced an acceptable grid on the morning of the race.

This drama prompted Bernie Ecclestone to remark that amateur timekeepers had become a menace to the sport. There was too much money involved in all the teams for this kind of chaos to be tolerated, and it made the circus look foolish, unprofessional. Thus Ecclestone determined to find a more reliable means of timing.

Meanwhile, the Compagnie des Montres Longines had already begun expensive research into the problem, drawing on experience gained as official timekeepers for other sports such as skiing, swimming, athletics and the Olympic Games. As long ago as 1910, the firm was producing timing boxes, either operated manually or by tape when broken by athletes. Motor sport was bound to follow, and the first instance that Longines handled the timing was at the 1933 Grand Prix of Brazil. By 1945, the company had developed a photo-electric cell to register the precise moment that competitors crossed the finish line. Then, with post-war revival of the sport, came Longines' ascendance in timing the Le Mans Twenty-Four-Hour Race.

Rallying benefited too, with the introduction in 1957 of the 'Printogines' clock used to stamp competitors' cards at time controls. Electronics became increasingly important in the 1970s, and peripheral equipment was evolved to display timing information direct to the spectator or television viewer. One outcome was the 'Timing by Coded Information' system, worked up by Longines in collaboration with Societa Ing C Olivetti SpA. It led to their appointment as official timekeepers of grand prix racing from 1981.

Ironically, six cars in that controversial 1978 Long Beach race had been fitted with early versions of the new equipment, and further trials took place at that year's Canadian Grand Prix. The following season, at the Long Beach and Spanish races, ten cars were thus equipped. At the Belgian Grand Prix the number had risen to sixteen; at Monaco, all twenty qualifiers had them. More testing was done at the Paul Ricard circuit in the south of France in November 1979, and only then was the system declared fully reliable.

On the Monday before each race Kaspar Arnet and a team of twelve Longines technicians arrive at the circuit to begin unpacking their thirty cases of equipment, weighing 1,5 tonnes and valued at about £150,000.

An electronic 'black box' about the size of a cigarette packet, is attached to each car and an aerial placed below the right-hand front suspension. This coder identifies a particular car by emitting a signal on a frequency (between 2 and 3,6 megaHertz) unique to it.

Each car retains its identification frequency throughout the season. However, the coders are only fitted on arrival at the circuit, and are removed after every race. Longines people keep a close guard on the secret inner working of these devices, and so they should be tamper-proof.

A double strip of metallic foil is laid across the track at the start-finish line, firmly attached to the surface with the aid of super-glue and a plastic mallet. As a car crosses the line, the foil strips pick up its signal, and passes it to filters. These identify the actual number of the corresponding car and send it, within 1/1000th of a second, to a timer. The number impulse and time are then fed to the first of four Olivetti P 6066 computers where it is memorized and its accuracy checked against the back-up system.

Also at the start-finish line is an infra-red light barrier, so sensitive that it will respond to an object 4 cm long, travelling at 300 km/h. As each car cuts the light beam a second impulse is sent, also within 1/1000th of a second, to a timer.

At the front of the timekeepers' box sit four Longines people, working together through intercom headsets. The first calls out the numbers of the cars as they cross the line, and he is tape recorded. The second man writes down the car numbers as he hears them. The third writes the car numbers against times being printed out on tape in response to impulses from the light barrier. The last man in the chain taps this information into the computer which checks it against the data coming from the metallic strip.

The third main function is carried out by a patented closed-circuit television system, focused continually on the start-finish line and running throughout qualifying sessions and the race. It records at the rate of 100 frames per second, which compares with the 50 to 60 frames per second of domestic television. As the recording proceeds, the time of each frame is included to 1/100th of a second.

If any dispute – maybe over a neck-and-neck finish or a false start – needs to be settled, the pictures are there for all to see, frame by frame, run slowly or frozen.

Millions of television viewers saw a replay of this to advantage when Elio de Angelis snatched victory by half a car's length – 1/20th of a second – in the Austrian Grand Prix. If you blinked at the instant of the actual finish, you missed the gap. Even those concentrating hard had difficulty in telling whether or not Rosberg had caught up sufficiently to win. Seeing the Longines replay was believing de Angelis's win.

Although the three systems – coders, photocells and video – of necessity all run to different time bases, they are synchronized to within 1/1000th of a second. And so great is the accuracy that, after twenty-four hours' continuous operation, the maximum additional variation that can occur is 1/1000th of a second.

Information from the computers is displayed immediately on TV screens at key points. Each of the teams subscribing to the service has a screen in its pit. During an official qualifying session, the fastest lap thus far of every driver is shown together with his speed across the start-finish line, and is updated the instant there is an improvement.

This cuts both ways. Everyone knows everybody else's progress during the session, and the pressure to grab the top places on the grid is that much greater. What's more, the times are accepted as being accurate to within 2/1000th of a second, which sorts out close times, and there is a lot less leeway for deception.

Places on the grid are allocated in order of the best times set by each *car* rather than driver. This is a fine distinction, but it should prevent a team, for instance, getting its two drivers qualified high up the grid when it has only been able to field one competitive car at the time and the others are nails. A trick of the trade was to put the front bodywork, bearing one car's number, on another car.

The first team to pull this stunt once the new timing system was in operation got a nasty shock. The driver came into the pits in one car, and went out again soon after in an apparently identical car. But visual identification did not then tally with the frequency now being sent from the black box. Kaspar Arnet enjoys the joke: 'Ordinary timekeepers had no proof, but the computer could tell they were different cars. That's when we go down quick and tell them, 'Listen, if you tried a little trick with us, we noticed it.' And they say, "Excuse us please, we didn't do it on purpose – our mechanics must have made a mistake." '

Although not exactly an outsider himself, Arnet still continues to be amazed by the intense competitiveness in grand prix racing. 'Nobody trusts each other, and they're always looking over their shoulders. But at least the timing now leaves no room for cheating. And, since we started doing it, we have never had an official protest.

'In 1982 there was one driver who complained that we had missed him on his last qualifying lap. He thought this was because he had crossed the line side by side with another car. But, when we printed out all his lap times and re-ran the video frame by frame, he was astonished to see that the other car was about 7 metres ahead, and we had all his times.

'Journalists got wind of this, and came to have a look too. That's why everyone is hesitant to say Longines are wrong. When I say we're not wrong, it's up to me to prove it.'

Even so the grand prix drivers are always trying to beat the system. 'But it's not our job to look out for every trick they try to play. There are stewards to do that.'

The revised Spa-Francorchamps circuit presented Keke Rosberg with a golden opportunity to make up for the lack of turbo power of his Williams while qualifying for the 1983 Belgian Grand Prix. The new Formula 1 start/finish line and pits had been placed just before La Source hairpin. Yet the timing line was downhill from the bend at the old start/finish line and pits.

As he came round to La Source Rosberg seemed to have trouble changing gear and overshot, continuing up the run-off area which is normally the main road into the town of Francorchamps. Turning the car and rushing full 'chat' downhill he was able to cross the timing line much quicker than if accelerating away from the slow corner.

He got what every driver wants – a fast time – but it was immediately disallowed. It had been tried before, a decade ago, by former world champion Denny Hulme.

After each qualifying session a large amount of Longines data is quickly made available to the teams. Each driver's progress is clearly printed out with times and start-finish line speeds for every lap completed. This has opened a lot of eyes.

Although the start-finish line is generally not on the quickest point of a circuit, the Longines speed data has brought home with a bang just how much advantage the turbo cars have over those that are normally aspirated. A Williams-Cosworth might cross the line at 220 km/h while a Ferrari does so at 234 km/h. As, say, only 70 to 80 per cent of top speed is attainable here, the difference between the two will be that much greater at the end of the longest straight. The answer becomes plain: go and buy a turbo engine, or lobby to have the rules changed and ban them.

The availability of all this instant information leaves less scope for a driver to explain away a mistake. But it can also help him a good deal by showing right away which combination of tyres, suspension settings and wing angles have been giving the best results. But it is not left at that. Teams now feed the Longines data into their own computers. The first request came from Lotus which found this took only an hour or so working from a floppy disc, as opposed to a week if the data was keyed in by an operator.

During the race itself, the system maintains a lap chart that records all lap times and every car's position lap-by-lap. This information is relayed to the screens with a choice of three channels: (1) showing the top eighteen cars; (2) the top six – for flashing up on the television picture being broadcast; (3) the cars in the order that they cross the line, but indicating overall positions. This can all be printed out afterwards.

To an extent it decreased enthusiasm for pre-planned pit stops to take on fuel (banned from the beginning of the 1984 season) and fresh tyres. The theory was that a driver starting with a half load of fuel and not having to worry about conserving tyres would be able to gain an advantage that would far outweigh time taken for a really slick pit stop.

The analysis available through the Longines set-up showed that the benefits were not as great as might be imagined. A well-drilled pit crew might take 9 to 14,5 seconds to refuel a car and change four wheels. But there was more to it than that – time taken in slowing to enter the pit lane and then accelerating away from a standstill was seen to be increasing the total time actually lost to 30 or even 40 seconds, worth maybe half a lap.

The teams do not have a monopoly on access to the Longines screens. The service is also made available to the fifteen to twenty television commentators who attend each race, and to the press. It gives them all plenty to chew on. In all, forty to fifty Longines monitor screens are installed at a circuit.

Although Longines very early on convinced everyone of the accuracy and reliability of the system, life for this globetrotting timing team is seldom dull. 'We cannot claim to be God on earth,' says Kaspar Arnet. 'Every time some new problem comes along. At the 1983 Montreal race, the electricity broke down. A year before, we would have been in a hell of a mess. If the power fluctuates by even fifteen to twenty per cent, the computer goes down, and you have to start again from the beginning. So now we have our own emergency generator which can be started within a minute.'

At Detroit in 1982, the first qualifying session on the Friday was delayed because the start-line light barrier could not be installed. 'No problem,' they had said when asked on the Monday for a 30 × 50 cm hole at the base of one of the large concrete blocks placed beside the grid to form a crash wall. Nothing was done until the Friday afternoon when the track was blocked by workmen with a compressor and pneumatic drills. 'They made a huge hole in the wall, not necessary for a little light beam, and I told them we use tunnels for trains in Switzerland. The Americans are up in space, but you ask them for a little hole and you don't get it.' Having windows fitted to the timekeepers' box proved problematical too.

It's not that the Americans are unfriendly or unwelcoming. On the contrary. 'They always say "no problem at all", but at the end you're in a damn mess. Whatever you need doing, you have to fight to the end to get it,' warns Arnet.

The British, it seems, are a different kettle of fish, exuding reasonableness and setting up facilities in good time. The only point of disagreement is that they have stuck, uniquely, to their guns in ruling that no race timing can be more accurate than to 1/100th of a second, despite Longine's faith in its ability to go to 1/1000th.

High standards are now taken for granted. Once, if a team thought it had set a new best qualifying time, it might have to wait a quarter of an hour for confirmation. Now this usually shows up on the screens within a minute.

'They have no more patience,' says Arnet, 'and they want to know immediately. We have to be so fast today that it's unbelievable. If for any reason we have to run a check and this takes two or three minutes, they are banging on the door and starting to quibble. Yet five years ago, they often had to wait hours.

'It's a bad life for us. The more we offer, the more they ask for. When we offered speeds across the start line, they said: "Great. What's next?" The question is always: "What's next?" And, every time, we must be absolutely sure that new features are efficient and accurate.'

In a fast-developing environment like grand prix racing, the pressure on the firm to expand the scope of the service is relentless. Swiss steadiness, a firm belief in getting things right first time, and cost keep the brakes on any such headlong rush. 'Technically, we could greatly increase the amount of information we provide,' admits Arnet. 'But there comes a point when we have to double our staff and, at the moment, this is not possible.'

A next, relatively straightforward step would be to provide each of the teams with a printer in its pit, instead of distributing copies of print outs at the end of each session. This would give them instant back-reference.

In the longer term, it is not inconceivable that grand prix circuits will be much more comprehensively monitored. Measurements of speeds – at critical points, such as just before the brakes go on at the end of the longest straight, and at exits from corners – would give designers lots of invaluable information about the behaviour of their creations, not to mention driver performance. Similar principles have already been applied by Longines for some years at Ferrari's Fiorano test track. Doing this at sixteen race circuits would take a long time and masses of money, a commodity to which the circus is well accustomed. Meanwhile, there is no fixed schedule for such innovations to be introduced.

'When, at Rio at the beginning of 1983, we first announced we would be showing speeds across the start-finish line, the teams said: "Well, that's not bad",' remembers Arnet. 'but, believe me, when they saw the difference between car A and car B, they were really astonished. Some were slow, and others had a hell of a lot of speed. It made them realize they were doing something wrong, and some immediately began altering wing angles to get more pace.'

Not always as quick on the uptake have been others who have been offered the service. Many of the regular television commentators understand its value, take the trouble to learn how to use it, and are only too glad to have the race order flashed on the broadcast picture from time to time. Others appear to dislike this, feeling the viewers will think them less knowledgeable.

In any event, the decision lies not with mere commentators but with the grand panjandrums of the television world whose sense of their own omniscience can sometimes be a trifle alarming.

This is where a diplomatic touch in negotiation can help. It's quite simple really, says Arnett. 'We offer them a service, and we'd like to get a little bit in return. The trouble arises when they believe that, because they are the biggest, they know best. When they get the results in a mess, nobody blames TV because the Olivetti-Longines name is at the bottom of the picture. And, if you are a TV commentator, you're not going to say "my boss is bloody stupid". That would be your last commentary. So it's up to us to convince them how to get it right.

'We had the same sort of problem at the World Cup skiing at Aspen. They said "We don't need you". So we switched them off completely for the women's downhill. They had no idea who was in the lead, who won, no intermediate times, no running clock, nothing. The tune was immediately changed for the men's downhill. We don't like to put pressure on someone – we just explain. If they don't believe it, well, they don't believe it. They have to find out for themselves that they made a big mistake.'

Providing the service is costly, even by grand prix standards. To perfect it took two years of intensive research. 'I'm glad we never calculated the cost. Otherwise the boss would never have even considered it. But today we are happy because we are the only ones in the world to have a system with this accuracy.'

The Longines budget for a grand prix season is about

£500,000, which covers transportation of people and equipment, but not salaries.

Ten per cent of this is recouped from the teams, each of which pays £200 per race for the service. The only exception has been Theodore which lacked the money. 'We are very sorry about this, and would feel more humane if we let them participate. But Bernie Ecclestone makes a very strict rule about it – he says all the others would be stupid to pay if we let Theodore in for nothing, even though it's true they have no money.'

The race promoter's contribution is to pay for six twin-bedded rooms for the Longines technicians during their stay, and to provide modest publicity on the circuit – space for two banners for Olivetti and two for Longines, each measuring 1 metre by 10 metres.

Strategically placed for the television cameras, these banners are where the firm starts to get value for its investment. Then comes the *quid pro quo* for providing television services and commentators with all that information free of charge – during the screening of each race, the European Broadcasting Union agrees that 'Olivetti-Longines' may appear in the picture for four seconds on ten occasions.

In the final analysis all this effort is directed towards selling wrist watches, although to measure its effectiveness is almost impossible. It is certainly about image – the speed and excitement of the sport – and provides strong additional sales arguments.

'A watch has a dial, second, minute and hour hands, the date, a bracelet. Okay every watch has those. But we can say we create the complete watch, instead of being an assembler of components bought in, and our styling is pure Longines. In addition people see our name on the TV screen, and when they learn that we time motor sport to 1/1000th of a second they know our watches can't be rubbish. Also, we can point to the grand prix coverage on television and our retailers can see just how much we are doing to help them sell by promoting our products.'

The timing service is not the firm's only involvement in grand prix racing. Its policy is to sponsor cars rather than drivers. 'We don't say we dislike the driver – after all, he's the man who wears the watch. But many things can happen to him. If he gets killed, people may think this happened because we gave him the money, even though he will drive anyhow, with or without our support.

'If a driver is badly injured halfway through the season, the sponsor's advertising stops. What does the company do then? Ask for half the money back? Impossible. However, you have to look at the driver not as a man but as an advertising hoarding, no different from a car. If you have prepared a big promotion in a country and then – bang! – the car crashes, there's no problem. You get another car. But a driver in hospital is much more difficult to replace.'

This explains why the Longines logo appears not on drivers' overalls, but on the Renaults and Ferraris; it's all the more significant to have space on the latter – until 1985 this was allowed only to firms whose technical support was used.

The firm has received many requests to supply its novel grand prix timing system in kit form to circuits for use in other forms of motor racing. But, even though the system has proved weather and crash proof as well as totally reliable, it is thus far too complicated for use in inexpert hands. 'We don't want to sell something, and have people coming back and telling us it's useless because they can't handle it,' remarks Arnet. This is not to say that, in five years' time, it won't have been perfected to a simple enough system to be sold outside.

12

BEAMING THE MESSAGE

The shark, dubbed the most efficient eating machine in the animal kingdom, goes on its predatory way with pilot fish always in attendance. The grand prix circus, the most voracious consumer of money in the sporting world, has the media instead.

As in other co-existent groups with a well-developed sense of self-importance, individuals in both camps have been known to fall for the delusion that they don't really need the other side which, equally, could not survive without them. The reality, of course, is mutual dependence.

The sponsors, whose money makes it all possible, are there for the excitement and exposure the media create. The media are there for the excitement and column inches or airtime the sport creates. Marshall McLuhan rules.

Typically, 1500 media men and women receive accreditation for a grand prix – writers, photographers, radio, television and public relations people, generating the Niagara of words and images that catalyse the whole performance.

During the race, maybe 500 journalists and photographers, lugging huge lenses and bags of heavy gear, distribute themselves at vantage points close to the action around the circuit. Others crowd into the press room, keeping a blow-by-blow record of events. After the chequered flag, probably 300 journalists have immediate deadlines to meet.

As they scramble to do so, typing with frantic speed, checking facts with colleagues, and yelling down crackling telephone lines to copy takers in distant offices, the atmosphere becomes a cacophonic blend of unruly schoolroom and the Tower of Babel. How anyone can concentrate on writing a coherent, accurate story, always with one eye on the clock, defies comprehension.

They are aided in telling the world about the race by a dozen telex machines and operators, a switchboard with eighteen telephone lines, and banks of pay phones. And, miraculously, one way or another, they get the news across on time.

One of the best organized – and most highly pressurized – is Paul Treuthardt, number-two man at the Associated Press bureau in Paris and known in the sport as 'the guy who covers motor racing and wars.' An Australian working from France for America's largest news agency that serves more than 100 countries, he admits that his material must reach an audience that is 'excessively, frighteningly large'.

Yet, for him, writing about grands prix comes almost as a hobby, a little light relief from a routine of stories on politics, wars, sport and crime that takes him around Europe, the Middle East and North Africa. 'It's pleasant to get away from the nasty run-of-the-mill copy – the wars and things – and write this sort of stuff. It's absolutely show business, and doesn't really have a bearing on anything else except a very small group of people who are making a lot of money.'

Instead of a typewriter, Treuthardt carries a portable word processor that connects with the AP communications network by telephone line. He taps out his story on the keyboard, and it shows up on a small TV screen while being stored in the memory. When this is done, he dials one of the AP computers in London, Paris, Frankfurt, Brussels or Rome, and, once the link is established, he places the receiver in a pair of cups on the machine.

At the press of a button, the copy is transmitted down the line at the rate of 300 words a minute. Depending on the codes keyed in at the top of the story, it is automatically switched through to other computers in the network, whence it can be available within minutes to more than 10,000 newspapers and television and radio stations around the world. Some still receive it at a traditional 60 words a minute, but the AP Sportswire out of New York runs at 1200 words a minute.

'I'm on deadline all the time. Our deadline is now,' says Treuthardt. 'The theory is that, at any one time, a newspaper somewhere is going to press or a radio station is going on the air because we are literally serving the whole world. The story just has to be gotten out as fast as possible.'

The basic requirement is for stories on Friday's practice for Saturday morning and afternoon papers, then on Saturday practice for Sunday papers, and on the race for Monday papers. The stories for afternoon papers tend to be fairly terse – about 500 words – while the morning ones are allowed the luxury of running to 600 to 750 words.

Adding to the pressure is the requirement to do two 40-second spots on each of the three days, with maybe a quote from a driver, for the AP radio service taken by more than 1000 stations in the USA.

The instant he has physically checked the winners across the line, Treuthardt presses a button to transmit copy giving the top six drivers and cars into the network. Within ten minutes, he sends a short report – no more than 300 words – outlining the top six finishers, championship leader and major incidents. And then he sets about finding drivers and others to get background for a fuller, more colourful report – 700 to 750 words – to appear in the Monday morning papers.

'It would be nice to get some quotes from the winner. In some places, he is interviewed over the loudspeakers. In others, he is brought to the press room – unfortunately that's rare. Sometimes, you have to run down to his motorhome, and be privileged to enter or not as the case may be.

'On one famous occasion when Alan Jones won at Paul Ricard, Williams had, for some reason, decided that they would allow him to be interviewed by three journalists at a time. So instead of simply standing there with a hundred journalists and saying it once, he had to keep doing so over and over again. All the time, the people on the outside were banging on the door, screaming and shouting that they were on deadline.'

This pattern can be disrupted if there is a major accident. 'If it's in the race or it is stopped because of a first-lap accident, I'll jump on the phone and do a short piece explaining the delay. If it's something like Gilles Villeneuve being killed in practice, you are there all night if necessary until you get the details.

'An interesting sidelight on the Villeneuve affair was that I had been under a certain amount of pressure, for various reasons, not to go to practice but simply to the races. Then I got a message on the wire from the person concerned saying: "Please send recipe for humble pie." That was very nice of him, but it pointed up the unfortunate fact that, as much as anything, we're there in case people get killed. That's the press, though I like to think we tell a good story when people aren't killed.'

Like many of his colleagues, Treuthardt finds relationships with drivers variable. Some can be very difficult, monosyllabic, to talk with. Much of their personality is lost because they hide away in motorhomes so much of the time. 'I don't necessarily blame the drivers. They have a lot on their minds. But I'm very curious about some of their sponsors because, if I was a sponsor, paying a driver a wadge of money, I would make exceedingly sure that, even if he didn't qualify, he was still up in the press room. Not "available in his motorhome", but dragged by his goolies and screaming up to the press room to see whomever was necessary.'

BBC Television's commentator, Murray Walker, remarks: 'Whatever vintage of drivers you're looking at, some are absolutely super – outgoing, helpful, constructive, prepared to talk to you whenever you want. Others are not going to be very helpful. But, in the end, you can get to anybody you really want because it's very important to them that you should. I'm not saying that big-headedly, but because I represent something that is very important to them, and the sponsors are paying a lot of money for them to do it.

'If some driver was so superior or unhelpful that he wasn't prepared to co-operate, you could say to his team manager: "Look, I want to talk to Smith, and he's being extremely difficult." "Oh, *is* he? Right. Be back. Five minutes." And the driver will be on parade.

'Now, I've never actually had to do that, but there are one or two drivers who are not most helpful, while there are others for whom I have nothing but praise.'

Walker himself has been immersed in motorised sport of one sort or another since childhood. His father was European motorcycle racing champion in the 1930s, editor of *Motorcycling* magazine, and also commentated for the BBC. Walker junior got his break in 1949 when a BBC producer heard him doing the public address at Shelsley Walsh hillclimb, and offered him an audition. He was given the second commentary post at that year's British Grand Prix at Silverstone, and also did his first television broadcast from a motorcycle hillclimb at Gnat's Valley in Kent.

'It's all I ever really wanted to do. I had to make a living which was why I was in the advertising business. But, since I retired from it in 1981, I've done nothing but think, dream, eat, sleep and drink motor sport. If there isn't a grand prix on, I go to another meeting. I cover motorcycles, trials, rallying, rallycross and all forms of circuit racing. Because you are expected to be able to talk about whatever aspect of motor sport the BBC decides to cover, you've damn well got to keep up, if for no other reason than, if you don't, somebody else will.'

To do the job, you must be able to talk *and* know what you're talking about. Enthusiasm is essential to putting across a fast-moving and exciting sport, and so is an ability to think quickly and instinctively on your feet.

Typically, the television outside broadcast set-up for coverage of a grand prix comprises about fourteen cameras placed around the circuit, a few hand-held cameras to cover the start and action in the pits, and perhaps a helicopter or the Goodyear airship. These feed pictures and sound to large mobile scanner units, one to seven cameras controlled by a producer responsible for following the cars round half the circuit before handing over to his opposite number.

In the other half of the scanner unit are technicians looking after sound and picture quality.

One of the two producers is the senior with ultimate control over what is broadcast. They sit facing banks of monitor screens showing what is continually coming through from each camera, and select what the viewer sees by punching buttons on a keyboard with the dexterity of a piano player. Simultaneously they are talking to the cameramen all the time, calling them to zoom in on a particular car or concentrate on a group of others.

The commentator hears all this through his headphones as well. He has to be able to keep talking while filtering out instructions to himself from those to the cameramen.

'There are all sort of pressures that people aren't aware of. And why should they be? It's not their problem. It's the commentator's. It's quite difficult because you've got to make the two halves of your brain operate independently.

'Lots of people seem to think that, in some magical way, the commentator decides what they are going to see. It isn't like that at all. He sees the picture being transmitted. So he's got to talk and give the story from that. At the same time, he must watch the lap chart and keep half an eye on the course for extra input.

'And you can be sure that if you're sitting talking from Rio, the master producer in London – as opposed to the local one controlling the cameras – will suddenly say: "Where's John Watson?" You can bet your boots that, the moment you look to check on the lap chart, something dramatic happens on the monitor – the leader bursts into flames, and stops – and you miss it altogether. And the public is wondering: "Didn't the bloody fool see what was happening?" Suddenly you realize Rosberg's not leading any more, and say so. Then the viewers think: "Big deal. He's woken up." '

That is minor compared with some of the horrors that can befall a commentator. At the San Marino Grand Prix in 1983, a local power failure meant that Walker's monitor screen went blank, but it did not affect the picture the viewers at home could see. 'Now that really is a problem.

So you have to busk it, and talk as you would if it were a radio commentary.'

To try and avert such disasters and leave Walker free to gather information and then concentrate fully on his commentary, he is accompanied to races by a BBC producer and an engineer. But most of his counterparts from other countries are left much more out on their own.

During the broadcast, Walker is assisted by journalist Mike Doodson who feeds him tidbits of information and maintains the lap chart, while former world champion James Hunt shares the chat. 'Broadly the understanding between us is that James Hunt does the comment while I do the commentary. That's not to say that we don't ever swap roles. I chatter away. James watches the monitor and, because he's not having to think about saying things, he can notice that somebody is coming up through the field while I concentrate on the top six. When he wants to say something, he gives me a tap, and then I take over again. Over the years, we've developed quite a rapport.'

Though the BBC's camera work on the grands prix run in Britain is widely regarded as the best in the world, it has little control over what the viewer sees – live at any rate – of a race abroad. For this is always provided by cameramen and producers employed locally, while the BBC's own man puts the words over the top.

It was from 1978 that the BBC decided to televize all grands prix. But it wasn't entirely plain sailing. One of the challenges during the Spanish Grand Prix was to extract half an hour's exciting viewing from a live feed during which the local producer had kept the cameras only on Mario Andretti for 62 of the 102 minutes it took him to win the race.

A hideously memorable race was the 1982 South African Grand Prix where everything went wrong technically. First, the BBC commentary trio were placed where they could only look at the start line as cars crossed at nearly 320 km/h, whereas the previous year they were on top of a grandstand and could see the whole circuit. The local producer was making an appalling job of the coverage, and the sound system was not working properly.

'Looking at the monitor didn't really tell you what was happening in the race because he was missing it all,' remembers Walker. 'This was compounded by the fact that I couldn't hear what James was saying, amd he couldn't hear me. The producer could hear neither of *us*, and we couldn't hear him. Worse still, I could hear myself a sentence late because it had gone to London and come back before I heard it. So, when I said: "There goes Prost into Crowthorne corner", I heard "Prost" as I said "corner". 'You've no idea how disconcerting that is. So you stop to wait for yourself to catch up, and then you don't hear anything. You think that's all right, and you start again. But all you've done is delay the evil moment. In desperation, I had to take off the cans and busk it.'

The live feed from that race was such a disaster that, back in London, it took them ten hours to put together the half hour to be shown in the evening.

Small wonder, then, that the least of Walker's worries is the possibility of being quoted in *Private Eye*'s 'Colemanballs' column. 'I would mind if I had made a dreadful error of fact. But most of things are a slip of the tongue like: "I'll just stop my startwatch." Anyway, a bloke who never makes mistakes is not human. If you're not big enough to accept it in good part when someone points one out, then you shouldn't be doing the job. When all's said and done, it's not the most important thing in life. I don't think anybody should get too uptight about it.'

Finding the right balance between highly technical and plain language is also part of the art. 'When I get criticism because I didn't draw attention to the fact that a car now has four valves per cylinder whereas, last week, it only had two, I say: "Look, mate, enthusiasts are perhaps five per cent of the audience. The other ninety-five per cent don't know, don't care, don't want to know. And it takes simpler terminology to make it meaningful to them, hopefully without antagonizing the enthusiasts." '

13

SETTING THE PACE

The bullshit stops here – for organizers and competitors alike. If they haven't got it together in time for the start of the two days of pre-race practice, the odds are it is too late to polish up their respective acts sufficiently.

The juggernaut is rolling, and nothing is going to stop it now. It is time to sort out the men from the boys. The punters throng through the turnstiles. And, though there will always be argument about whether or not their true reason for being there is to see blood, they certainly expect a good show, for which they have paid serious readies.

For drivers and teams, it is time to come up with the goods, prove that all the money and midnight oil has been worth it. For those who are established, it is an opportunity to face their peers. But they must also face the possibility that they may be humbled if only by some quirk of circumstance or automotive temperament.

The first hurdle is to get among the thirty actually allowed to attempt to qualify for a place on the starting grid. Priority is given to a closed shop of twenty-six cars from the teams, maximum two cars each, that have put up the best showings in the constructors' championship during the two previous half-seasons.

The opportunity to qualify is open to four additional cars from teams that have yet to attain membership of the club. If there are no more than thirty-four entries for the race, all can participate in the first one-and-a-half-hour untimed practice session. And the quickest four outsiders will be allowed to go forward with the 26 to run during qualifying. If there are more than thirty-four entries, the outsiders must fight it out for those four places during a pre-qualifying session.

At Monaco, where only twenty cars may start, qualifying is limited to twenty-six cars. If the entry is greater than that, twenty-two places in qualifying are guaranteed to the best insider teams. Two places are reserved for 'cars designated by the organizing committee of the event', and two more are open to the best of the pre-qualifiers. However, at Monaco and the other races, getting into qualifying is no guarantee of a place on the grid, no matter how good the previous record of team or driver.

A further obstacle to newcomers trying to break in is that, if during their initial season they are not going to enter the world championship but are going to try their luck at a few races, they must put down a deposit of $30,000 with FISA.

Even if there are fewer entries than places available on the grid, each driver must run in at least one of the qualifying sessions in a car of the type he intends to race.

During the three days of a grand prix weekend competitors have a total of only five and a half hours' running time to shake down their cars and qualify prior to the start. Each of the first two days allows an untimed practice session from 10.00 to 11.30 and timed qualifying from 13.00 to 14.00. And there is a half-hour 'warm-up' only hours before the race starts.

It is a time to keep a close eye on your rivals and, knowing they are watching you just as carefully, not to give too much of the game away all at once. And a lot of tactical psyching-out takes place.

Much of this has to do with the temperaments of the drivers and the people controlling the teams. If they feel they have a definite edge and are cock-a-hoop about this, a driver may be sent out on sticky tyres to pulverize opposition morale with some blindingly quick times. Then the word may be put about that he had a lot of fuel on board and he wasn't running on qualifying rubber.

However, this can so easily backfire. The perpetrators may lull themselves into a false sense of security. They can only fool some of the people some of the time. And older, wiser hands have been given a pretty clear indication about just how far they must pull out the stops to do better.

The more sanguine view is that the only fast times that matter are the four or so posted during the two qualifying periods. Once the best set-up for qualifying has been found, untimed practice is best spent running full tank tests to check consumption and thus ascertain the minimum fuel load necessary at the start. This is also the time to run tyre wear rate checks so as to arrive at the stickiest permutation of rubber that will go the distance during the race.

The ideal situation for a team is to have two drivers who complement one another by liking their cars set up the same way, both for qualifying and for the race. During untimed practice, one can concentrate on the qualifying set-up while the other plays around with race settings. When the time comes they swap information, and get the best of both worlds.

Real life is never that simple. One or both drivers may battle throughout the sessions without finding the answers and getting nowhere. They may not go as far even as that – some high-tech malady may have the engineers foxed for hours on end, and the bloody thing has no power, won't run at all.

Or, just as he thinks he is really getting it together, the driver feels a sickening jolt and the car begins to slow. A glance in the mirror confirms the frustrating truth – dense smoke and perhaps flames billow from the engine. It could mean a window in the cylinder block but as likely as not these days a turbo-charger has blown to pieces.

If that is not exciting enough, there may be a bonus: sudden loss of power in a high-speed corner makes a car a handful to control – it was the urge through the back wheels that was keeping it stable. But a generous spray of oil over the rear tyres will ensure a spin of gut-churning violence. With luck all this kinetic energy will be dissipated harmlessly as the car ploughs across open spaces of grass or sand. Without luck, there will be a neck-snapping, head-ringing slam into a steel barrier or wall.

Adrenalin is a great panacea – if no bones are broken. The only thought is to curse one's luck, and leg it back to the pits so as to climb into the spare car and get on with the job. Always assuming the other driver in the team has not pulled the same trick earlier and has first call on the spare.

The sharing of the third car varies from team to team. Some have a pecking order, where a number-one driver gets priority, and number two has to sit it out if they're both in trouble, though things would be really serious if they both were continually.

However, Renault's policy, for instance, is to give both drivers the same status with èqual call on the third car. For the start of the 1984 season, it was made clear to Patrick Tambay and Derek Warwick that this was so. But, from mid-season, whichever was best placed in the championship would assume a degree of number-one status, and his partner would be expected not to get in the way, as had happened as a result of the acrimony between Alain Prost and René Arnoux during 1982.

McLaren's attitude, similarly, is that if a team is to double its costs by running a second car, it is madness not to make the most of both by giving each of the two drivers the best available support. Nevertheless, Niki Lauda shrewdly has a contract that allows him the bulk of the test mileage – which has to give him the sharper edge, even if subsequently deposed partner John Watson pulled more race points.

To avert the dangers of slower cars creating traffic jams by obstructing the leaders, a driver is not supposed to start unless he has qualified with a lap time less than or equal to 110 per cent of the average of the fastest three on the grid. No Wallies, please.

Force majeure is the get-out. It allows the stewards discretion to start the maximum number of cars, even if some have not come within the percentage limit. It could be that torrential rain turned practice into a *casino* (Italian term for a situation where cars are spinning off all over the place) before everyone had a chance to go for a quick time.

208

This sort of situation can crop up even in countries renowned for non-stop scorching sunshine. For example, the South African Grand Prix at Kyalami traditionally takes place in March – high summer – though, recently, the race has been moved to the other end of the calendar. On the highveldt, summer – not winter – is the great provider of rainfall. And it is usually accompanied by the full Wagnerian number with darkening skies, thunder, lightning and torrents of water.

The object of the whole needle-match is to snatch as high a placing as possible on the starting grid so as to have the initiative when it comes to the race. The fastest driver to emerge from the two official qualifying sessions takes pole position – theoretically the best from which to spring for the lead into the first corner – on the front row. This gives an immense psychological, as well as actual, advantage. Though it also puts the pole driver under great pressure not to screw up his start and throw away a hard-won gain. And, for some, the stress of holding the lead, while rivals 'climb all over the back of the car' and try to force a way past, can prove too much.

For the start, the cars are drawn up two by two on the grid, in descending order of qualifying pace, the slowest being at the back. A good grid position is crucial because the nearer a driver is to the front, the fewer cars he will have to overtake during the race while attempting, like everyone else, to finish first.

The danger has always been that, without competent supervision, qualifying would become a free-for-all won by the team that cheats most successfully, has most political muscle or shouts loudest. Taking that to its logical conclusion, the rule book might as well be tossed away, allowing the circus to degenerate into a form of high-priced banger racing. Nowadays, however, there is evidence of the authorities' increasing technical competence to ensure that the rules are followed, though the rules themselves are seldom so clear-cut as to be totally resistant to probing by fertile inventiveness. But, at least, there has been a serious attempt at policing to ensure that the minimum weight limit is not circumvented and to control use of qualifying tyres.

At the beginning of each half season, every driver entered in the championship must be weighed, complete with his fireproof clothing and crash helmet. The resulting data are programmed into the computerized electronic weighing system in operation at the entrance to the pit road during every qualifying session.

As each car comes into the pits, an official interrogates a computer with secret software. This will, at random, flash a red light, whereupon the car must be weighed, or a green light, four times as often, which allows cars to proceed straight to their pits.

The scales consist of four sensor pads under the wheels, and these flash an all-up weight to the computer which deducts the driver's weight. If a car is then shown to be under-weight, it is disqualified. And no team is deliberately going to risk that.

Use of qualifying tyres is controlled insofar as a driver may run on no more than two sets of four tyres in each of the two one-hour official timed pre-race practice sessions. Half an hour beforehand, the eight tyres must be presented to an official who marks them with special colour-coded paints, so that it can be seen at a glance whether a driver is using tyres from his allocation. Should he be caught out, his times will be nullified, and he won't be able to start the race.

The problem with qualifying tyres is that, although they have been known to last for ten or twelve laps, they generally have a very short life, reaching their peak effectiveness on the second lap, and deteriorating rapidly thereafter. The moment of departure from the pits must be carefully chosen so that he won't be baulked by other cars on the circuit – either not inherently as fast as he is or slowing down after a quick lap. It is a period of great watchfulness, waiting to see who is quicker and, if a driver has a set of tyres left, going out again as late as possible to try to redress the balance.

It was this compulsion that was blamed for Gilles

Villeneuve taking the risk that led to his death during qualifying for the 1983 Belgian Grand Prix.

If qualifying tyres were unlimited, the track would be chock-a-block all the time with competitors driving their hearts out at blistering speed in two-lap bursts between tyre changes, all trying for the ultimate time until the very last minute. Very worrying for organizers fearful of horrendous shunts, and also for drivers, mindful of their own safety.

As it is, the present system is by no means perfect. For, at any one moment, there is likely to be a big speed differential with some cars warming up tyres, others going for a quick lap, and some slowing down.

The pressure on the driver is titanic. He knows he has only two opportunities during each qualifying period to make his mark, and must wind himself up to absolute peak performance, mentally and physically, for so brief a time. Part of the art is to find a gap in the traffic, preferably having the circuit to himself, but at least chosing a moment to go out when slower cars are unlikely to be in the way when all the road is needed at crucial corners.

One method is to opt for a belt-and-braces approach, nominating one set of 'quallies' and one of rather harder rubber with more laps in them. That way, if a driver is baulked or makes a mistake, he knows he has four more tyres that will allow him several laps during which to post a quickish time. Then, if the second qualifying is washed out, he at least is sure to start the race.

Certainly, this does reduce the risk that a driver, only too aware that this is his last shot on a second set of tyres, will come up on a slower car, and overtake at a stupid place, while imbued with a sense of immortality.

One of the current issues is how to ensure that qualifying bears some relationship to the race and that, once started, it will in turn be close-fought. In the days when the Cosworth ruled, the twenty-six places on the grid would be covered by possibly less than one second, while those that did not get in counted their failures in 1/100ths of a second.

The coming of the turbo blew all this to pieces. A turn of a screw lopped off two seconds a lap, and the gap between

211

pole position and the fastest Cosworth car widened to three seconds and greater. As more and more teams go turbo the time spread across the grid should close up once again. However, assuming the limit on tank sizes and the ban on re-fuelling stops stay in force, the difference between grid times and those achieved in the race will become increasingly unrealistic as the power of qualifying engines goes up.

One solution put forward is to dispense with the present means of qualifying. Instead, grid positions would be based on the finishing order of the previous race with the proviso that the top twenty cars in the championship of the year before would be guaranteed places. The remaining entries would have to qualify for the six slots left over.

It is an idea that could help keep Cosworth teams in the running, that is if fuel restrictions do limit turbo power. But it would greatly reduce the spectacle to be seen during the two days before the race – not that this would worry those who consider that the televizing of the race is the only thing that matters.

Proposals for changes in the qualifying procedure have also included basing grid positions on an average of each driver's best five or ten practice laps, as an alternative to placings in the race before. Nelson Piquet is sceptical of such ideas, saying he thinks they do not represent any better solution than trying to qualify in a series of single very quick laps with short-lived super-sticky tyres.

'The risk', he explains, 'is not in the tyres but the traffic. You come with everything for the lap, and you find somebody in front of you. If it's one or ten laps, it's the same because you're trying a hundred per cent. And the more laps you have to do, the greater the risk.'

Indianapolis-style qualifying – where each driver is allocated time on the track all to himself – would not answer Piquet's objections either. To begin with, a temperature change of only two or three degrees during the day can mean a considerable disparity between performances of the cars. 'Also, between the first guy and the last guy, a lot of rubber will have been put on the road, and that makes a big difference. And, when somebody's engine blows up and

212

drops a line of oil, this is cleaned up immediately if there are five or ten cars on the track. But a driver out there alone would have a big problem with this for four or five laps.'

As for basing the grid for one race on the results of the previous one, Piquet is scornful. 'When a grand prix is finished, it's finished. You have to start another one.'

Others take the view that, short of slamming the brakes on expensively achieved technical progress, there is nothing that can — or should — be done about the direction qualifying has been taking. They feel the problem now is not one of safety, but of the increasing cost involved in running different cars for qualifying and the race. However, fatalistically, they argue that, in the real world, if you want to play the game, it's up to you to find a way to keep up.

14

GREEN MEANS GO!

The aphrodisiac effect of grand prix racing is extraordinary. Whatever the primeval thread that links power, speed, mortal danger and the reproductive urge, it certainly brings out the groupies, dressed up in their best posing attire, to witness the jousting.

Their lustful reverie is blown away by the ever louder commotion as, one by one, engines stutter into angry life. It is time for the half-hour untimed warm-up session – a form of foreplay that sharpens up drivers' minds to racing pitch and checks that all is well with their cars.

So unobtrusively has each driver slipped into his protective overalls and then his car, close-fitting as an outer skin, that onlookers are taken by surprise, rather miffed they were not warned. Somewhere a commentator realizes he has less than three minutes in which to try to explain what on earth this is all about.

Nobody really hears, not that they care all that much. For the brilliance of the images and the sounds of this scene are overwhelming. Even the old hands thrill with anticipation, and all but the most determined of bar-flies are drawn by the spectacle.

Newcomers are baffled by the sheer pace at which everything on the track happens: the way cars are hurled into hairpin bends, scrabbling round faster than most country's speed limits; the neck-snapping squirt of acceleration and rapid-fire gear changes away from corners; the dodging and darting of the cars on the limits of adhesion, sensitive to every little ripple in the track surface; long spurts of orange flame and the base crackle of high-revving engines on the over-run; squeals of protest from high-stressed brakes, glowing red as they convert immense kinetic energy into heat to be dissipated into thin air; the shock-waves of noise as the cars come barrelling flat-out along the straights; the furnace aroma of heat laced with oil, rubber and exhaust gases rich in half-burned fuel.

When, after thirty minutes, all this is abruptly halted, the world seems very bright, sharply in focus, but now slow moving and echoing quiet. It takes a while for revved-up minds to come down, and turn to gentler earthbound thoughts of lunch and available talent. The majority refresh themselves on the hoof. A fortunate but growing minority in cool marquees with crisp table cloths and sparkling cutlery, tuck in to cold buffet and chilled champagne. And the feast is occasionally interrupted as they go out to gaze up in awe at the Red Arrows or some other aeronautically heroic display.

Meanwhile, behind the smoked glass windows of air-conditioned motorhomes parked behind the pits, drivers relax, counting themselves down mentally and physically for the coming moment of truth. For Niki Lauda, for one, this process continues throughout the year under the super-vision of Willi Dungl, Austrian super-physiotherapist.

It was he who brought Lauda back to fitness with amazing speed after his fiery accident at the Nürburgring in 1976. Dungl's regime comprises an arduous programme of running, swimming, cycling and exercises – all aimed at stamina rather than brute strength – and a strict diet that includes muesli, whole-wheat black bread, cheese, herb tea, herb soup, salads, yogurt, and meat only twice a week. The aim is to give the right balance of protein and calories, easily digestible.

It is also vital to drink adequately before the start. During the coming one and a half to two hours drivers, subjected to cockpit temperatures of around 50°C and changing gear possibly 700 times, will sweat off 4 to 5 kg. This presents the very real risk of dehydration which, at best, blunts a driver's competitive edge, and can dangerously affect his stamina and concentration.

As the time for the start looms nearer, drivers respond

in different ways to the inevitable tension. Some talk of 'throwing a mental switch', concentrating on the task to come and setting aside any apprehension. But a certain uptightness is necessary to get the adrenalin flowing. Sometimes a driver becomes so knotted up that he is physically sick.

'I think in general, that I keep pretty calm and cool because that's the way you operate to the best degree,' says Nigel Mansell. 'If you're on the first or second row of the grid and you feel you have a chance of winning the race, you tend to think more deeply about it. Obviously, you get revved up a bit, but, in general, I feel very good – no problems.'

Derek Warwick remarks: 'I'm quite fortunate. But I think I'm only not nervous because I keep active before a race. The most nervous time for me is two minutes before the start. You're sat there in the car with a little bit of a wobble going, invariably wanting a pee, and wishing you'd had one ten and not fifteen minutes ago.'

Whatever the outward signs of inner calm, the driver's body is less easy to fool. Subconscious nervous activity, over which he has little control, prepares him for the coming ordeal by speeding up the heart and breathing. Maybe hours before the race, the driver's heart rate is likely to be up from a normal 70 beats per minute to 100, and may reach 175 once he gets into the car. During the race itself, his pulse will probably top 200 beats per minute, way above the rate of 150 beats per minute normally induced by energetic exercising.

Half an hour before the off comes the time for the drivers to step daintily into their cockpits, snuggling down into the confines, ready to be firmly strapped in by mechanics. Now it is time to set off on a reconnaissance lap round to the 'dummy grid' where the cars are drawn up in order behind the actual starting grid.

Any car that has not left the pits twenty minutes before the start will be kept there until the last minute, and will have to start from the back of the grid.

Final countdown to the race begins with the display of

the 5 minute board. At 3 minutes, the grid must be cleared of everyone except officials and mechanics there to start the engines which is done with 1 minute to go. And, at 30 seconds, a green flag is displayed, sending the drivers on their way slowly round one lap to the starting grid proper.

One man not proceeding round with the field but sharing in the drivers' tension, is the official starter, Derek Ongaro. He has the complex split-second task of trying to ensure that the show gets on the road in an orderly fashion. In this he has to act as ringmaster and read the minds of the drivers whom he categorizes under three main headings: complete rock apes, the sensible ones, and the old ladies sitting at the back.

Like many other aspects of the sport, the starting procedure has undergone much change. It used to be what Ongaro calls 'a one-man ego trip' for a local big wheel brandishing his country's national flag. Lights were eventually substituted for this; however, the accident at the start of the 1978 Italian Grand Prix, after which Ronnie Peterson died, lent weight to moves to have a cadre of full-time officials who would travel from race to race looking after safety.

As a result Ongaro's role was expanded from concern with circuit safety to starting the races as well. From his researches emerged the present grid system with the cars two to a row, separated by at least 7 metres, and staggered (theoretically at any rate) so that each driver has more open space on either side of him and thus a better chance of avoiding a stalled car.

Past grid layouts have included alternate rows of three and two cars, and rows of two and one. Rolling starts kept in check by a pace car at the head of the field were also considered. But, when accidents have happened while using this method, half the cars have been involved.

One advantage Ongaro had was that because of his circuit safety work he and most of the drivers already knew one another and there was continual feedback, whereas a locally appointed starter would handle only one grand prix a year.

Part of Ongaro's function is to check that all the cars have rolled correctly into position on the grid, assure himself that none of the drivers is waving his arms to indicate that his engine has stalled, and make a quick decision on whether or not to abort the start. He is aided in this by a marshal standing by each row holding aloft a numbered board which is lowered as soon as those two cars are in position. Also, he tries to count the cars in, and notes distinctive colours of those at the back of the grid.

Making provision to abort the start if necessary is seen as a big step forward because it can help avert a major start line accident as it did at Spa in 1983 where two cars were stalled side by side. Though it can be open to abuse: 'It's difficult to know if somebody's playing up. If a driver goes round on his warm-up lap and finds he has a problem, the thing to do is sit there and wave his arms about. Then he's got at least another five minutes. It would be very difficult to prove if anybody's playing that game.'

Getting the race off to a clean start depends on everyone's co-operation, a mighty tall order. For, once that green flag is out, nerves are stretched to within an ace of snapping, and a great deal of self restraint is required if a disorderly gallop to the line is to be prevented. Sometimes the temptation is too much, as it was for Andrea de Cesaris when he had claimed his first pole position at Long Beach in 1982. He rushed off from the dummy grid as though the race had already started, while the others crept round as expected, and had to stand there for 23 seconds before everyone was in place and ready to go.

It is very much up to the man on pole to keep the field closed up by cruising round slowly as the cars weave crazily from side to side warming tyres up to working temperature. On a hot day, a grand prix car, relying only on high-speed air flow alone and not fans for cooling, will tolerate being at a standstill for only 15 to 20 seconds before it starts to overheat. So a front-runner who lets his eagerness get the better of him is asking for trouble.

Seen in close-up, it is plain why this finely balanced situation demands a practised hand on the start-light button, someone the drivers can trust. As the front cars arrive, the drivers may knock them out of gear to avoid the risk of stalling or cooking their clutches. But, if they are to do this, they must be sure that, once the red light comes on, indicating that all the other cars are ready behind them, they will be given time to get back into gear – maybe two or three seconds.

Now, twenty-six engines cry out to be unleashed, and cars creep, straining to be away. As 75,000 spectators crane forward to witness this moment of truth, the drivers pray that one man will get it over with quickly, and slip the hair trigger to release this slingshot of breathtaking force.

The rule book says he must do the deed – give the signal to start – 4 to 7 seconds after showing the red light, but he has probably beaten four: 'If they're all sitting there, why hold them?'

The green light comes on, signal for an overwhelming mechanized orgasm as 19,000 horsepower is loosed. The din is cataclysmic. Furiously spinning wheels lay fat black stains along the track. Back markers elbow their way past slower starters in mid-field, snatching a split-second initiative. Everyone is ducking and diving, maybe four abreast, jockeying to force the other man to chicken out and beat him into the first corner. It all happens much too fast for most onlookers to comprehend fully.

Within 5 or 6 seconds of the green light being shown – less time than it takes to read this sentence aloud – the last cars have shot across the line, still accelerating hard. With about 270 metres to run from rest, they have reached more than 200 km/h by now. This is the flashpoint for disaster. If a front-runner stalls while trying to get away, he is helpless to move out of the path of the back-markers. And there is little that can be done at this stage to warn them, let alone abort the start.

A hard-charging hero may come rushing through from the back of the grid, have scant time to react to the obstacle, and be catapulated into the path of other cars. Luckier drivers weave through the debris, but the fiasco is instantaneous, though the race is up and going. May the devil take the hindmost.

During the next 60 seconds, either the track must be cleared or the decision taken to stop the survivors, and try again for a fresh start. When, miraculously, the start is clean, little more than a minute ticks by before the cars storm across the line, hustling hard for advantage. But the race is not considered official until two laps have been run. And, by then, the choices lie with the clerk of the course, and not the official starter.

15

ELUSIVE CHAMPION

Winning the Formula 1 World Championship is about money, team work, consistency and staying lucky.

The driver needs more than his fair share of talent, intelligence, determination, stamina and courage. He must maintain these at a high pitch, remaining unfazed by immense psychological pressures, right from the start of the first race through to the chequered flag of the last. He never gives up, never loses his will to race.

But he is nothing if the team behind him is not 110 per cent together or the machinery is not competitive and reliable.

If one takes the fifteen grands prix of 1983 as an example, drivers made 384 individual starts, but an average of only half were still running at the finish. Of those eliminated, one-fifth were involved in accidents, half suffered failures of engines or directly related systems, and the rest had other mechanical troubles.

In thirty-four years, the world championship has been won by twenty drivers, representing ten nationalities. Most successful individual was the legendary Juan Manuel Fangio with five titles, the first taken when he was forty years old and the last at the ripe old age of forty-six in the year before his retirement in 1958.

Only two drivers won the championship three times: Sir Jack Brabham and Jackie Stewart. And grand prix racing increasingly became a younger man's game. Brabham was thirty-three when he first became champion, and Stewart was thirty when he took the first of his three.

Six drivers won the title twice: Albert Ascari, Graham Hill, Jim Clark, Emerson Fittipaldi, Niki Lauda and

Nelson Piquet. Fittipaldi was only twenty-five when, in 1972, he claimed his first. But the age graph has since moved up again to the early thirties.

This trend may be explained by the ever greater competitiveness of the sport. It is so difficult for aspiring young drivers to break in early in their careers, and thus put in the time necessary to reach championship-winning potential while really young.

Nelson Piquet, World Champion of 1981 and 1983, makes the point that a large part of the problem stems from the widening difference in power between Formula 1 and Formula 2 or Formula 3, the training grounds for up-and-coming drivers. The jump is now so big that team managers are reluctant to test young talent from Formula 3, he says. And they prefer an experienced Formula 1 driver, even though he may not be all that quick.

Piquet's own experience highlights just how tough it is to make the transition. His grand prix debut came in 1978, the year he won the British Formula 3 Championship. And he had to come to grips with the then 475 bhp of the Ford Cosworth DFV engine which was almost three times the 170-odd bhp he had been used to. Formula 3 power has remained in much the same ballpark. But Piquet's Brabham-BMW turbo now has 850 bhp on tap, five times the power of the lesser formula.

'I was very lucky,' said Piquet. 'When I first tested a Formula One car – a McLaren M23 – at Silverstone, I had been used to lapping a Formula Three car there in around one minute twenty-eight seconds. I sat in the McLaren, and it was so much different. All that tremendous power was unbelievable. And it was heavy – but nice – to drive. I went round in maybe one minute nineteen point seven seconds, the same day that Patrick Tambay did one minute nineteen point three seconds in the new McLaren M26.

'We were eight seconds quicker than Formula Three cars then. Today, the Formula Three guy is doing maybe one minute twenty-six seconds. But, in Formula One, you do one minute ten seconds now. So the difference has doubled to sixteen seconds.'

As Piquet recalls, during his early days Formula 1 was very heavy going for the novice. Yet today it must be far worse. 'To sit in an F1 car for ten laps and show all your talent is easy. Testing all day or driving through a race is something else. To start to do this takes many, many years.'

During his first three grands prix, his prayers that his car would not go the distance were answered. 'I couldn't do more than fifteen laps in a row. I was not strong enough. The first race that I finished was in Italy, but that had been shortened after Ronnie Peterson's fatal accident. And, afterwards, I realized that I could hardly walk. The Canadian race was very easy because it was wet. When it is wet, you do not have too much force in the car, and you drive much slower.

'But it's not only a physical problem. It's a mental one. You have to realize that a Formula Three race lasts maybe twenty minutes. In Formula One, you really have to drive for nearly two hours. And you have to get used to it.'

This is something the Brazilian managed to do fairly fast, despite an unpromising start. In 1980, his second full season in Formula 1, he came second in the world championship. And the following year he was number one.

With a second championship, won so coolly in the final round of 1983, to his name, he is ungrudgingly admired by rival teams – not only for his racecraft, but his mature demeanour and his skill as a test driver. Of his first championship he says: 'There was a lot of pressure. I enjoyed the second one much more – I knew what to do. But to be world champion is very difficult. You have to be the right guy in the right year in the right team with the right engine, tyres and designers. It's all these things together. But I think we're in a condition to repeat it. I hope so.'

What makes the Brabham team tick so well? 'Gordon Murray – our designer,' comes the unhesitating reply, and then: 'Well, Bernie Ecclestone's not stupid. He's a very clever man. He realizes immediately if something is going badly, and he tries very hard. People say he always is looking just for the money. That's not true. He makes sure the team is running very well. It is very small, very organized, very clean. You know it's fantastic to work with. I have to fight every year a little bit the money and this and that. But I never want to leave. Bernie knows about that.'

Piquet's recipe for success seems to lie in the way in which he handles the pressures of his own role. He largely shuns the razzmatazz associated with the title, though he is affable and approachable enough. 'I love boats, and I spend a lot of time on mine. That's the reason I have a lot of privacy. Nobody can find me. Even Brabham I only call once a week to have news of this or that. And that's the reason when I come to the race I'm fresh and I want to race.

'I don't read any magazines about motor racing, so I don't know much about it. In my Formula Three days, they would write such a lot of bullshit. And I got so annoyed that I told myself never read nothing about motor racing. Now I have a very good relationship with all the journalists because, even if they write something that would annoy me, I don't know. And they are happy.'

Like many of his peers, Piquet has been learning to fly, though the fact that he has been taking these lessons in Italy should not be a sign that he has been fishing for a Ferrari drive. England's winter makes lessons out of the question, and the summer is taken up with racing. One and a half months in the USA is also not on. But, in Italy, conveniently close to his Monte Carlo home, he can fly from Monday to Friday, leaving the weekend free to visit England or work at home.

Back at the racing circuit, Piquet unembarrassedly enjoys himself like a kid let loose in an expensive toy shop and revels in his good fortune. What's more, the toys go on improving. His reckoning of his own is that, in only one season, progress with the engine and aerodynamics had already made up what had been lost to lap times with the ban on ground effect.

Reducing fuel capacity to 220 litres and abolishing mid-race refuelling should be a tempering influence for 1984, though maybe not all that much. 'Now we have to take more care with the tyres. And – not very often but in some of the races – we may have to stop to change tyres. It will not be quite the same, but it does at least mean there will be pit stops.'

Piquet's prediction is that the cars will be no slower than they were in 1983, though without the fuel restrictions they would have been quicker. However, he feels that, if the 195-litre fuel tank limit proposed for 1985 goes through, it could have a drastic effect. 'After that, the drivers cannot go and race all the way. I don't think it will be very nice. We have to start to slow down to save fuel for the end. You will have to have a big computer to tell you what to do because it will be very difficult to know how much fuel you have left and how much quicker you can go. It's the only way to do it.'

If anything, this will increase pressure on drivers to qualify for a high placing on the starting grid. Already, there are great advantages to being on the first two rows. 'I prefer to be on the front row than the second one because you have nobody in front of you for the race. You can really get away from the others because you don't have trouble with accidents if you are in front. I never do a good start from the second row because I wait for the first guy. I don't start from the light. I always start *after* the first car because, otherwise, it's a big risk – not to get hurt but to damage the car for the race.'

Hardly surprisingly, his favourite race is the Brazilian Grand Prix. 'But, if I finish second there now, they will kill me. They're very spoiled by having so many wins by home drivers. Emerson Fittipaldi won there twice, Carlos Pace once, and I won two. And I would like to win again, even though they took my points away in 1982.'

Britain is also high on the champion's list. 'There are the world's most brilliant drivers here. I like to come to England to race partly because of the people. They love and really follow racing. It's nice to come to a place where people really enjoy the technical part and understand the sport.'

While the fashion among previous world champions has often been to quit while they were ahead, Piquet, retaining an almost boyish enthusiasm, has no such intentions. If he has his way, he will be more than 40 before he does retire. 'I hope I can stay in motor racing for a long, long time – the next 10 years. You know I really don't enjoy anything else, and I think it's really a very easy life. And, every time I think to myself about when I stop, I wonder: "Shit – what am I going to do?" '

DRIVERS'BIOGRAPHIES

Kenny ACHESON: British; born 27 November 1957; lives in Abingdon, England. Debut with RAM March during practice for 1983 British Grand Prix, but failed to qualify for that and subsequent five races. Finally succeeded in South Africa at the end of the season, and finished 12th.

Michele ALBORETO: Italian; born 23 December 1956; lives in Milan, Italy. European Formula 3 Champion, 1980. Grand prix debut with Tyrrell, for whom he drove from 1981 to 1983. GPs driven: 41. Wins: 2. Moved to Ferrari for 1984. Placed 12th in 1983 World Championship.

Elio de ANGELIS: Italian; born 26 March 1958; lives in Monte Carlo. Grand prix debut in 1979 with Shadow (now defunct) in Argentina. Then to Lotus, for whom he drove throughout 1980–3, and remained there for 1984. GPs driven: 72. Wins: 1. Placed joint 17th in 1983 World Championship.

René ARNOUX: French; born 4 July 1948; lives in London, England. European Formula 3 Champion, 1977. Grand prix debut in Belgium with Martini in 1978; also drove two races for Surtees at the end of that season. With Renault from 1979 to 1982, winning four times. Joined Ferrari for 1983; remained there for 1984. GPs driven: 79. Wins: 7. Placed 3rd in 1983 World Championship.

Mauro BALDI: Italian; born 31 January 1954; lives in Reggio Emilia, Italy. European Formula 3 Champion, 1981. First grand prix with Arrows in Brazil in 1982. Moved to Alfa Romeo for 1983, but displaced at season's end. GPs driven: 26. Wins: nil. Placed 16th in 1983 World Championship.

Stefan BELLOF: German; born 20 November 1957; lives in Giessen, West Germany. Placed 4th in 1983 World Endurance Championship for Drivers, driving for Porsche, and setting fastest lap in each of the 8 rounds. GPs driven: nil.

Raul BOESEL: Brazilian; born 4 December 1957; lives in Vichy, France. Brazilian Karting Champion, 1975. Grand prix debut with March in South Africa in 1982. Moved to Ligier for 1983, but left at end of season. GPs driven: 23. Wins: nil.

Thierry BOUTSEN: Belgian; born 13 July 1957; lives in Brussels, Belgium. European Formula 2 Championship – second in 1981, and third in 1982. Grand Prix debut with Arrows in Belgium in 1983. GPs driven: 10. Wins: nil.

Martin BRUNDLE: British; born 1 June 1959; lives near Kings Lynn, England. Placed second in 1983 British Formula 3 Championship. GPs driven: nil.

Johnny CECOTTO: Venezuelan; born 25 January 1956; lives in Treviso, Italy. 350 cc Motor Cycle World Champion, 1975. 750 cc Motor Cycle World Champion, 1978. Placed second in 1982 European Formula 2 Championship. Grand prix debut with Theodore in Brazil in 1983. GPs driven: 9. Wins: nil. To Toleman for 1984. Placed joint 19th in 1983 World Championship.

Andrea de CESARIS: Italian; born 31 May 1959; lives in Rome, Italy. Grand prix debut with Alfa Romeo in Canada in 1980. Drove for McLaren throughout 1981. Returned to Alfa Romeo for 1982–3, then moved to Ligier for 1984. GPs driven: 47. Wins: nil. Placed 8th in 1983 World Championship.

Eddie CHEEVER: American; born 10 January 1958; lives in Monte Carlo. Grand prix debut with Hesketh in South Africa in 1978; then returned to Formula 2. First full GP season with Osella in 1980; Tyrrell – 1981; Ligier – 1982; Renault – 1983. Moved on to Alfa Romeo for 1984. GPs driven: 54. Wins: nil. Placed joint 6th in 1983 World Championship.

Corrado FABI: Italian; born 12 April 1961; lives in Milan. European Formula 2 Champion, 1982. Grand prix debut with Osella in Brazil in 1983. GPs driven: 10. Wins: nil.

Teo FABI: Italian; born 9 March 1955. First grand prix season with Toleman in 1982. GPs driven: 7 Wins: nil. Placed second in the CART (Championship Auto Racing Teams) 1983 Indycar championship in America.

Emerson FITTIPALDI: Brazilian; born 12 December 1946. Grand prix debut in Britain in 1970 with Lotus, for whom he drove until the end of 1973 before transferring to McLaren for 1974–5; Copersucar – 1976–9. Retired at the end of 1980 after a season driving for the same team (renamed Fittipaldi) which continued until near the end of 1982. GPs driven: 144. Wins: 14. World Champion, 1972 and 1974.

Piercarlo GHINZANI: Italian; born 16 January 1952; lives in Bergamo, Italy. Italian Formula 3 Champion, 1979. First grand prix with Osella in Belgium in 1981. Returned for a full season with the team in 1983, but struggled to qualify. GPs driven: 8. Wins: nil.

Bruno GIACOMELLI: Italian; born 10 September 1952; lives in Monte Carlo. European Formula 2 Champion, 1978. First grand prix in 1977 in Italy with McLaren, and drove five races with the team in 1978. With Alfa Romeo for 1979–82, and then Toleman for 1983. GPs driven: 69. Wins: nil. Placed joint 19th in 1983 World Championship.

François HESNAULT: French; born 30 December 1936; lives in Plaisir les Gatines, France. Placed second in the 1983 French Formula 3 Championship, and 12th in the European Formula 3 Championship. Grand prix debut with Ligier in 1984.

Jean-Pierre JARIER: French; born 10 July 1946; lives in Paris, France. European Formula 2 Champion, 1973. Grand prix debut in Italy in 1971 with March; first full season with this team in 1973, followed by Shadow – 1974–6; ATS – 1977–8; Lotus – two races at the end of 1978; Tyrrell – 1979–80; Ligier – two races early in 1981; Osella – 1981–2. GPs driven: 136. Wins: nil.

Stefan JOHANSSON: Swedish; born 8 September 1956; lives in London, England; British Formula 3 Champion, 1980. Grand prix debut in Britain in 1983 with Spirit-Honda. GPs driven: 6. Wins: nil.

Alan JONES: Australian; born 2 November 1946; lives in Yea, Victoria, Australia. First grand prix in Spain with Hesketh in 1975. Drove for Surtees in 1976; Shadow – 1977; Williams – 1978–81. Comeback in 1983 for one race, US GP West, with Arrows. GPs driven: 97. Wins: 12. World Champion, 1980.

Jacques LAFFITE: French; born 21 November 1943; lives in Stoke Poges, England. French Formula 3 Champion, 1973. European Formula 2 Champion, 1975. Grand prix debut in Germany with ISO in 1974, and continued to drive for Frank Williams throughout 1975. Went to Ligier for 1976–82. Returned to Williams in 1983, and remains there for 1984. GPs driven: 136. Wins: 6. Placed 11th in 1983 World Championship.

Niki LAUDA: Austrian; born 22 February 1949; lives on Ibiza. John Player Formula 3 Champion, 1972. Grand prix debut with March in Austria in 1971, and continued with this team throughout 1972; BRM – 1973; Ferrari – 1974–7;

Brabham – 1978–9, and then retired. Comeback in 1982 at McLaren with whom he continues for 1984. GPs driven: 141. Wins: 19. World Champion, 1975 and 1977. Placed 10th in 1983 World Championship.

Nigel MANSELL: British; born 8 August 1954; lives on the Isle of Man. Brush Fusegear Formula Ford Champion, 1977. First grand prix in Austria in 1980 with Lotus, for whom he drove throughout 1981–3, and where he continues in 1984. GPs driven: 43. Wins: nil. Placed 13th in 1983 World Championship.

Dr Jonathan PALMER: British; born 7 November 1956; lives near Reading, England. British Formula 3 Champion, 1981. European Formula 2 Champion, 1983. First GP: Grand Prix of Europe, Brands Hatch, in 1983 with Williams.

Riccardo PATRESE: Italian; born 17 April 1954; lives in Monte Carlo. European Formula 3 Champion, 1976. Grand prix debut in Monaco in 1977 with Shadow, for whom he drove 9 races that year; Arrows – 1978–81; Brabham – 1982–3. Moved to Alfa Romeo for 1984. GPs driven: 96. Wins: 2. Placed 9th in 1983 World Championship.

Nelson PIQUET: Brazilian; born 17 August 1952; lives in Monte Carlo. Brazilian Super Vee Champion, 1976. British Formula 3 Champion, 1978. First grand prix in Germany with Ensign in 1978, during which year he also drove for McLaren and Brabham. Continued with the latter ever since. GPs driven: 78. Wins: 10. World Champion, 1981 and 1983.

Didier PIRONI: French; born 26 March 1952; lives in Paris, France, and Geneva, Switzerland. First grand prix in Argentina with Tyrrell, for whom he drove throughout 1978 and 1979; Ligier – 1980; Ferrari – 1981–2. Seriously injured in accident during practice for 1982 German Grand Prix, but hopeful of comeback. GPs driven: 70. Wins: 3.

Alain PROST: French; born 24 February 1955; lives near Lausanne, Switzerland. French Formula 3 Champion, 1978. European Formula 3 Champion, 1979. First grand prix in Argentina in 1980 with McLaren, for whom he drove throughout that year. Moved to Renault for 1981–3, then returned to McLaren for 1984. GP's driven: 57. Wins: 9. Led 1983 World Championship, but beaten at the finish by Nelson Piquet.

Carlos REUTEMANN: Argentinian; born 12 April 1942; lives Santa Fe, Argentina, and Cap Ferrat, France. First grand prix in Argentina with Brabham, for whom he drove from 1972 to 1976. Joined Ferrari for last race of 1976, and continued there to end of 1978; Lotus – 1979; Williams – 1980–2. Quit after first two races of 1982. GPs driven: 146. Wins: 13.

Keke ROSBERG: Finnish; born 6 December 1948; lives Cookham Dean, England, and Ibiza. First grand prix in South Africa with Theodore in 1978, during which year he also drove for ATS and Wolf. Continued with the latter in 1979; Fittipaldi – 1980–1; Williams – 1982–3; and remains there for 1984. GPs driven: 66. Wins: 2. World Champion, 1982. Placed 5th in 1983 World Championship.

Ayrton SENNA DA SILVA: Brazilian; born 21 March 1960; lives in Reading, England. British Formula 3 Champion, 1983. First grand prix season with Toleman in 1984.

Danny SULLIVAN: American; born 9 March 1950; lives in Paris, France. Placed 2nd in British Formula 3 Championship, 1975; 3rd in the CanAm (Canadian-American) Championship, 1982. First grand prix season in 1983 with Tyrrell. GPs driven: 15. Wins: nil. Placed joint 17th in 1983 World Championship.

Marc SURER: Swiss; born 18 September 1951; lives in Basel, Switzerland, and Kidlington, England. European Formula 2 Champion, 1979. First grand prix with Ensign in 1979 US GP East. Drove for ATS in 1980; Ensign, then Theodore – 1981; Arrows – 1982–3. GPs driven: 50. Wins: nil. Placed 15th in 1983 World Championship.

Patrick TAMBAY: French; born 25 June 1949; lives in London, England. CanAm Champion, 1977 and 1980. First grand prix season with Ensign in 1977; McLaren – 1978–9; Theodore, then Ligier – 1981; Ferrari – 1982–3. Moved to Renault for 1984. GPs driven: 70. Wins: 2. Placed 4th in 1983 World Championship.

Derek WARWICK: British; born 27 August 1954; lives in Four Marks, England. European Formula Ford Champion, 1976. Vandervell Formula 3 Champion, 1978. First grand prix in 1981 in Las Vegas with Toleman, for whom he drove until the end of 1983. Moved to Renault for 1984. GPs driven: 27. Wins: nil. Placed 14th in 1983 World Championship.

John WATSON, MBE: British; born 4 May 1946; lives in London and Bognor Regis, England. First grand prix in 1973 in Britain with Brabham, for whom he drove throughout 1974; Surtees, then Lotus, then Penske – 1975; Penske – 1976; Brabham – 1977–8; McLaren – 1979–83. GPs driven: 151. Wins: 5. Placed joint 6th in 1983 World Championship.

Manfred WINKELHOCK: German; born 6 October 1952; lives in Berglen-Steinach, West Germany. First grand prix season in 1982 with ATS, where he continued throughout 1983. GPs driven: 27. Wins: nil.

Author's Note
With regard to who drives what in 1984, these thumbnail biographies are as accurate as we could make them at the time of going to press. Drivers' records (grands prix driven and wins) are to the end of the 1983 season.

APPENDIX B

TEAMS

Alfa Romeo – Euroracing
via Piemonte 29, 20030 Senago, Milan, Italy
Tel: 02 9986 722

Arrows Racing Team Ltd
Unit 39, Barton Road, Water Eaton Industrial Estate,
Bletchley, Milton Keynes, Buckinghamshire, England
Tel: 0908 70047

ATS Engineering Ltd
Unit 2, Telford Road Industrial Estate, Bicester,
Oxfordshire, England
Tel: 08692 4577

Brabham – Motor Racing Developments Ltd
Roebuck House, Cox Lane, Chessington, Surrey, England
Tel: 01 391 0121

**Ferrari – Società per Azioni Esercizio. Fabbriche
Automobili e Corse**
41053 Maranello, Italy
Tel: 0536 949111

Automobiles Ligier
105 route d'Hauterive, 03200 Abrest, France
Tel: 70 989248

Team Lotus International Ltd
Ketteringham Hall, Wymondham, Norfolk, England
Tel: 0603 811190

McLaren International Ltd
Boundary Road, Woking, Surrey, England
Tel: 04862 22721

Osella Squadra Corse
via Brandizzo 245, 10088 Volpiano, Torino, Italy
Tel: 011 988 16 88

RAM Automotive
Unit 5 Telford Road Industrial Estate, Bicester,
Oxfordshire, England
Tel: 08692 46244

Renault Sport
Usine Amedee Gordini, 15 avenue du President Kennedy,
91170 Viry-Châtillon, France
Tel: 1 996 9110

Spirit Racing Ltd
243 Gresham Road, Slough Trading Estate, Slough,
Berkshire, England
Tel: 0753 71122

Toleman Group Motor Sport
Unit 9, Witney Trading Estate, Station Lane, Witney,
Oxfordshire, England
Tel: 0993 74221

Tyrrell Racing Organisation Ltd
Long Reach, Ockham, Woking, Surrey, England
Tel: 04865 4955

Williams Grand Prix Engineering Ltd
Basil Hill Road, Didcot, Oxfordshire, England
Tel: 0235 818161

APPENDIX C
CIRCUITS

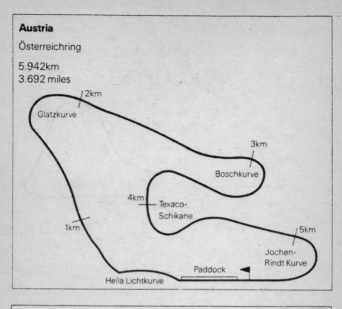

Austria

Österreichring

5.942km
3.692 miles

Glatzkurve

2km

3km

Boschkurve

4km — Texaco-
Schikane

1km

5km

Jochen-
Rindt Kurve

Paddock

Hella Lichtkurve

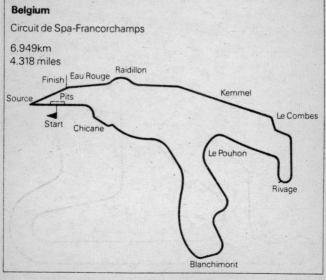

Belgium

Circuit de Spa-Francorchamps

6.949km
4.318 miles

Finish | Eau Rouge   Raidillon

Source

Pits

Kemmel

Start   Chicane

Le Combes

Le Pouhon

Rivage

Blanchimont

238

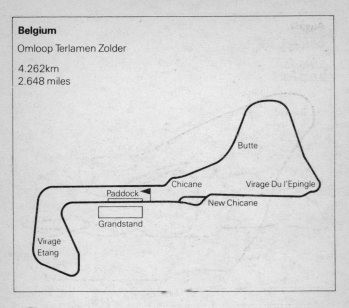

Belgium

Omloop Terlamen Zolder

4.262km
2.648 miles

Butte

Chicane

Paddock

Virage Du l'Epingle

New Chicane

Grandstand

Virage
Etang

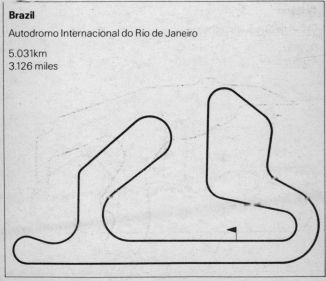

Brazil

Autodromo Internacional do Rio de Janeiro

5.031km
3.126 miles

Canada

Circuit Gilles Villeneuve, Montreal

4.41km
2.74 miles

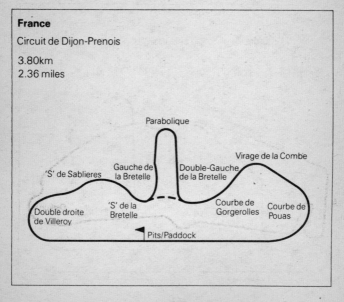

France

Circuit de Dijon-Prenois

3.80km
2.36 miles

France

Circuit Paul Ricard

5.81km
3.61 miles

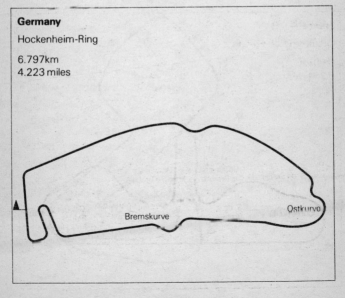

Germany

Hockenheim-Ring

6.797km
4.223 miles

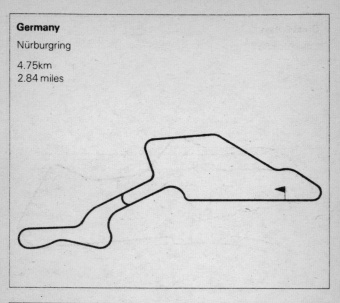

Germany

Nürburgring

4.75km
2.84 miles

Great Britain

Brands Hatch Circuit

4.206km
2.612 miles

Derek Minter Straight

Westfield Bend

Dingle Dell

Hawthorn Bend

Dingle Dell Corner

Pilgrims Drop

Stirlings Bend

Druids Hill Bend

Graham Hill

McLaren

Clearways

Hailwood Hill

Graham Hill Bend

Cooper Straight

Surtees

Paddock Hill Bend

Pits

Clark Curve

Brabham Straight

Grandstand

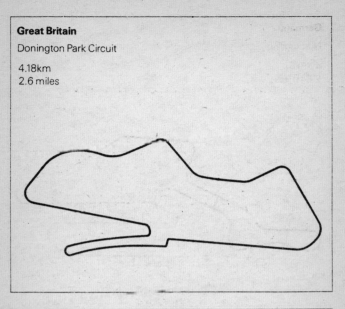

Great Britain

Donington Park Circuit

4.18km
2.6 miles

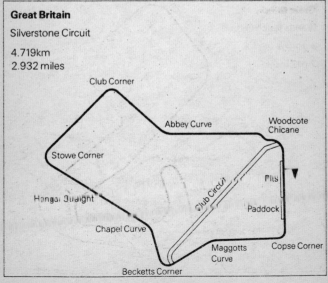

Great Britain

Silverstone Circuit

4.719km
2.932 miles

Club Corner

Abbey Curve

Woodcote
Chicane

Stowe Corner

Club Circuit

Pits

Hangar Straight

Paddock

Chapel Curve

Maggotts
Curve

Copse Corner

Becketts Corner

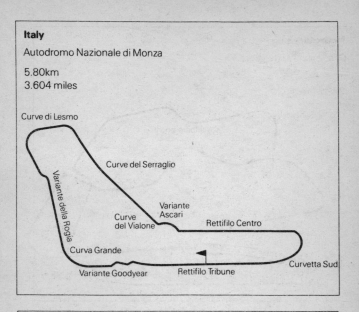

Italy

Autodromo Nazionale di Monza

5.80km
3.604 miles

Curve di Lesmo

Curve del Serraglio

Variante della Rogia

Variante Ascari

Curve del Vialone

Rettifilo Centro

Curva Grande

Variante Goodyear

Rettifilo Tribune

Curvetta Sud

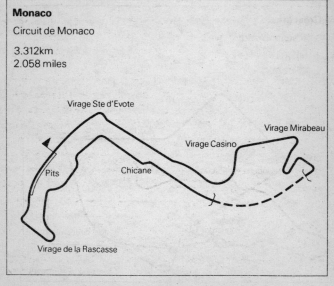

Monaco

Circuit de Monaco

3.312km
2.058 miles

Virage Ste d'Evote

Virage Mirabeau

Virage Casino

Pits

Chicane

Virage de la Rascasse

Netherlands

Circuit van Zandvoort

4.252km
2.642 miles

Scheivlak

Marlboro-bocht

Panoramabocht

Hunserug

Gerlachbocht

Tarzanbocht Pits Hugenholtzbocht

'Bos uit'

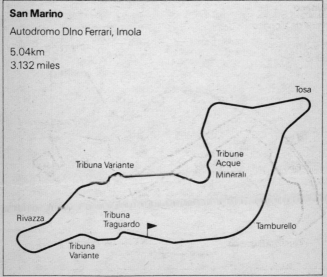

San Marino

Autodromo Dino Ferrari, Imola

5.04km
3.132 miles

Tosa

Tribune
Acque
Minerali

Tribuna Variante

Rivazza

Tribuna
Traguardo

Tamburello

Tribuna
Variante

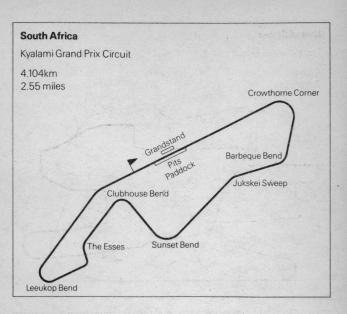

South Africa

Kyalami Grand Prix Circuit

4.104km
2.55 miles

Crowthorne Corner

Grandstand

Pits
Paddock

Barbeque Bend

Jukskei Sweep

Clubhouse Bend

The Esses   Sunset Bend

Leeukop Bend

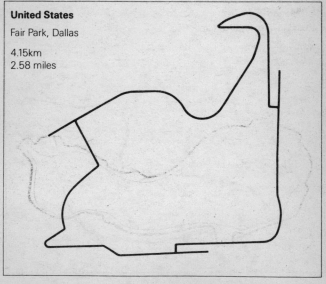

United States

Fair Park, Dallas

4.15km
2.58 miles

United States

Detroit Grand Prix Circuit

4.12km
2.56 miles

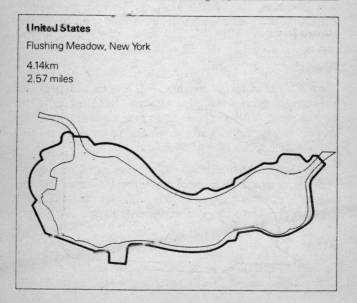

Atwater
Street Tunnel

Pits

United States

Flushing Meadow, New York

4.14km
2.57 miles

APPENDIX D

GLOSSARY

Aerodynamics:

Aerofoil – a body or wing shaped to create lift by virtue of its motion through air. On a car, it is mounted upside down to produce 'negative lift' or downforce, increasing tyre grip and stability.

Ground effect – creation of much greater downforce by shaping the underside of the car like an aerofoil. Passage of air through the venturi thus formed between the car and the road sucks the car downwards. Side skirts are used to seal in the vacuum. From 1983, the practice was largely dispensed with in Formula 1 by a rule stipulating flat bottoms.

Engines:

Naturally aspirated – relying entirely on atmospheric pressure to fill the cylinders with air. In Formula 1, the engine capacity limit is 3000 cc, and the maximum number of cylinders is twelve. Turbine, Wankel (rotary), Diesel and two-stroke engines are not allowed.

Turbo-charged – using forced induction of air into the cylinders by means of a compressor turbine/s driven by the engine's exhaust gasses. In Formula 1, the maximum capacity of a turbo-charged engine is 1500 cc.

FISA:

la Fédération Internationale du Sport Automobile, in effect international motor sport's governing body, in which the 'national sporting authorities', representing member countries, pool their powers.

Formula 1:

Set of rules governing specifications of cars designed solely for use on circuits or closed courses and eligible to compete in Formula 1 World Championship Grand Prix races. In addition to aerodynamics and engines, there are criteria for safety features, dimensions, weight and fuel capacity.

FOCA:

the Formula One Constructors' Association. This represents most of the teams (largely British-based and formerly Cosworth DFV-engined for the most part). It negotiates financial packages with grand prix promoters, and distributes prize funds among all the competing teams.

Flag signals:

Blue – stationary: another car is close behind.
Blue – waved: another competitor is trying to overtake.
White: slow vehicle is on the circuit.
Yellow – stationary: danger; no overtaking; slow down.
Yellow – waved: great danger; be prepared to stop.
Yellow with red stripes – stationary: slippery surface ahead.
Yellow with red stripes – waved: slippery surface imminent.
Green: the hazard has been cleared; or proceed on warming-up lap; or proceed on slow lap from dummy grid to the start.
Red: stop racing immediately.
Black – at individual marshal's posts: the race has been stopped.
Black – with orange disc and white number: warns the driver concerned of fire or apparent mechanical failure.
Black and white – split diagonically and displayed with number: warns the driver concerned about his behaviour.
Black – displayed with white number: tells the driver

concerned to stop at his pit within one lap and report to the clerk of the course.

Black and white chequered: end of race.

'Garagistes':

patronising term used to describe the 'kit car' constructors. They design and build their own chassis, but fit proprietory major components – such as engines and gearboxes – from outside suppliers.

'Grandes Marques':

or *'grandees'*. The teams – such as Alfa Romeo, Ferrari and Renault – supported by major car manufacturers. They consider themselves one up because they make their own engines and gearboxes as well as chassis. However, the distinction between them and the *garagistes* has become increasingly blurred with the participation of companies such as BMW, Honda and Porsche as engine suppliers.

Handling:

This is the product of weight distribution, tyre characteristics, suspension geometry, spring, damper and anti-roll bar stiffnesses, and the settings of front and rear wings. Terms frequently used include:

Neutral steer: when a car goes round corners 'on rails'.

Oversteer: when the back wheels are sliding more than those at the front, and 'the tail is hanging out'.

Traction: a measure of how well the driven wheels 'put the power down on the road'. If it is poor, the wheels will spin under hard acceleration, wasting power, and the car will slide about, losing time.

Turn-in: a measure of how well the car follows its front wheels when the driver turns the steering into a corner. If turn-in is good the driver can leave his entry into a corner late, and confidently go in hard. If turn-in is poor, he will have to begin steering into a corner early and more gently.

Understeer: when the front wheels are sliding more than those at the back. The tendency is for the car to plough straight ahead when the driver turns the steering.

Measures:

Lengths, speeds, weights and volumes are so much part of the sport that the problem is how to avoid driving the reader barmy with a mish-mash of Imperial and metric units. In the full knowledge that you can't please all of the people all of the time, the decision went in favour of metrication. For although the British still drive in miles per hour, they buy their bread, salt, sugar, petrol and curtain fabric in metric quantities. Younger readers will have no problem with this. However, to help those educated in the days of avoirdupois and twelve inches to the foot (or caught, like the author, in the middle of the generation gap), here is a ready reckoner:

Dimensions:

10 mm/1 cm	= 0,39 inches
100 mm/10 cm	= 3,9 inches
500 mm/50 cm	= 19,5 inches
1000 mm/100 cm/1 metre	= 39 inches

Distances:

100 metres	= 328 ft
500 metres	= 1640 ft
1000 metres/ 1 km	= 0,62 miles
2 km	= 1,24 miles
3 km	= 1,86 miles
4 km	= 2,48 miles
5 km	= 3,1 miles
10 km	= 6,21 miles

Pressures:

0,5 bar	= 7,25 lbs/sq in
1,0 bar (1 atmosphere approx)	= 14,5 lbs/sq in

251

2,0 bar	= 29 lbs/sq in
3,0 bar	= 43,5 lbs/sq in

Speeds:

50 km/h	= 31 mph
100 km/h	= 62 mph
120 km/h	= 75 mph
160 km/h	= 100 mph
200 km/h	= 124 mph
250 km/h	= 155 mph
300 km/h	= 186 mph
325 km/h	= 202 mph
350 km/h	= 217 mph
375 km/h	= 233 mph

Temperatures:

0° Celsius	= 32° Fahrenheit
10° C	= 50° F
20° C	= 68° F
30° C	= 86° F
40° C	= 104° F
50° C	= 122° F
100° C	= 212° F
200° C	= 392° F
300° C	= 572° F
400° C	= 752° F
500° C	= 932° F
1000° C	= 1832° F

Volumes:

1 litre	= 1,76 pints
10 litres	= 2,2 gallons (Imperial)
50 litres	= 11 gallons
100 litres	= 22 gallons
195 litres	= 43 gallons
200 litres	= 44 gallons
220 litres	= 48 gallons
250 litres	= 55 gallons

Weights:

1 kg	= 2,2 lbs
2 kg	= 4,4 lbs
3 kg	= 6,6 lbs
4 kg	= 8,8 lbs
5 kg	= 11 lbs
10 kg	= 22 lbs
100 kg	= 220 lbs
500 kg	= 1100 lbs

N.B.: For the sake of clarity, many of these figures have been rounded up or down to the nearest whole number, and should not be used for making highly accurate calculations.

Tyres:

Compound: the mix of rubber and other constituents applied to the circumference of a tyre and providing contact between car and track surface. A wide variety of compounds are used in response to factors such as ambient and track temperatures and surface abrasiveness.

Slicks: tyres without a tread pattern. These maximize the contact patch, as well as creating less heat.

Wets: tyres with a tread pattern, the channels of which help to disperse water that would otherwise form a 'bow wave' and prevent the tyre from contacting the track.

Formula 1 World Championship:

There are two titles to be gained, one for the drivers and the other for the constructors of the cars. Up to sixteen grands prix count towards a year's championship, each race being 300 to 320 km in length and with a maximum duration of two hours.

Constructors: each may count all points scored in every race by a maximum of two cars which it must nominate before the start of the season.

Drivers: the number of results each driver may count is equal to half the number of races plus three. So, if there are sixteen races, a driver's championship placing at the end of the season is based on his eleven best scores.

Points: points towards both the constructors' and drivers' titles are awarded for each race as follows:

First place	nine points
Second	six
Third	four
Fourth	three
Fifth	two
Sixth	one

APPENDIX E

TICKET OFFER

Motor Circuit Developments
Brands Hatch   Oulton Park   Snetterton

and

Countdown to a Grand Prix
Arrow Books

invite you to come to watch motor racing — *free*. First select your date below. Then turn the page for details of this offer and booking form.

*May 27	Oulton Park	Holiday Car Races: Formula Ford 1600, Sports, Saloons (entry worth £3)
*June 17	Snetterton	Championship Car Races: FF1600, Sports, Saloons (entry worth £3)
*July 28	Oulton Park	Star of Tomorrow Car Races: FF1600, Sports, Saloons (entry worth £3)
*July 29	Snetterton	Championship Car Races: Sports 2000, FF1600, FF2000, Saloons (entry worth £3)
*August 5	Brands Hatch	Clubmans Car Races: FF1600, Sports, Saloons (entry worth £3)
*August 26	Snetterton	Championship Car Races: FF1600, Sports, Saloons (entry worth £3)
*September 2	Brands Hatch	GM Dealer Sport Motor Race Day: Saloons, Sports, FF1600 (entry worth £3)

255

*September 16	Oulton Park	Historic Car Races: Historic Single Seaters and Sports Cars (entry worth £3.50)
*September 16	Snetterton	Championship Car Races: FF1600, Sports, Saloons (entry worth £3)
*October 13	Oulton Park	Clubmans Car Races: FF1600, Sports, Saloons (entry worth £3)
*October 14	Brands Hatch	Championship Car Races: Sports 2000, FF2000, FF1600, Saloons (entry worth £3)
*December 2	Brands Hatch	Champion of Brands Car Races: FF1600, FF2000, Sports 2000, Saloons (entry worth £3)

VOUCHER

This voucher can be exchanged for a single circuit admission ticket for any one of the race meetings listed on the previous page, and can also be used to book additional tickets for the same meeting.

Please complete the form in block capitals, and depending on the meeting you have selected, mail to:

"Countdown Offer"

at

Brands Hatch Circuit Ltd
Fawkham
Dartford
Kent DA3 8NG

or

Oulton Park Circuit Ltd
Little Budworth
Tarporley
Cheshire CW9 9BW

or

Snetterton Circuit Ltd
Norwich
Norfolk NR16 2JU

Name: _____

Address: _____

_____

_____ Postcode: _____

As a reader of **Countdown to a Grand Prix**, I accept your offer of one free admission ticket for:

Circuit: _____

Date: _____

Race meeting: _____

I would also like _____ (number) additional

tickets at £_____each (prices on previous

page), and enclose my cheque/postal order/Money

order/cash (delete where not applicable) to the value

of £_____payable to Brands Hatch Circuit

Ltd/Oulton Park Circuit Ltd/Snetterton Circuit Ltd.

or Please charge my Access/Barclaycard/Trustcard/ American Express account.

My number is: _____

Signed: _____

Date: _____

Children under 16 admitted free to meetings listed in this offer.

This booking must arrive by first post, Monday preceding the meeting of your choice. Otherwise tickets cannot be guaranteed.